MW00629449

954-341-4478

WALKING
WITH
JESUS

90 DEVOTIONALS ON THE LIFE OF CHRIST

WALKING
—WITH—
JESUS

DAVID A. GLOCK

ECS
MINISTRIES
The Word to the World

Walking with Jesus: 90 Devotionals on the Life of Christ

David A. Glock

Published by:
 ECS Ministries
 PO Box 1028
 Dubuque, IA 52004-1028
 phone: (563) 585-2070
 email: ecsorders@ecsministries.org
 website: www.ecsministries.org

First Edition 2011

ISBN 978-1-59387-146-8

Code: B-WWJ

Copyright © 2011 ECS Ministries

Cover painting by Robert Zünd (1827-1909) – *Der Gang nach Emmaus* (The Road to Emmaus)

Cover design by LambCreek, www.lambcreek.com

Printed in the United States of America

Dedicated to my wife

Melsie

Remembering the excitement of our youth,
the challenge of our education,
the joy of our family,
the fullness of our service together
before God . . . "keeping on!"

Jesus! the Very Thought of Thee

Jesus! the very thought of Thee
With sweetness fills my breast;
But better far Thy face to see,
And in Thy presence rest.

No voice can sing, no heart can frame,
Nor can the mem'ry find
A sweeter sound than Thy blest name,
O Savior of mankind!

O hope of ev'ry contrite heart,
O joy of all the meek,
To those who fall, how kind Thou art;
How good to those who seek!

But what to those who find? Ah, this
No tongue, or pen can show,
The love of Jesus! What it is
None but His loved ones know.

Savior, our only joy be Thou,
As Thou our crown shalt be;
Be Thou, O Lord, our glory now,
And through eternity.

–Bernard of Clairvaux

Table of Contents

PREPARING TO GO TO JERUSALEM

THE LATER JUDEAN MINISTRY

CHRIST'S RESURRECTION AND ASCENSION

Introduction

For over forty years I have had the privilege of teaching the course *Life of Christ* to the students of Emmaus Bible College. Based on this wonderful experience, I have written *Walking with Jesus* to share insights into the ministry of the Lord Jesus in His life, death, burial, resurrection, and ascension.

And without controversy great is the mystery of godliness:
God was manifested in the flesh. (1 Timothy 3:16)

The goal of *Walking with Jesus* is

➤ to enhance our understanding of the historical development of the life of Christ

➤ to establish the theological development of the life of Christ

➤ to discern and practice principles for living from the life of Christ

➤ to enable us to worship Christ in a greater way

Walking with Jesus is arranged in a format suitable for both private and family devotions. Chapters are short in length for ease in reading. It is based on a harmony of the Gospels in which all of the events recorded in the Gospels are integrated and arranged in chronological order. Each chapter includes the gospel references, the specific gospel text under consideration, and related devotional thoughts.

May God bless you as you contemplate the life of Christ!

David A. Glock
Faculty, Bible and Theology, Emmaus Bible College

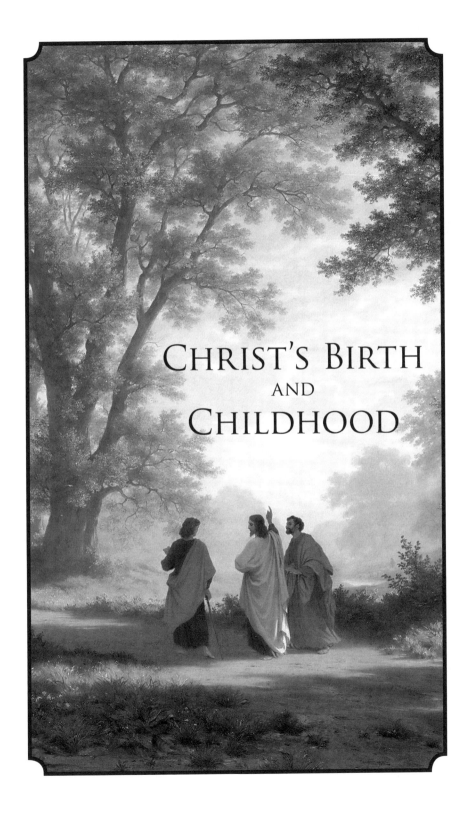

CHRIST'S BIRTH
AND
CHILDHOOD

1

God Has Spoken

Matthew 1:1-17; Mark 1:1; Luke 1:1-4; 3:23-28; John 1:1-18

In the beginning was the Word, and the Word was with God, and the Word was God. He was in the beginning with God. All things were made through Him, and without Him nothing was made that was made. In Him was life, and the life was the light of men. And the light shines in the darkness, and the darkness did not comprehend it. . . . No one has seen God at any time. The only begotten Son, who is in the bosom of the Father, He has declared Him. (John 1:1-5, 18)

God had not spoken for over four hundred years. He had warned Israel about dispersion, about being without king or prince (Hosea 3:4), and so it was. But an eternal plan was being executed with precision. Daniel had prophesied of a series of world empires—Babylon, Persia, Greece, Rome, and the millennial kingdom of Christ. He was very specific in establishing a date marking out 483 years to Triumphal Entry Sunday, the first Palm Sunday. This time span was to be marked from the issuing of the decree to build the wall of Jerusalem under Artaxerxes (Daniel 9:25; Nehemiah 2:1). About 450 years had now elapsed, and whispers from God were being heard. The intensity was increasing! Simeon had been told that he would not die before seeing the Messiah (Luke 2:26), and Anna was looking forward to the redemption of Jerusalem (Luke 2:38). The intensity was increasing! Gabriel was commissioned to announce the birth of the forerunner of the Messiah, John the Baptist, to Zacharias, and the message of the miraculous conception of Jesus to Mary (Luke 1:13, 30). Joseph was instructed by an angel in a dream to marry Mary (Matthew 2:20-21). The intensity was increasing!

And suddenly there was with the angel a multitude of the heavenly host praising God and saying: "Glory to God in the highest, and on earth peace, goodwill toward men!" (Luke 2:13-14)

The shepherds hurried to the manger to see a newborn baby, to hear God speak! Thirty-three years would remain before the triumphal entry—the years of the life of Christ here on earth. Thirty-three years of God speaking through His Son!

The way each respective gospel account begins is significant. In Mark the introduction is brief, without genealogy, because Jesus is a Servant. In

Matthew, Jesus is linked with Joseph, David, and Abraham because Jesus is the King of the Jews. In Luke, Jesus is linked with Mary, David, and Adam because Jesus is the Second Man. In John He is the Word, God!

A twenty-foot-high polished stone cross dominates the beautiful Marble Chapel at Emmaus Bible College. As you face the cross you will notice a symbolic figure at the end of each member of the cross. At the foot of the cross is an ox; at the right member, the face of a lion; at the left member, the face of a man; and at the top member, the head of an eagle. These are ancient symbols concerning the revelation of God in Jesus Christ. God speaks and tells us that

> ➤ Jesus Christ is the perfect Servant—The gospel of Mark
> ➤ Jesus Christ is the perfect King—The gospel of Matthew
> ➤ Jesus Christ is the perfect Man—The gospel of Luke
> ➤ Jesus Christ is fully God—The gospel of John

God, who at various times and in various ways spoke in time past to the fathers by the prophets, has in these last days spoken to us by His Son. (Hebrews 1:1-2)

<u>Thou Art the Everlasting Word</u>

Thou art the everlasting Word, the Father's only Son,
God manifestly seen and heard and heaven's Beloved One.

Worthy, O Lamb of God, art Thou, that every knee to Thee should bow!

In Thee most perfectly expressed, the Father's glories shine,
Of the full deity possessed, eternally divine!

Worthy, O Lamb of God, art Thou, that every knee to Thee should bow!

True image of the Infinite, whose essence is concealed;
Brightness of uncreated light, the heart of God revealed.

Worthy, O Lamb of God, art Thou, that every knee to Thee should bow!

But the high myst'ries of His Name the creature's grasp transcend;
The Father only (glorious claim!) the Son can comprehend.

Worthy, O Lamb of God, art Thou, that every knee to Thee should bow!

Yet loving Thee, on whom His love ineffable doth rest,
Thy members all, in Thee above, as one with Thee are blest!

Worthy, O Lamb of God, art Thou, that every knee to Thee should bow!

Throughout the universe of bliss, the center Thou, and Sun,
Th' eternal theme of praise is this, to heaven's Beloved One:

Worthy, O Lamb of God, art Thou, that every knee to Thee should bow!

—Josiah Conder

2

John and Jesus, Miracle Children

Luke 1:5-56

But the angel said to him [Zacharias], "Do not be afraid, Zacharias, for your prayer is heard; and your wife Elizabeth will bear you a son, and you shall call his name John. . . . And he will turn many of the children of Israel to the Lord their God. He will also go before Him in the spirit and power of Elijah, 'to turn the hearts of the fathers to the children,' and the disobedient to the wisdom of the just, to make ready a people prepared for the Lord." . . . Then the angel said to her [Mary], "Do not be afraid, Mary, for you have found favor with God. And behold, you will conceive in your womb and bring forth a Son, and shall call His name JESUS. He will be great, and will be called the Son of the Highest; and the Lord God will give Him the throne of His father David. And He will reign over the house of Jacob forever, and of His kingdom there will be no end." (Luke 1:13 16-17, 30-33)

Gabriel, the angel sent by God to Daniel with the prophecy of the Seventy Weeks (Daniel 9:22-27), is now sent by God to Zacharias, and then to Mary. Four hundred and fifty years of the prophecy have passed and thirty-three years remain—the years of the life of our Lord here on earth. So Gabriel comes with the message of the miraculous conception of John the Baptist, and the even more miraculous conception of Jesus.

First, John the Baptist. It was the high, holy day for Zacharias. By custom, a priest could only serve once in a lifetime. Zacharias had waited long for this singular day. The privilege of offering the sacrifice was decided by lot, and by God's design the lot fell to him this time. Gabriel waited as Zacharias entered the Holy Place with the ascending incense representing the prayers of Israel. He stood by the altar of incense, and his presence troubled Zacharias. Angels often begin their conversations with, "Do not be afraid." While Gabriel's appearing frightened Zacharias, his message *shocked* him.

> *"Do not be afraid, Zacharias, for your prayer is heard; and your wife Elizabeth will bear you a son, and you shall call his name John." (Luke 1:13)*

This is the part of the message that Zacharias heard, as his delayed question will show. The rest of the message states the reason for the miraculous conception of John.

"And he will turn many of the children of Israel to the Lord their God. He will also go before Him in the spirit and power of Elijah, 'to turn the hearts of the fathers to the children,' and the disobedient to the wisdom of the just, to make ready a people prepared for the Lord." (Luke 1:16-17)

The ministry of John would be to prepare the nation of Israel for the coming King. In about thirty years his message would be, "Repent, for the kingdom of heaven is at hand!"

Zacharias missed the theological importance, the kingdom importance, of Gabriel's message. He would have nine months to contemplate this with his impending loss of speech. He would then speak with great clarity as the priest becomes a prophet—but that, later.

Zacharias's delayed question was not about theology, but biology.

And Zacharias said to the angel, "How shall I know this? For I am an old man, and my wife is well advanced in years." (Luke 1:18)

With delicacy the man who is old refers to the advanced age of his wife, Elizabeth. They had prayed long for a child, but they were now beyond the age of childbearing.

What do angels know? With astonishment at being questioned as a messenger sent by God, Gabriel responded curtly with a sentence of nine months of silence. Unbelief yielded, and John the Baptist was conceived in the womb of aged Elizabeth.

Gabriel's second assignment relating to the birth of a child was even more amazing! It was to be a birth without a human father. It was to be a birth that would be a harmonious union of all the infinite attributes of God and all the limited attributes of perfect humanity in the one God-Man—the Savior, Christ, the Lord! This mystery of God manifest in the flesh remains a mystery to angels and humans alike. And yet faithful Gabriel comes with this message of amazing grace to a young maiden of Israel, Mary: "You have found favor with God."

The message was full of kingdom theology. This is important. What kingdom? The answer in the text is very clear.

"He will be great, and will be called the Son of the Highest; and the Lord God will give Him the throne of His father David. And He will reign over the house of Jacob forever, and of His kingdom there will be no end." (Luke 1:32-33)

This was the beginning of the fulfillment of the Davidic Covenant (2 Samuel 7:12-13). It would be a literal, earthly, political kingdom—an eternal house, and throne, and kingdom. It was to be that fifth kingdom of Daniel's prophecy, contained in that earlier message from Gabriel. The child to be born was from the kingly line of David; it was his throne He was to occupy. He was to reign over the nation of Israel. And His kingdom on earth would be permanent. This truth is restated on Triumphal Entry Sunday:

> *"Hosanna! 'Blessed is He who comes in the name of the LORD!' Blessed is the kingdom of our father David that comes in the name of the Lord! Hosanna in the highest!" (Mark 11:9-10)*

Like Zacharias, Mary responds to Gabriel with a question—not a question of doubt, but a question requesting more information. The answer of Gabriel describes the special act of creation by the Holy Spirit within Mary.

> *"The Holy Spirit will come upon you, and the power of the Highest will overshadow you; therefore, also, that Holy One who is to be born will be called the Son of God." (Luke 1:35)*

Mary accepts this explanation and sweetly submits to the role that will make her the blessed of all women.

> *Then Mary said, "Behold the maidservant of the Lord! Let it be to me according to your word." And the angel departed from her. (Luke 1:38)*

Mary is an example to all believers of submission to God's purpose in our lives, with all the joys and sorrows entailed, even as blessed Mary the mother of Jesus experienced.

Two ladies, miraculously with child—the forerunner to the King and the King Himself!

3
Mary's Visit to Elizabeth and Return to Joseph

Luke 1:29-56; Matthew 1:18-25

Now Mary arose in those days and went into the hill country with haste, to a city of Judah, and entered the house of Zacharias and greeted Elizabeth. And it happened, when Elizabeth heard the greeting of Mary, that the babe leaped in her womb; and Elizabeth was filled with the Holy Spirit. . . . And Mary remained with her about three months, and returned to her house. (Luke 1:39-41, 56)

Then Joseph her husband, being a just man, and not wanting to make her a public example, was minded to put her away secretly. But while he thought about these things, behold, an angel of the Lord appeared to him in a dream, saying, "Joseph, son of David, do not be afraid to take to you Mary your wife, for that which is conceived in her is of the Holy Spirit. And she will bring forth a Son, and you shall call His name JESUS, for He will save His people from their sins." (Matthew 1:19-21)

The passage of time, though precise in measurement, varies enormously in emotional experience. Time can "fly" or it can "drag." Mary decides to make a quick trip to visit Elizabeth, the only other woman on earth who could understand what God was doing. It was a trip of eighty to a hundred miles by foot, which was the means of transportation for the poor. It would take the best part of a week for the journey—but joy makes time fly, and with joy she anticipates being with Elizabeth. About three months later Mary is going to make the return trip to home, to Nazareth, to Joseph. What a long trip that would be! Would Joseph believe her? Dread makes time drag by.

It was the information Gabriel supplied to Mary that initiated the journey. Her relative Elizabeth was with child. The effort of the confirming journey was immediately rewarded. Upon entering the home, the babe in the womb of Elizabeth leapt for joy. The unborn forerunner salutes the unborn Messiah! Already John was bearing witness to the Messiah, initially to his mother. (Please notice the term "baby" used of a second trimester baby and the emotion of joy being expressed by that unborn baby.) It was a time of great joy in the home of Zacharias and Elizabeth and the unborn forerunner, for Mary and the unborn Messiah were with them. The ladies are exuberant—there is joy and rejoicing and loud cries and praise and blessings. What a godly celebration on their part. Zacharias, however, is silent.

But the response was more than godly emotion; it was full of equally exciting theology. Elizabeth speaks of the fulfillment of the word of the Lord. In the *Magnificat* Mary recognizes God as her Savior as well as His holiness, mercy, omnipotence, sovereignty, and omniscience. Beyond all of this she claims the Abrahamic Covenant to be her own. She did indeed have a unique relationship to it:

> Now to Abraham and his Seed were the promises made. He does not say, "And to seeds," as of many, but as of one, "And to your Seed," who is Christ. . . . What purpose then does the law serve? It was added because of transgressions, till the Seed should come to whom the promise was made; and it was appointed through angels by the hand of a mediator. . . . *But when the fullness of the time had come, God sent forth His Son, born of a woman,* born under the law, to redeem those who were under the law, that we might receive the adoption as sons. (Galatians 3:16, 19; 4:4-5)

The fullness of time *had* come, and it focused on Mary and the coming birth of Jesus. For three months Mary remained with Elizabeth, who was to give birth shortly. Mary, now over three months pregnant, began her trip back home while travel was a healthy choice.

This return trip of equal distance would seem so much longer. No joy was anticipated at the end of *this* trip. How Mary must have prayed on the long walk. How she must have rehearsed her explanation to Joseph. How she must have anticipated Joseph's response. How she must have weighed her future situation of life. How she must have feared the loss of her reputation. Sometimes it's hard being the servant of the Lord. It took longer to get home! Upon meeting Joseph her worst fears are realized—*divorce.*

> Then Joseph her husband, being a just man, and not wanting to make her a public example, was minded to put her away secretly. (Matthew 1:19)

Engagement was binding according to the Jewish practice of that day and could be dissolved by divorce for immorality. Godly Joseph, a just man, would not tolerate the supposed immorality. Tender Joseph, a loving man, would then divorce her secretly. Mary was telling the truth, but Joseph would not believe her. Who could? She had left over three months ago, and now was returning when it would soon be obvious that she was with child. And now this fiction of a virgin conception, a baby to be born without a human father, a conception by the supernatural creative act of the Holy Spirit! *Mary?*

Mary was telling the truth as the handmaiden of the Lord. Joseph was acting in a truthful way as a just man. What mutual hurt was experienced by these two godly people as they submitted to the revelation of God—Mary from the words of the angel Gabriel, and Joseph from God's written word.

Why did God do it this way? Could He not have sent two angels simultaneously, one to Mary and one to Joseph, with the wonderful and amazing news? He certainly has enough angels. Then this godly, happy, soon-to-be-married couple would not have had this emotionally devastating confrontation. Sometimes it's hard being the servant of the Lord.

As always, God had a purpose in His actions. The supernatural act of conception within the womb of Mary broke the human connection with sin. Jesus could not say as His father David, "In sin did my mother conceive me" (Psalm 51:5). Hence, the virgin conception of Jesus protected Him from sin when He entered the sinful race of mankind.

> *For we do not have a High Priest who cannot sympathize with our weaknesses, but was in all points tempted as we are, yet without sin. . . . For such a High Priest was fitting for us, who is holy, harmless, undefiled, separate from sinners, and has become higher than the heavens. (Hebrews 4:15; 7:26)*

The virgin birth is, therefore, of great theological significance.

The human experience in the conflict of Mary and Joseph protects the miraculous conception of Jesus from being a myth that develops into a legend that becomes dogma. The virgin conception accounts for a Human without sin. The discord of Mary and Joseph accounts for the truthfulness of Mary's explanation. *She* would not yield! *He* would not yield! Theology is reinforced by practice of life.

God intervenes to bring joy and reconciliation to the couple. In a dream, Mary's explanation is confirmed to Joseph by an angel. I wonder if he looked like Gabriel.

> *Behold an angel of the Lord appeared to him in a dream, saying, "Joseph, son of David, do not be afraid to take to you Mary your wife, for that which is conceived in her is of the Holy Spirit." . . . Then Joseph, being aroused from sleep, did as the angel of the Lord commanded him and took to him his wife, and did not know her till she had brought forth her firstborn Son. And he called His name Jesus (Matthew 1:20, 24-25).*

Mary's long journey home finally ended happily.

4

The Birth of John the Baptist, the Forerunner to the King

Luke 1:57-80

Now Elizabeth's full time came for her to be delivered, and she brought forth a son. . . . And he [Zacharias] asked for a writing tablet, and wrote, saying, "His name is John." So they all marveled. . . . "And you, child, will be called the prophet of the Highest; For you will go before the face of the Lord to prepare His ways, to give knowledge of salvation to His people by the remission of their sins, through the tender mercy of our God, with which the Dayspring from on high has visited us; to give light to those who sit in darkness and the shadow of death, to guide our feet into the way of peace." (Luke 1:57, 63, 76-79)

Jesus Himself gave testimony to the birth of John the Baptist.

"Assuredly, I say to you, among those born of women there has not risen one greater than John the Baptist; but he who is least in the kingdom of heaven is greater than he." (Matthew 11:11)

Being the forerunner to the King elevated John above all people—he was in a category of one. But all who see Christ's millennial kingdom established will occupy a higher place. To be there will be greater than to proclaim its coming. Christ's teachings about John throughout His ministry are complex, but we'll come to that later, as John's life unfolds parallel to the life of Christ. Now, to observe his birth.

The miraculous conception of John resulted in a normal, full-term delivery—after all, he had been filled with the Holy Spirit from his mother's womb. He was equipped for a special task. God, who begins good works, will accomplish them!

The first complication comes as a committee of friends and relatives decide to name him Junior. Will the father, Zacharias, have any say in the matter? He has not been able to contribute anything verbally for nine months. That was about to change in a forceful way. He writes, and then he speaks. He writes, "His name is John." It was more important that his name should point forward to the future King than backward to an old priest. Then he speaks—the priest becomes a prophet. Just as John had been filled with the Holy Spirit from the womb, so now his father, Zacharias, is likewise filled with the Spirit to prophesy. And what a prophecy it is! Notice the content of his prophecy:

> The Lord is the Lord God of Israel.

> He has visited and redeemed His people, Israel.

> Salvation has come through the house of David.

> Deliverance from the world empire, Rome, has come for Israel.

> The Abrahamic Covenant is being fulfilled.

> A holy and righteous kingdom is being offered.

> Salvation and forgiveness of sins are being offered.

In naming the child "John," Zacharias also commissions the eight-day-old forerunner with his message. To understand this commission is to understand the ministry of John and the nature of the kingdom to be offered. Notice, help had come for the nation of Israel through a king from the house of David to deliver Israel from the ruling empire in fulfillment of the Abrahamic Covenant to provide a holy kingdom. Zacharias sounded like his namesake, the prophet of old, when he spoke of that coming kingdom.

> *Thus says the LORD: "I will return to Zion, and dwell in the midst of Jerusalem. Jerusalem shall be called the City of Truth, the Mountain of the LORD of hosts, the Holy Mountain." . . . Thus says the LORD of hosts: "Behold, I will save My people from the land of the east and from the land of the west; I will bring them back, and they shall dwell in the midst of Jerusalem. They shall be My people and I will be their God, in truth and righteousness." (Zechariah 8:3, 7-8)*

The Abrahamic and Davidic Covenants are referenced in the prophecy of Zechariah. The Abrahamic Covenant promised Abraham a people, the land of Israel, and a seed (Genesis 12:1-3). The Davidic Covenant promised David a house (the house of David), a throne, and a kingdom (2 Samuel 7:16). The ministry of John was to prepare the people of Israel for their coming King and the establishment of that literal, earthly kingdom.

If we rush to the end of the story we will hear the nation of Israel say, "We will not have this man to reign over us." They will reject John the Baptist, they will reject Jesus, and they will reject the kingdom. As we have already noted, Jesus will refer to John throughout His ministry. Notice the following comments Jesus made concerning John:

> *"For all the prophets and the law prophesied until John. And if you are willing to receive it, he is Elijah who is to come." (Matthew 11:13-14)*

"Indeed, Elijah is coming first and will restore all things. But I say to you that Elijah has come already, and they did not know him but did to him whatever they wished. Likewise the Son of Man is also about to suffer at their hands." Then the disciples understood that He spoke to them of John the Baptist. (Matthew 17:11-13)

Christ makes the first comment before John's death, and the second after it. Notice the potential nature of John fulfilling his unique role: "If you are willing to receive it . . ." The second quote shows that they did *not* receive it. Potential fulfillment of the role available, but never realized. At least, not yet! This is a spiritual "could've, would've" with eternal consequences. God's gracious plan was being worked out without the parties involved even knowing it. Peter made reference to this as an Old Testament problem.

Of this salvation the prophets have inquired and searched carefully, who prophesied of the grace that would come to you, searching what, or what manner of time, the Spirit of Christ who was in them was indicating when He testified beforehand the sufferings of Christ and the glories that would follow. To them it was revealed that, not to themselves, but to us they were ministering the things which now have been reported to you through those who have preached the gospel to you by the Holy Spirit sent from heaven—things which angels desire to look into. (1 Peter 1:10-12)

Herein is the paradox. The rejections of John and of Christ were as certain as tomorrow's sunrise—more certain. Christ is the Lamb slain before the foundation of the earth! Yet John and Christ go about their ministries with validity and sincerity in the offer of the kingdom. Rejection will come, but glory will follow—in time. Jesus *shall* reign!

Hindsight brings understanding; we comprehend God's providential dealings better *after* the fact. Job and James and Peter and Paul all address the principle of "suffering first, glory later."

For I consider that the sufferings of this present time are not worthy to be compared with the glory which shall be revealed in us. (Romans 8:18)

This principle finds varied but certain applications in the lives of each one of us. We can trust God and experience the peace that passes understanding as we realize that He works all things according to the counsel of His own will (Ephesians 1:11), even those things that we don't understand.

5

The Greatest of All Miracles: The Incarnation (part 1)

Luke 2:1-20

And it came to pass in those days that a decree went out from Caesar Augustus that all the world should be registered. . . . Joseph also went up from Galilee, out of the city of Nazareth, into Judea, to the city of David, which is called Bethlehem, because he was of the house and lineage of David, to be registered with Mary, his betrothed wife, who was with child. (Luke 2:1, 4-5)

God becoming man is the greatest of all miracles! Paul calls it a great mystery in introducing an early hymn of the church.

And without controversy great is the mystery of godliness:
<u>God was manifested in the flesh</u>,
Justified in the Spirit,
Seen by angels,
Preached among the Gentiles,
Believed on in the world,
Received up in glory. (1 Timothy 3:16)

God manifested in the flesh! God with us—Emmanuel. Unto us a Son is given, a child is born. In Him dwells all the fullness of the Godhead bodily. My Lord and my God! Let all the angels of God worship Him. The Word was with God, the Word was God! God and man in one Person. We can define it, we can describe it, we can defend it—this mysterious theology of the God-Man. But we cannot understand it. It calls us to worship.

Once man, it was fitting for Him to suffer, to be tempted, to be rejected, to die. This is the plight of the human condition. If He was going to represent us as our Great High Priest, He must experience humanity—it is a qualification for priesthood; it is becoming, suitable; it is to be expected in being human. But it was not expected that God should become man. That's not fitting! That's not usual. It was totally and uniquely unusual. It was a miracle—the greatest of all miracles, giving birth to all the rest of the miracles in which God intervenes in the affairs of men. Let us draw near in awe as that miracle takes place—the birth of Jesus.

There are a number of players in this great drama: Caesar Augustus, Mary and Joseph, the shepherds, the angels, and the Babe.

The first on stage was Caesar Augustus, Octavian (27 BC - AD 14), the first Roman emperor, an able administrator. As such, he decreed an empire-wide registration to be implemented by regional officials, of whom Quirinius, governor of Syria, was one. This census would take years to conduct, as the entire empire was on the move home.

Caesar was doing what politicians do well—he was taxing the people. But he was doing far more than that—he was fulfilling God's eternal decree. The prophetic clock that led eventually to Triumphal Entry Sunday began ticking with the decree of Artaxerxes. Caesar's decree led to Mary and Joseph relocating to the prophesied city of Bethlehem, the birthplace of the coming Messiah.

Neither Artaxerxes in 445 BC nor Caesar Augustus in 0 BC/AD comprehended the enormity of their acts. The powers-that-be—and their decisions—are ordained of God. The emperors of Persia prepare Jerusalem, the emperors of Greece propagate a language, and the emperors of Rome provide the place of Messiah's birth, the means of the Savior's death, and the roads for the evangelization of the world. The former emperor, Nebuchadnezzar of Babylon, stated it correctly after his conversion:

> "I, Nebuchadnezzar, lifted my eyes to heaven, and my understanding returned to me; and I blessed the Most High and praised and honored Him who lives forever: for His dominion is an everlasting dominion, and His kingdom is from generation to generation. All the inhabitants of the earth are reputed as nothing; He does according to His will in the army of heaven and among the inhabitants of the earth. No one can restrain His hand or say to Him, 'What have You done?'" (Daniel 4:34-35)

> ". . . in order that the living may know that the Most High rules in the kingdom of men, gives it to whomever He will, and sets over it the lowest of men." (Daniel 4:17)

Next on stage were Joseph and Mary. From the highest in the empire, Caesar Augustus, to a poor couple, descendants of King David, but inhabitants of an occupied nation. We join them in a slow journey to their place of origin, Bethlehem of Judea.

> But you, Bethlehem Ephrathah, though you are little among the thousands of Judah, yet out of you shall come forth to Me the One to be Ruler in Israel, whose goings forth are from of old, from everlasting. (Micah 5:2)

Mary and Joseph had already endured heart-breaking emotional stress. Remember Mary's return from visiting Elizabeth four months into her pregnancy. The first steps of divorce were followed by the relief of angelic revelation and subsequent reconciliation of the couple. Now, five months later, by edict of government, the soon-to-be mother struggles along with Joseph in their journey to register at home, at Bethlehem.

Can it get more difficult? Yes! The time for the greatest of miracles has come! Mary is about to give birth. But where? There is no room in the inn, and there's only one inn as Bethlehem is a small town. God, who moved the empires for this moment of history, did not make provision for an elaborate birthing suite. Rather, a barn, a manger, and animals. Deity arrives in a strange place. And no help! It is Mary who gives birth, it is Mary who wraps Him is swaddling clothes, and it is Mary who lays Him in the manger.

What a lowly beginning for the Christ Child. He did not consider the prerogatives of deity a thing to be clutched to Himself, but emptied Himself by being born in a barn and laid on hay in a feeding trough. His emptying will entail far more.

> Let the same mind be in you that was in Christ Jesus, who, being in the form of God, did not consider it robbery to be equal with God, but made Himself of no reputation, taking the form of a bondservant, and coming in the likeness of men. And being found in appearance as a man, He humbled himself and became obedient to the point of death, even the death of the cross. (Philippians 2:5-8)

Paul commands each one of us to have this same attitude as we pattern our lives after the Servant Savior. There is no room for power, pride, or ego as we follow Christ! As He emptied Himself of the *real* prerogatives of deity that He possessed, we must empty ourselves of the *supposed* rights and prerogatives of our humanity in following Him.

> Therefore, when He came into the world, He said: "Sacrifice and offering You did not desire, but a body You have prepared for Me. . . Then I said, 'Behold, I have come to do Your will, O God.'" (Hebrews 10:5, 7)

Servants have very few rights!

6
....

The Greatest of All Miracles:
The Incarnation (part 2)

Luke 2:1-20

Now there were in the same country shepherds living out in the fields, keeping watch over their flock by night. And behold, an angel of the Lord stood before them, and the glory of the Lord shone around them, and they were greatly afraid. . . . And they came with haste and found Mary and Joseph, and the Babe lying in a manger. (Luke 2:8-9, 16)

Perhaps they were the lowest of the shepherds doing night duty watching the sheep. Perhaps they were the owner shepherds guarding the sheep at lambing time. Sheep were necessary for food, for clothing, and for religious ceremony in Israel. Being a shepherd was an honorable profession. It is fitting that shepherds should hear the angelic annunciation. After all, the Lamb of God is about to arrive on the scene, the Good Shepherd who will give His life for the sheep is about to take His first breath of humanity. Thirty-three years later He will breathe His last. The shepherds were faithfully executing the routine of their livelihood, but that routine was soon to be interrupted by an angel, by the manifestation of the glory of God, and by a multitude of angels.

The darkness of night is overwhelmed by the brightness of the glory of God and the appearance of an unnamed angel. Gabriel had been the select angel to Zacharias and to Mary, perhaps here as well to the shepherds. The message of the angel is important, as is his confirming prophecy. Introduced by the common "Do not be afraid" is the glorious message of salvation through the coming Messiah.

> *"For there is born to you this day in the city of David a Savior, who is Christ the Lord." (Luke 2:11)*

As in the previous angelic communications the connection with the nation of Israel is stressed. Gabriel had already said:

- ➤ John will turn many of the sons of Israel to the Lord.
- ➤ John will prepare Israel for the coming of the Lord.

- ➢ Jesus will receive the throne of His father David.
- ➢ Jesus will reign over the house of Jacob.
- ➢ There will be no end to the kingdom.
- ➢ His people will be saved from their sins.

Here, the location of the birth is once again identified as "the city of David." The Davidic Covenant of 2 Samuel 7 is never very far from the life of Christ. This Son of David, unlike those of the connecting lineage, will be the Savior and the Messiah, and very God! If David calls Jesus "Lord," how is He his Son? (Matthew 22:45). The answer? The greatest miracle of all, the Incarnation.

The angel becomes prophetic with a promised sign to confirm the message just delivered. The sign? "Therefore the Lord Himself will give you a sign: Behold, the virgin shall conceive and bear a Son, and shall call His name Immanuel" (Isaiah 7:14). The sign? A Babe wrapped in swaddling clothes in a manger. Whenever did anyone see an event like this? God, in a manger!

The message is confirmed by the sudden appearance of a multitude of angels praising God and speaking of the glory of God and the subsequent peace on earth with the coming of the Messiah-King. Then the angels disappear, darkness returns, and the shepherds rush to see the predicted sign fulfilled. Just as the angel said, they find Mary and Joseph, and the Babe lying in a manger.

The Babe! Sweet, little Jesus boy; they made Him be born in a manger. We do well to bring theology to the manger scene. Contemplate as we gaze on a baby boy in a manger.

> *In the beginning was the Word, and the Word was with God, and the Word was God. He was in the beginning with God. All things were made through Him, and without Him nothing was made that was made. . . . He was in the world, and the world was made through Him, and the world did not know Him. . . . And the Word became flesh and dwelt among us, and we beheld His glory, the glory as of the only begotten of the Father, full of grace and truth. (John 1:1-3, 10, 14)*

> *He is the image of the invisible God, the firstborn over all creation. For by Him all things were created that are in heaven and that are on earth, visible and invisible, whether thrones or dominions or principalities or powers. All things were created through Him and for Him. And He is before all things, and in Him all things consist. . . . For in Him dwells all the fullness of the Godhead bodily. (Colossians 1:15-17; 2:9)*

God . . . has in these last days spoken to us by His Son, whom He has appointed heir of all things, through whom also He made the worlds; who being the brightness of His glory and the express image of His person, and upholding all things by the word of His power, when He had by Himself purged our sins, sat down at the right hand of the Majesty on high. . . . But when He again brings the firstborn into the world, He says: "Let all the angels of God worship Him." (Hebrews 1:2-3, 6)

"I am the Alpha and the Omega, the Beginning and the End," says the Lord, "who is and who was and who is to come, the Almighty. . . . I am the Alpha and the Omega, the First and the Last, Do not be afraid; I am the First and the Last. I am He who lives, and was dead, and behold, I am alive forevermore. Amen." (Revelation 1:8, 11, 17-18)

The person of the incarnate Christ possesses undiminished deity and perfect humanity in one Person forever. We neither divide the Person nor confuse the natures. There is a mysterious communion of attributes working in harmony without conflict: omnipotence and weariness; omnipresence and bodily limitations; omniscience and growing in knowledge; eternality and a birthday; life and death, existing at once in Jesus Christ.

Mary struggled to put all these things together. We ponder as well, and with the shepherds praise and glorify God.

7

Looking for the Messiah— Simeon, Anna, and the Wise Men

Luke 1:21-39; Matthew 2:1-12

And when eight days were completed for the circumcision of the Child, His name was called JESUS, the name given by the angel before He was conceived in the womb. Now when the days of her purification according to the law of Moses were completed, they brought Him to Jerusalem to present Him to the Lord (as it is written in the law of the Lord, "Every male who opens the womb shall be called holy to the LORD"), and to offer a sacrifice according to what is said in the law of the Lord, "A pair of turtledoves or two young pigeons." And behold, there was a man in Jerusalem whose name was Simeon, and this man was just and devout, waiting for the Consolation of Israel, and the Holy Spirit was upon him. And it had been revealed to him by the Holy Spirit that he would not see death before he had seen the Lord's Christ. . . . Now there was one, Anna, a prophetess, the daughter of Phanuel, of the tribe of Asher. She was of a great age, and had lived with a husband seven years from her virginity. . . . And coming in that instant she gave thanks to the Lord, and spoke of Him to all those who looked for redemption in Jerusalem. (Luke 2:21-26, 36, 38)

Now after Jesus was born in Bethlehem of Judea in the days of Herod the king, behold, wise men from the East came to Jerusalem, saying, "Where is He who has been born King of the Jews? For we have seen His star in the East and have come to worship Him." . . . And when they had come into the house, they saw the young Child with Mary His mother, and fell down and worshiped Him. And when they had opened their treasures, they presented gifts to Him: gold, frankincense, and myrrh. (Matthew 2:1-2, 11)

Gabriel had given the name for the Child in his communication to Mary. Joseph had been given the same name by the angel in his dream. In obedience to the commands from heaven mediated by angels, and in obedience to the law of Moses put into effect through angels, the obedient couple presents Him to God. He in whom all of the fullness of the Godhead dwells bodily, although a small body, is presented to God by His servants, Mary His mother and Joseph. Sacrifice is made, the sacrifice of poverty— two young pigeons. Mary, not able to bring a lamb?

> *"This is the law for her who has borne a male or a female. And if she is not able to bring a lamb, then she may bring two turtledoves or two young pigeons—one as a burnt offering and the other as a sin offering. So the priest shall make atonement for her, and she will be clean." (Leviticus 12:7-8)*

Mary brings the Lamb of God that bears away the sin of the world. She brings God's Lamb and presents Him to God. She brings the Lamb slain before the foundation of the world. But she also brings two pigeons.

Simeon, a righteous man, was longing for the restoration of Israel. As Jesus would later say, "Blessed are those who hunger and thirst for righteousness, for they shall be filled." When the kingdom comes, Simeon's longings will be satisfied. The Holy Spirit was upon him. By special revelation of the Holy Spirit, Simeon was told that he would not die until he had seen the Messiah. By the Holy Spirit, Simeon is directed to go to the temple at the exact time Mary and Joseph with Baby Jesus arrive there. Picture Baby Jesus in the arms of godly Simeon. Capture the smile of delight as Simeon gazes on the infant Messiah. Deliverance for Israel is coming because the Messiah has come. It is appropriate that Simeon begins his response with the word *despot*, meaning "Sovereign Lord." God the Holy Spirit had personally intervened in the life of Simeon and brought him to his Messiah. More so, God was intervening in the affairs of all peoples in bringing light to the Gentiles and glory for the nation of Israel—as it will be when Jesus reigns—when the longings of Simeon will be fully satisfied.

Aged Anna the prophetess had chosen a life of extreme piety. Widowed early in her marriage, she gave herself to fasting and prayer, remaining in the temple day and night ever since. She was a widow indeed, worthy of special honor! Anna spoke of the Child in relationship to the capital city of Israel, Jerusalem. With the coming of the Messiah, Jerusalem would be redeemed. And she told all of that glorious time when Jesus will reign.

The wise men from the East endured a very long journey in seeking the Messiah, the King. Natural revelation of God, the stars and His star, brought them to Jerusalem. As Herod summons the scribes (the experts in the law of Moses) special revelation from God gives detailed direction.

> *"But you, Bethlehem Ephrathah, though you are little among the thousands of Judah, yet out of you shall come forth to Me the One to be Ruler in Israel, whose goings forth are from of old, from everlasting." (Micah 5:2)*

Herod sends the wise men to Bethlehem, and the Messiah's star reappears to conclude the journey of the wise men to the King. They find Mary and the Child and they fall down and worship Him. This was the purpose of their long journey—to find and worship the King of the Jews. They bring gifts, appropriate gifts.

"Born a King on Bethlehem's plain: gold I bring to crown Him again."
"Frankincense to offer have I; incense owns a Deity nigh."
"Myrrh is mine; its bitter perfume breathes a life of gathering gloom."

Two dreams follow. The wise men are warned in a dream not to return to Herod and they depart back to the East by another way—no star guidance on the return trip, only obedience to the special revelation of God. They were truly wise men. In a second dream, Joseph is warned by an angel to flee to Egypt, and they flee in the darkness of night.

Herod was troubled, and when Herod was troubled, all Jerusalem was troubled. What's more, that trouble would engulf Bethlehem! Herod saw in Jesus a rival king with a competitive throne—a threat to his kingdom. Herod was the king of the Jews; who was this Jesus who had been born King of the Jews? There was a simple political solution: kill the baby! Kill all the baby boys under two years of age in Bethlehem! Thus began the open opposition and rejection of Jesus that would conclude some thirty years later with the answer of the priests, "We have no king but Caesar." Yet Jesus shall reign.

Simeon, Anna, the wise men, and even Herod saw in the Christ-child the King of the Jews, the Messiah. These responses, combined with the messages of Gabriel, the statements of Mary, and the prophecy of Zechariah all point to a literal, earthly kingdom, the nation of Israel, with Jesus ruling from Jerusalem on the throne of His father David.

Once again, we are reminded of the precision of God's execution of His eternal plan. Faithful Jews, Gentile wise men from the East, antagonistic rulers—all move through life within God's purpose and redemptive plan. The movement of our lives is no less directed by God within that same grand plan:

"And He has made from one blood every nation of men to dwell on all the face of the earth, and has determined their preappointed times and the boundaries of their dwellings, so that they should seek the Lord, in the hope that they might grope for Him and find Him, though He is not far from each one of us." (Acts 17:26-27)

8

The Childhood of Jesus

Matthew 2:19-23; Luke 2:40-52

An angel of the Lord appeared to Joseph in a dream saying, "Arise, take the young Child and His mother, and go to the land of Israel, for those who sought the young Child's life are dead." . . . And he came and dwelt in a city called Nazareth that it might be fulfilled which was spoken by the prophets, "He shall be called a Nazarene." (Matthew 2:20, 23)

His [Jesus'] parents went to Jerusalem every year at the Feast of the Passover. And when He was twelve years old, they went up to Jerusalem according to the custom of the feast. . . . After three days they found Him in the temple, sitting in the midst of the teachers, both listening to them and asking them questions. And all who heard Him were astonished at His understanding and answers. So when they saw Him, they were amazed; and His mother said to Him, "Son, why have You done this to us? Look, your father and I have sought you anxiously." And He said to them, "Why did you seek Me? Did you not know that I must be about My Father's business?" (Luke 2:41-42, 46-49)

Then He went down with them and came to Nazareth, and was subject to them, but His mother kept all these things in her heart. And Jesus increased in wisdom and stature, and in favor with God and men. (Luke 2:51-52)

A hasty flight to Egypt, a return to Israel and Nazareth, a visit to Jerusalem at Passover, and return to Nazareth—these comprise the scant biblical account of a few events in the childhood of Jesus. We can also surmise from Scripture that other children were born into the family:

After this He went down to Capernaum, He, His mother, His brothers, and His disciples; and they did not stay there many days. . . . Now the Jews' Feast of Tabernacles was at hand. His brothers therefore said to Him, "Depart from here and go into Judea, that Your disciples also may see the works that You are doing.". . . For even His brothers did not believe in Him. (John 2:12; 7:2-3, 5)

We know two brothers by name; they wrote the epistles named after them, James and Jude. They were not believers during the Lord's life on earth. Strange!

Following the temple account before us, Joseph disappears from the pages of Scripture. He is not at the cross when Jesus entrusts His mother Mary to John—an act hardly fitting if her husband was still alive. There was no doubt a time when Jesus was the "head of the home" in Nazareth. But back to our story of this little family.

God's favorite way of communicating to Joseph was in dreams, four of them in total.

An angel had appeared in a dream warning him to flee to Egypt. Now he appears in a dream and instructs him to return to Israel. And then he is warned in a fourth dream to go to Galilee. The current ruler in Judah is Archelaus, a man much like his father, Herod the Great. So Mary, Joseph, and Jesus return home to Nazareth, a humble town in Galilee. The Son of God would be ridiculed by being called a Nazarene. In Nazareth the baby Jesus grew physically, developed mentally, and found favor with God. The same summary statement occurs at His baptism, ". . . with whom I am well pleased."

The holy calendar of Israel provided for a number of days of celebration in Jerusalem. Faithful Jews would travel up to the Holy City from all points in the nation, family and friends going up by custom and tradition, thus fulfilling the law. The journey would be on foot, traveling in groups from the scattered towns and villages. Join up with the small group from Nazareth, who are no doubt singing from the Psalms of Ascent, Psalms 120 to 134.

> *I was glad when they said to me, "Let us go into the house of the LORD."*
> *Our feet have been standing within your gates, O Jerusalem!*
>
> *Pray for the peace of Jerusalem: may they prosper who love you.*
> *Peace be within your walls, prosperity within your palaces. For*
> *the sake of my brethren and companions, I will now say, "Peace be*
> *within you." Because of the house of the LORD our God I will seek*
> *your good. (Psalm 122:1-2, 6-9)*

Jesus is now twelve years of age. It is the year prior to the one when, according to Jewish tradition, a boy becomes personally responsible for his own religious commitments. Jesus is ahead of schedule—an eternity ahead of schedule. In fact, He *made* the schedule! The Feast of Passover is concluded and the traveling village folk return home—minus one. Mother and father assume that Jesus is with the crowd of relatives and friends—after all, they are in the habit of taking care of one another. "Have you seen Jesus?" "No." "Have *you?*" "No." A frantic search, followed by a return to Jerusalem by Mary and Joseph. I doubt they were singing this time!

After three days they find Him in the temple—with the teachers, asking and answering questions. Amazing! Earlier we read that "He was filled with wisdom." At the conclusion of this segment we will read, "He increased in wisdom."

Clearly aware of His messianic role, the unfettered intellect of the boy Jesus was a source of astonishment to all.

The confrontation! "Son, why have You done this to us?" It seems such an irresponsible act. Jesus habitually did the right thing; He knew better. "Your father and I have been looking for You anxiously." Don't get upset with Mary for calling Joseph Jesus' father. Mary understood the theology of the virgin birth better than anybody. It was a natural accommodation to living as a family. But it was more than that at this point. It was the lead into the "father debate"—a debate that would become even stronger in coming days. Mary says, "Your father . . ."; Jesus says, "My Father." The religious commitment of Jesus was being demonstrated as He moves from submission to His earthly parents into submission to His Father's things, here in His Father's house, the temple! The parents did not understand, but Jesus did!

The return trip to Nazareth was resumed, and the lesson for life is obvious.

Then He went down with them and came to Nazareth, and was subject to them, but His mother kept all these things in her heart. (Luke 2:51)

He was obedient to them! The perfect child, obedient to imperfect parents. In this single recorded incident in the childhood of Jesus, the single lesson that children must learn is obvious—submission, obedience to a higher authority. It is the lesson for childhood. Children now, as in the life of Jesus, are taught this by godly parents.

Children, obey your parents in the Lord, for this is right. "Honor your father and mother," which is the first commandment with promise: "that it may be well with you and you may live long on the earth." (Ephesians 6:1-3)

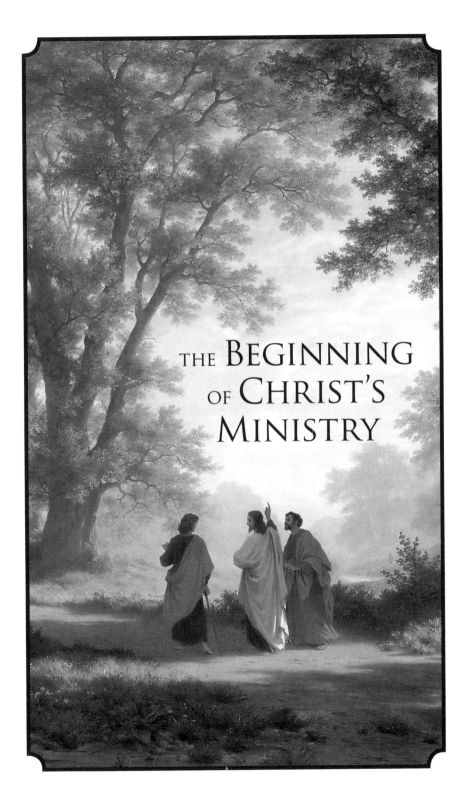

THE BEGINNING OF CHRIST'S MINISTRY

9

John, the Voice Crying in the Wilderness

Matthew 3:1-12; Mark 1:2-8; Luke 3:1-18

Now in the fifteenth year of the reign of Tiberius Caesar, Pontius Pilate being governor of Judea, Herod being tetrarch of Galilee, his brother Philip tetrarch of Iturea and the region of Trachonitis, and Lysanias tetrarch of Abilene, while Annas and Caiaphas were high priests, the word of God came to John the son of Zacharias in the wilderness. (Luke 3:1-2)

In those days John the Baptist came preaching in the wilderness of Judea, and saying, "Repent, for the kingdom of heaven is at hand!" . . . Then Jerusalem, all Judea, and all the region around the Jordan went out to him and were baptized by him in the Jordan, confessing their sins. But when he saw many of the Pharisees and Sadducees coming to his baptism, he said to them, "Brood of vipers! Who warned you to flee from the wrath to come? Therefore bear fruits worthy of repentance, and do not think to say to yourselves, 'We have Abraham as our father.' For I say to you that God is able to raise up children to Abraham from these stones. And even now the ax is laid to the root of the trees. Therefore every tree which does not bear good fruit is cut down and thrown into the fire." (Matthew 3:1-2, 5-10)

So the people asked him, saying, "What shall we do then?" . . . Then tax collectors also came to be baptized, and said to him, "Teacher, what shall we do?" . . . Likewise the soldiers asked him, saying, "And what shall we do?" (Luke 3:10, 12, 14)

We turn the page of the Gospels and we rush into the beginning of the public ministries of John the Baptist and of Jesus. Both of them are about thirty years old. Luke, the precise historian of the gospel accounts, gives us the political and religious hierarchy, the names that will become commonplace: Pontius Pilate, Herod Antipas of Galilee, Jewish priests Annas and Caiaphas. He mentions the multitudes, the tax collectors, and the soldiers as well. Matthew introduces the Jewish religious groups of the Pharisees and the Sadducees. Later we will meet the Zealots and the Herodians.

The scene is set. An Elijah-like figure, John the Baptist emerges from his hermit wilderness home. Strange dress and strange diet attract attention. But the message and the method bring all Jerusalem and Judea to the River Jordan. The message was, "Repent, for the kingdom is at hand!" That same kingdom of the birth annunciations is at hand—the King of Israel, David's greater Son, Jesus, had come to reign. The method connected with the message—a strange new thing, a way of public identification and acceptance of the message—a baptism of repentance. After all, he was John the Baptizer. Prophecy is being fulfilled!

> *The voice of one crying in the wilderness: "Prepare the way of the LORD; make straight in the desert, a highway for our God. Every valley shall be exalted, and every mountain and hill brought low; the crooked places shall be made straight and the rough places smooth; the glory of the LORD shall be revealed, and all flesh shall see it together; for the mouth of the LORD has spoken." (Isaiah 40:3-5)*

> *"Behold, I send My messenger, And he will prepare the way before Me. And the Lord, whom you seek, will suddenly come to His temple, even the Messenger of the covenant, in whom you delight. Behold, He is coming," says the LORD of hosts. ". . . Behold, I will send you Elijah the prophet before the coming of the great and dreadful day of the LORD. And he will turn the hearts of the fathers to the children, and the hearts of the children to their fathers, lest I come and strike the earth with a curse." (Malachi 3:1; 4:5-6)*

Prophecy is being fulfilled. Or is it? Remember, Jesus will say, ". . . If you are willing to accept it, he is Elijah who is to come" (Matthew 11:14). Read carefully the prophecies recounted above and the conclusions predicted remain unfulfilled—the Covenant was *not* established, the temple was *not* entered, and the glory of the Lord was *not* revealed. "If" is an important word!

The "if" is conditional: "If you are willing to accept it. . ." The Pharisees and Sadducees come, the orthodox and the liberal, that mixed body of the Sanhedrin. This is official Judaism coming out of curiosity to keep up with the religious rumblings in *their* nation. There is no repentance! The Baptist responds in hermit boldness, "You brood of vipers!" To them, their lineage as sons of Abraham is their deliverance. John confronts them with their faulty presumption, states that the stones could become sons of Abraham if God desired, and threatens them with coming judgment. They and the nation will be cut down as with the swing of an ax. And so it will be with the coming of the Roman armies under Titus! "If?"

Luke identifies another group made up of the multitudes, tax collectors, and soldiers. Upon hearing the message of repentance, each group asks,

"What shall we do?" It is a question that arises out of conviction of sin, and John identifies the reality of conviction and conversion—fruit worthy of repentance. John speaks with Sermon-on-the-Mount expressions before the Sermon on the Mount is given. It must run in the family!

> He answered and said to them, "He who has two tunics, let him give to him who has none; and he who has food, let him do likewise." . . . And he said to them, "Collect no more than what is appointed for you." Likewise the soldiers asked him, saying, "And what shall we do?" So he said to them, "Do not intimidate anyone or accuse falsely, and be content with your wages." (Luke 3:11, 13-14)

Two groups—the religious leadership and the people—with different responses to John's message of repentance. In time both would say the same thing: "We will not have this man to reign over us."

John's message was so messianic that some thought John was the Messiah. This problem of faulty interpretation would persist so that Jesus would later say,

> "Who do men say that I, the Son of Man, am?" So they said, "Some say John the Baptist, some Elijah, and others Jeremiah or one of the prophets." (Matthew 16:13-14)

To John, however, his role was clear. He was the forerunner to the Messiah. He confesses that he is not worthy to carry or untie His sandals. Later he will say, "He must increase, but I must decrease." Later still he will be beheaded!

John the Baptist introduces yet another important truth. He initiates water baptism, nowhere found in the Old Testament. Yes, there were the ceremonial washings and baths, but not baptism (which means "immersion"). In addition to introducing water baptism, John is the first to identify that other baptism— the baptism of the Holy Spirit. Here, at the beginning of the preaching of the kingdom message, a ministry of the Holy Spirit uniquely linked to the church is introduced by the Baptizer. This is a clear reference to the events of the day of Pentecost recorded in Acts 1 and 2, which were unknown to John! The offer and rejection of the kingdom are often in strange juxtaposition.

The life of John the Baptist shouts out the life lesson for all of us: each person has a role to play for the glory of God.

> But to each one of us grace was given according to the measure of Christ's gift. Therefore He says: "When He ascended on high, He led captivity captive, and gave gifts to men" . . . . For the equipping of the saints for the work of ministry, for the edifying of the body of Christ, till we all come to the unity of the faith and of the knowledge of the Son of God, to a perfect man, to the measure of the stature of the fullness of Christ. (Ephesians 4:7-8, 12-13)

10
:

The Baptism of Jesus, and the
Inauguration of His Ministry

Matthew 3:13-17; Mark 1:9-11; Luke 3:21-23

Then Jesus came from Galilee to John at the Jordan to be baptized
by him. And John tried to prevent Him, saying, "I need to be baptized
by You, and are You coming to me?" But Jesus answered and said to
him, "Permit it to be so now, for thus it is fitting for us to fulfill all
righteousness." Then he allowed Him. When He had been baptized,
Jesus came up immediately from the water; and behold, the heavens
were opened to Him, and He saw the Spirit of God descending
like a dove and alighting upon Him. And suddenly a voice came
from heaven, saying, "This is My beloved Son, in whom I am well
pleased." (Matthew 3:13-17)

We last saw Jesus when He was twelve, in His Father's house and about
His Father's business. We saw Him go home to Nazareth and be
subject to His father Joseph and His mother Mary, and go about the business
of being a carpenter. That was eighteen years ago. Luke tells us that He was
about thirty years of age when He began His ministry. Out of the shadows of
a small town in Galilee, Nazareth, Jesus steps into the spotlight of religious
activity. All of Jerusalem and Judea were going out to be baptized by John
in the Jordan River. Now Jesus comes from Galilee to be baptized by him as
well!

It was an awkward moment for John. How could Jesus be baptized with a
baptism of repentance—He who knew no sin! But Jesus was identifying with
the message and movement of John in bringing the nation to repentance and
the Messiah to the nation. Thus it was fitting that He who would provide both
individual and national righteousness should be identified with that message
by baptism. And John consents.

If you would see the Trinity act at once in unity, go to the Jordan! The Son
is there, baptized and praying. The Holy Spirit is there in bodily form,
descending like a dove and alighting on Him. The Father is there in the voice
from heaven, speaking. Three years later that same unity of action was seen
when salvation was secured.

... How much more shall the blood of Christ, who through the eternal Spirit offered Himself without spot to God, cleanse your conscience from dead works to serve the living God? (Hebrews 9:14)

The message of the Father is significant. The surface meaning is an evaluation of the eighteen years of silence. The statement conveys the perfections of Jesus as a teenager, as a workman, as a son and brother, as an oldest son in His role as head of the home. God was well pleased—an eloquent testimony to years without written record.

But there is deeper meaning! Two Old Testament passages are referred to by the Voice from heaven:

"I will declare the decree: The LORD has said to Me, 'You are My Son, today I have begotten You. Ask of Me, and I will give You the nations for Your inheritance, and the ends of the earth for Your possession. You shall break them with a rod of iron; You shall dash them to pieces like a potter's vessel.'" (Psalm 2:7-9)

"Behold! My Servant whom I uphold, My Elect One in whom My soul delights! I have put My Spirit upon Him; He will bring forth justice to the Gentiles. He will not cry out, nor raise His voice, nor cause His voice to be heard in the street. A bruised reed He will not break, and smoking flax He will not quench; He will bring forth justice for truth. He will not fail nor be discouraged, till He has established justice in the earth; and the coastlands shall wait for His law." (Isaiah 42:1-4)

Matthew records the Voice from the perspective of the observers, "This is My Son . . ."; Mark and Luke do so from the perspective of Jesus, "You are My Son . . ." Psalm 2 is being referred to as the Father speaks to the Son. Psalm 2 is a poetic setting of 2 Samuel 7, in which the Davidic Covenant is established promising David an eternal house and throne and kingdom. Mary heard of that same Covenant from the angel Gabriel. Zacharias referred to the Covenant when his tongue was loosed. The many Bethlehem references relate to the city of David, who was the first of the kingly line of the Messiah. Here at the beginning of His public ministry, the Father identifies Jesus as His only begotten Son as well as the Son of David who would inherit the throne. All He needs to do is ask! He is the King!

The second reference made by the Voice from heaven is found in Isaiah 42. This is the first of the Servant Songs in Isaiah. In this setting the Servant is the *elect* or *beloved* One. He is the object of delight of the Father's soul. He receives the Spirit from the Father. His servant-like ministry is described. The passage from Isaiah finds fulfillment in the baptism of Jesus.

The Servant Songs in Isaiah also include Isaiah chapters 52 and 53.

> *Behold, My Servant shall deal prudently; He shall be exalted and extolled and be very high. Just as many were astonished at you, so His visage was marred more than any man, and His form more than the sons of men. . . . All we like sheep have gone astray; we have turned, every one, to his own way; and the LORD has laid on Him the iniquity of us all. (Isaiah 52:13-14; 53:6)*

The servanthood of Jesus will lead Him to the cross, where He will "pour out His soul unto death." He is the Servant of Jehovah.

At the beginning of His public ministry, at the baptism, Jesus is reminded by the Father of His dual role: He is both King and Servant. He must be the Suffering Servant before He can be the Ruling King. The baptism of Jesus brings the divine approval of heaven to the Person and ministry of Jesus, the King!

Just as Jesus identified with the movement and message of John through His baptism, Christians identify with Jesus through baptism in the name of the Father, and the Son, and the Holy Spirit. Jesus commanded this after He was raised out from among the dead. This baptism acknowledges that we have died with Christ and have been raised with Him to walk in newness of life, which is the servant-like life of Jesus Christ. Jesus will address His disciples in this way in a few years in the Upper Room:

> *"Do you know what I have done to you? You call me Teacher and Lord, and you say well, for so I am. If I then, your Lord and Teacher, have washed your feet, you also ought to wash one another's feet. For I have given you an example, that you should do as I have done to you. Most assuredly, I say to you, <u>a servant is not greater than his master</u>; nor is he who is sent greater than he who sent him. If you know these things, blessed are you if you do them." (John 13:12-17)*

11

The Temptation of Jesus

Matthew 4:1-11; Mark 1:12, 13; Luke 4:1-13

Then Jesus was led up by the Spirit into the wilderness to be tempted by the devil. And when He had fasted forty days and forty nights, afterward He was hungry. Now when the tempter came to Him, he said, "If You are the Son of God, command that these stones become bread." But He answered and said, "It is written, 'Man shall not live by bread alone, but by every word that proceeds from the mouth of God.'" Then the devil took Him up into the holy city, set Him on the pinnacle of the temple, and said to Him, "If You are the Son of God, throw Yourself down. For it is written: 'He shall give His angels charge over you,' and, 'In their hands they shall bear you up, lest you dash your foot against a stone.'" Jesus said to him, "It is written again, 'You shall not tempt the LORD your God.'" Again, the devil took Him up on an exceedingly high mountain, and showed Him all the kingdoms of the world and their glory. And he said to Him, "All these things I will give You if You will fall down and worship me." Then Jesus said to him, "Away with you, Satan! For it is written, 'You shall worship the LORD your God, and Him only you shall serve.'" Then the devil left Him, and behold, angels came and ministered to Him. (Matthew 4:1-11)

Temptation immediately follows the baptism. Jesus is directed by the Holy Spirit into the wilderness to be tempted by the devil. Matthew and Luke say the Holy Spirit "led" Him; Mark says He "drove" Him. Surely Jesus was recalling His own experience when He taught His disciples to pray:

". . . and do not lead us into temptation, but deliver us from the evil one . . ." (Matthew 6:13)

The baptism shows the approval of the Father that His Son should be King. The temptation demonstrates that He is morally qualified to be the King. Luke tells us that the temptation lasted for forty days. He also states at the end of the account that additional unrecorded temptations would follow. One other *is* recorded—Gethsemane! The temptation before us today is the climax of the forty days of temptation. For forty days Jesus fasted, by which time He was, understandably, very hungry.

Satan had been an observer at the baptism, where he had heard the Voice from heaven, witnessed the descent of the Dove, and seen the King. "You are My Son. Ask, and I will give you the nations for Your inheritance." Satan devises a way for Jesus to gain the inheritance of the nations without being the Suffering Servant. This would be the third and final thrust in his temptation strategy.

In the first temptation, Satan does not doubt the deity of Christ—he challenges it. Satan does not deny the deity of Christ—only His followers do.

> Now when the tempter came to Him, he said, "If You are the Son of God, command that these stones become bread."

If as John stated, "God is able to raise up children to Abraham from these stones" (Matthew 3:9), it would be no challenge for the Son of God to turn a few stones into simple bread—no challenge at all! Jesus, in His forty days of temptation, in own His personal wilderness, was no doubt thinking of the forty days that Moses and Israel spent at Sinai and the forty years of wilderness wanderings when the nation of Israel was tested by God. All of His quotations come from that Old Testament setting. Israel failed the test of faith! They did not learn from the regular and repeated provision of manna to trust God in the wilderness. They would have made it to the land if they had believed. Jesus would not repeat that failure by taking things into His own hands and acting in His own will. He would trust His situation of life into the hands of His Father, the One who had given instruction to the Holy Spirit to lead Him into the wilderness to be tempted by the devil. He responds,

> "It is written, 'Man shall not live by bread alone, but by every word that proceeds from the mouth of God.'"

In the second temptation, Satan advances his argument based on Jesus' response. Jesus avows His faith in God, that He is trusting God for His wilderness situation, for His lack of food, for the very attack of Satan. The devil takes Him to a pinnacle of the temple in the Holy City and challenges that faith to action:

> And he said to Him, "If You are the Son of God, throw Yourself down. For it is written: 'He shall give His angels charge over you,' and, 'In their hands they shall bear you up, lest you dash your foot against a stone.'"

Again, Jesus responds from Israel's history. The story is the Rock and Water event, when Moses contended with Israel because they were thirsty. Moses smote the rock and water was provided. God's complaint against Israel was that they questioned His presence—"Is the Lord among us or not?" Moses countered with, "Why do you tempt the Lord?" Just as Jesus would not take things into His own hands by turning stones into bread, He would not as an act of faith thrust Himself onto God's hands for a promised deliverance. He would not ask for a miraculous display of God's presence. So He responds,

"It is written again, 'You shall not tempt the LORD your God.'"

Now, the final phase of the devil's strategy.

Again, the devil took Him up on an exceedingly high mountain, and showed Him all the kingdoms of the world and their glory. And he said to Him, "All these things I will give You if You will fall down and worship me."

Receive Your inheritance of all of the nations and the associated glory without being the Servant, without the cross, without bearing the iniquities of all! Could Satan make such an offer? Notice Luke's addition:

And the devil said to Him, "All this authority I will give You, and their glory; for this has been delivered to me, and I give it to whomever I wish. Therefore, if You will worship before me, all will be Yours." (Luke 4:6-7)

Jesus would not yield. The path to the kingdom would be through the cross! And to think that God would worship the creature—what theological insanity! But this is the quest of Satan and his great lie, that the creature *is* God. With the command of Deity and the authoritative quotation of Scripture, Satan is dismissed:

"Away with you, Satan! For it is written, 'You shall worship the LORD your God, and Him only you shall serve."

The King has demonstrated His moral qualifications for the kingdom and His determination to be pleasing to the Father by being the Suffering Servant.

Jesus gives us the guidelines for overcoming the temptations of the devil and his hosts in everyday life. We must understand that the settings of temptations are not outside the purposes of God, and that the contextual understanding and obedient application of the Word of God will insure deliverance from any temptation. In addition,

We do not have a High Priest who cannot sympathize with our weaknesses, but was in all points tempted as we are, yet without sin. Let us therefore come boldly to the throne of grace that we may obtain mercy and find grace to help in time of need. (Hebrews 4:15-16)

12

• • •

Disciples of John
Become Disciples of Jesus

John 1:19-51

Now this is the testimony of John, when the Jews sent priests and Levites from Jerusalem to ask him, "Who are you?" He confessed, and did not deny, but confessed, "I am not the Christ." And they asked him, "What then? Are you Elijah?" He said, "I am not." "Are you the Prophet?" And he answered, "No." Then they said to him, "Who are you, that we may give an answer to those who sent us? What do you say about yourself?" He said: "I am 'The voice of one crying in the wilderness: "Make straight the way of the LORD,"' as the prophet Isaiah said." . . . The next day John saw Jesus coming toward him, and said, "Behold! The Lamb of God who takes away the sin of the world!" . . . "And I have seen and testified that this is the Son of God." Again, the next day, John stood with two of his disciples. And looking at Jesus as He walked, he said, "Behold the Lamb of God!" The two disciples heard him speak, and they followed Jesus. . . . One of the two who heard John speak, and followed Him, was Andrew, Simon Peter's brother. He first found his own brother Simon, and said to him, "We have found the Messiah" (which is translated, the Christ). And he brought him to Jesus. Now when Jesus looked at him, He said, "You are Simon the son of Jonah. You shall be called Cephas" (which is translated, A Stone). The following day Jesus wanted to go to Galilee, and He found Philip and said to him, "Follow Me." Now Philip was from Bethsaida, the city of Andrew and Peter. Philip found Nathanael and said to him, "We have found Him of whom Moses in the law, and also the prophets, wrote—Jesus of Nazareth, the son of Joseph." And Nathanael said to him, "Can anything good come out of Nazareth?" Philip said to him, "Come and see." (John 1:19-23, 29, 34-37, 43-46)

John the Baptist was aware of his role: he was to prepare the way for the Messiah. By the nature of his task, his role was transitional, and that transition was about to take place. The baptism of Jesus becomes a decisive refocusing of attention from John to Jesus. The Sanhedrin inquires of John as to his own identity. And his response to their questions? "I am not the Christ . . . I am not Elijah . . . I am not the prophet . . . I am a voice . . . ." The next day he directs attention to the One who is the reason for his ministry—the Lamb of God, the Passover Lamb who would bear away the sin of the world. John refers back to the baptism of Jesus and testifies of his growth in grace in reference to Jesus. While he understood his role well, he came to understand who Jesus was in an increasing way.

> "After me comes a Man who is preferred before me, for He was before me. I did not know Him; but that He should be revealed to Israel, therefore I came baptizing with water. I did not know Him, but He who sent me to baptize with water said to me, 'Upon whom you see the Spirit descending, and remaining on Him, this is He who baptizes with the Holy Spirit.' And I have seen and testified that this is the Son of God." (John 1:29-34)

John's extended hermit-like existence accounts for not knowing Jesus personally. It also insures the identification of Jesus at the baptism to be of heavenly origin involving Father, Son, and Holy Spirit, and not a product of a conspiracy of relatives. This is similar to the delay in communicating to Joseph concerning the virgin birth.

John came to understand the humanity of his relative, Jesus, and the deity of this One who was before him in rank and time. Only those of miraculous birth could enter into this depth of spiritual experience concerning the incarnation.

There are three movements as some of John's disciples become disciples of Jesus.

In the first movement, John again states, "Behold, the Lamb of God." Two disciples follow Jesus and inquire as to His place of abode. Jesus invites them to come and stay with Him, and they do! Andrew is one of them—the Andrew who can find helpers like the boy with the lunch of bread and fish.

In the second movement, Andrew, in character, goes for help—for his brother Simon. He does this first. Introducing Simon to the Messiah is important! At that first meeting, Jesus gives Simon a new name—Peter, Rock. That choice of name will be clearer at Peter's confession of Christ, and Paul will expand on this concept in his epistles.

> "And I also say to you that you are Peter, and on this rock I will build My church, and the gates of Hades shall not prevail against it." . . . Having been built on the foundation of the apostles and prophets, Jesus Christ Himself being the chief cornerstone . . . (Matthew 16:18; Ephesians 2:20)

Peter becomes the spokesman for the apostles, the initial preacher at the inception of the church, the first contact with the Roman centurion Cornelius (thus bringing the church to the Gentile world), and an author of Scripture. He follows Christ in crucifixion! Andrew first finds Simon. It was important!

In the third movement, Jesus decides to go to Galilee, no doubt as a result of a wedding invitation that included His family. Jesus was sociable! Jesus summons Philip, and Philip searches out Nathanael with amazing news: the writings of Moses and the Prophets have been fulfilled in the coming of Jesus of Nazareth, son of Joseph! Nathanael scoffs at lowly Nazareth being the source of any good thing. Nathanael speaks his mind without hesitancy. This characteristic is identified when he meets Jesus: "Behold, an Israelite indeed, in whom is no deceit!" Without guile, Nathanael questions the ability of Jesus to know his character having never met him. But Jesus had been with him that day when he was having devotions under the fig tree. Upon this demonstration of deity—omniscience—Nathanael, without guile, speaks his mind:

> "Rabbi, You are the Son of God! You are the King of Israel!" (John 1:49)

Jesus responds by referring to an even greater revelation of God seen by Jacob in a dream, to be fulfilled when the Abrahamic Covenant is fulfilled in the kingdom.

> "Most assuredly, I say to you, hereafter you shall see heaven open, and the angels of God ascending and descending upon the Son of Man." (John 1:51)

> Then he dreamed, and behold, a ladder was set up on the earth, and its top reached to heaven; and there the angels of God were ascending and descending on it. And behold, the LORD stood above it and said: "I am the LORD God of Abraham your father and the God of Isaac; the land on which you lie I will give to you and your descendants. Also your descendants shall be as the dust of the earth; you shall spread abroad to the west and the east, to the north and the south; and in you and in your seed all the families of the earth shall be blessed. (Genesis 28:12-14)

> "In that day," says the LORD of hosts, "Everyone will invite his neighbor under his vine and under his fig tree." (Zechariah 3:10)

Perhaps these were the passages being considered by Nathanael in his devotions under the fig tree. John's disciples—John (unnamed here) and Andrew—are becoming the disciples of Jesus, as are Peter, Philip, and Nathanael. More will follow!

In His Great Commission recorded in Matthew 28:19, Jesus commands His followers to make disciples in all the nations. They are to become disciples of Jesus Christ. Paul exhorted *his* "disciples" by saying, "Imitate me, just as I also imitate Christ" (1 Corinthians 11:1). Like John the Baptist we are to point to Another and not draw attention to ourselves. He must increase, but I must decrease. It is difficult to glorify self and God at the same time!

13

:
:
•

New Wine at Cana, and
a New Home at Capernaum

John 2:1-12

*On the third day there was a wedding in Cana of Galilee, and the
mother of Jesus was there. Now both Jesus and His disciples were
invited to the wedding. And when they ran out of wine, the mother of
Jesus said to Him, "They have no wine." Jesus said to her, "Woman,
what does your concern have to do with Me? My hour has not yet
come." His mother said to the servants, "Whatever He says to you,
do it." Now there were set there six waterpots of stone, according to
the manner of purification of the Jews, containing twenty or thirty
gallons apiece. Jesus said to them, "Fill the waterpots with water."
And they filled them up to the brim. And He said to them, "Draw
some out now, and take it to the master of the feast." And they took
it. When the master of the feast had tasted the water that was made
wine, and did not know where it came from (but the servants who had
drawn the water knew), the master of the feast called the bridegroom.
And he said to him, "Every man at the beginning sets out the good
wine, and when the guests have well drunk, then the inferior. You
have kept the good wine until now!" This beginning of signs Jesus
did in Cana of Galilee, and manifested His glory; and His disciples
believed in Him. After this He went down to Capernaum, He, His
mother, His brothers, and His disciples; and they did not stay there
many days. (John 2:1-12)*

Jesus had returned to Galilee, no doubt to attend the wedding at Cana, a
neighboring town to Nazareth. It could have involved relatives. Perhaps
Mary was on the serving committee; it seems she had some responsible
connection to the refreshments. The weddings in that day were of extended
duration with specific customs as to timing of events, presentation of gifts,
participation of attendants, and the provision of food and drink. And the wine
fails! An embarrassment to the host and an insult to the guests! But Jesus is
there, and Mary seeks His help.

As in the temple confrontation at twelve, so here: Jesus is about His Father's business on His Father's schedule. Mary was aware of the recent events in the life of Christ—the baptism, the temptation. It was apparent that He was about to begin a public ministry. Perhaps this wedding crisis would present an opportunity to "go public" in Galilee. The verbal exchanges are short and obviously edited, but the sense is clear.

> *The mother of Jesus said to Him, "They have no wine." Jesus said to her, "Woman, what does your concern have to do with Me? My hour has not yet come." (John 2:3-4)*

Mary was looking for some kind of help, but receives a gentle rebuke. Maybe she was thinking of the incident in the temple when He was twelve. Now that Jesus was to begin His public ministry it was appropriate that His relationship with Mary would be less family oriented. He would later say when His family was near:

> *Then His mother and brothers came to Him, and could not approach Him because of the crowd. And it was told Him by some, who said, "Your mother and Your brothers are standing outside, desiring to see You." But He answered and said to them, "My mother and My brothers are these who hear the word of God and do it." (Luke 8:19-21)*

His address to Mary—"woman"—seems harsh to our sensitive ears, but it was not then, and neither was it at the cross when He entrusted Mary to John, the beloved disciple. True, an address to a mother would usually be more personal, but a different relationship is being established as Jesus breaks into His Father's business in a public way.

He is on His Father's schedule, and He says, "My hour has not yet come." That hour scheduled in a past eternity was still future. It was not at twelve years of age; it is not here in Cana; it will not be later in His Judean ministry when He repeats the same thought. On Tuesday of Passion Week He will say, "My hour has come."

The miracle that Jesus performs to relieve embarrassment and insult is of great theological importance. It also produces a great wedding celebration. Jesus is a social person and His miracles usually produce happiness. With a mother's twinkle in her eye, Mary tells the servants to do whatever Jesus says. That's still good advice! She knew that He would do something, but she knew not what. Six ceremonial urns were at hand, of twenty to thirty gallon capacity each—perhaps 150 gallons of water all told, soon to be the best wine the earth has ever witnessed. When Jesus turned the water into wine He demonstrated His deity. He is *Lord of creation*—He created the earth, the water, the vines, the grapes, and now the wine out of water. He is also the *Lord of time.* Wine takes time. This wine was seconds old and the best of wine!

Only the servants understood what Jesus had done. They participated in the miracle and were instruments for the glory of God. They filled the water-pots to the very brim. They did all that they could do in obeying Jesus. I wonder if any of the water that spilled over the top of the pots was turned to droplets of wine. Servants understand what Jesus does! This first sign was done in Cana, and His disciples believed in Him. Their faith was a growing one.

Jesus, Mary, and the family return from Cana to Nazareth for a short while. We see them next in Capernaum.

> *After this He went down to Capernaum, He, His mother, His brothers, and His disciples; and they did not stay there many days. (John 2:12)*

Capernaum will become the base of operation for the first phase of the public ministry of Christ—the Galilean Ministry. Many trips will be made throughout Galilee for evangelization, and to Jerusalem and back for worship. Capernaum will become "home" for Jesus. The crowds will say, "He is at home" (Mark 2:1). The little company from Nazareth came with all of the earthly belongings of Jesus to set up home in Capernaum. Perhaps they took out a short lease on an apartment.

Jesus had many addresses on earth. For two years or so He was in Bethlehem; then in Egypt; then in Nazareth for an extended time; then in Capernaum for the Galilean ministry; then in Bethany of Judea for the Judean and Perean ministries and Passion Week.

The wedding at Cana was a joyful experience for all, thanks to the first miracle of the Messiah. By the end of the Galilean ministry, life will not be so joyful.

There are many lessons for life from this segment of the Lord's life:

> ➤ Jesus celebrates at joyful events with other celebrants.
> ➤ Heavenly relationships are higher than family relationships.
> ➤ Jesus is Lord of creation and Lord of time.
> ➤ The timing of the events of life—the hour—is part of God's plan.

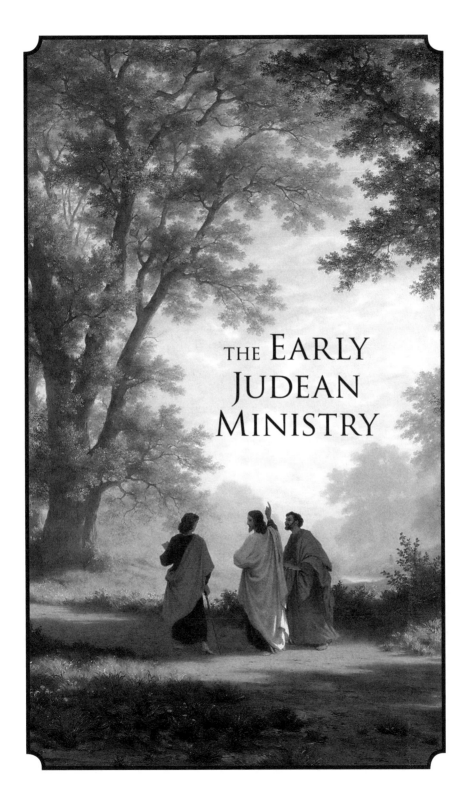

THE EARLY
JUDEAN
MINISTRY

14

Jesus Cleanses the Temple

John 2:13-25

Now the Passover of the Jews was at hand, and Jesus went up to Jerusalem. And He found in the temple those who sold oxen and sheep and doves, and the moneychangers doing business. When He had made a whip of cords, He drove them all out of the temple, with the sheep and the oxen, and poured out the changers' money and overturned the tables. And He said to those who sold doves, "Take these things away! Do not make My Father's house a house of merchandise!" (John 2:13-16)

The customs of childhood continued in the adult life of Jesus. He observed the Jewish religious calendar, and the Passover of the Jews was now at hand. By spiritual habit Jesus went up to Jerusalem. Spiritual habits are good; life choices do not require ongoing personal debates.

The temple was a scene of commerce! For the convenience of the populous, oxen and sheep and pigeons were available for sale—with a considerable profit for the religious establishment. Money changers were at their business. Roman coin of the realm had to be exchanged for untainted Jewish shekels to purchase the required certified sacrificial animals. Talk about supply and demand—worship was for sale! No mention is made of the detail of practice prescribed by Moses for the children of Israel—the selection of a lamb, the examination over a period of time, the sharing of a lamb with neighbors, the blood-markings on the door posts, eating it with bitter herbs, the dress of an exiting pilgrim—none of this. This was drive-through religion!

Jesus finds this scene in the temple courtyard; three years later He finds the same scene. Nothing changed! He is angry now, and then. His righteous anger grows as He stoops to pick up the discarded cords, as He weaves the cords into a whip. With a shouting voice and a lashing whip He drives out the animals. With strong carpenter muscles He overturns the merchants' wooden tables, and their religiously corrupted unrighteous mammon scatters across the courtyard ground. He would not harm the pigeons, so He commands the pigeon sellers to remove them. It is a strong command: "Do not make My Father's house a house of merchandise!"

In this command Jesus identifies the temple as His Father's house. It was a center of worship for Israel. It was the place where Gabriel met Zacharias, where Simeon and Anna greeted Jesus, where Jesus questioned the teachers of Israel when He was twelve, where He now returned for Passover. The holy temple! But it was built by Herod the Great to appease the Jews over whom he ruled. Herod was an Idumean who ruled over Israel by direction of Caesar. He married ten times and had fifteen children. His sons are scattered over the pages of the Gospels and Acts as regional rulers. He began the building of the temple in 19 BC but it was not completed until AD 64. It was patterned after Solomon's temple of old.

Here we see another indication of the way God works through human rulers for His purposes. David was not permitted to build a house for God because he was a man of the sword. Yet Herod the Great builds a temple for Israel as an astute politician and it becomes the house of God. God moves through the rulers of earth in strange ways and according to His own counsel. Yes, the temple built by Herod the Great becomes the house of God!

"Do not make My Father's house a house of merchandise!" The quotation ascribed to Christ's response comes from Psalm 69—a lament of the reproached!

> *Because zeal for Your house has eaten me up, and the reproaches of those who reproach You have fallen on me. . . . You know my reproach, my shame, and my dishonor; my adversaries are all before You. Reproach has broken my heart, and I am full of heaviness; I looked for someone to take pity, but there was none; and for comforters, but I found none. They also gave me gall for my food, and for my thirst they gave me vinegar to drink. (Psalm 69:9, 19-21)*

Even at this early point in His ministry, Jesus is anticipating the reproach He will bear at Calvary.

The response of Judaism is predictable.

> *"What sign do You show to us, since You do these things?"(John 2:18).*

His authority is being questioned, and they ask for a sign to justify this authoritative cleansing of the temple. The sign is the greatest of signs—His resurrection!

> *Jesus answered and said to them, "Destroy this temple, and in three days I will raise it up." (John 2:19)*

Neither the Jewish opposition nor the true disciples understood what Jesus meant. The opposition thought He was referring to Herod's temple, which was in a forty-six year building process. They scoffed at destroying it and rebuilding it in three days. In reality, Jesus was speaking of His death and resurrection. His disciples understood this after the event. "My Father's business . . . My hour has not yet come . . . Destroy this temple . . ." The crucifixion was ever before Jesus; He hints at it in these statements. Later, following Peter's great confession, He will state it clearly.

There are great lessons for Christian living that arise out of the cleansing of the temple. First, the relationship of money and ministry. When ministry is motivated out of profit, the voice of the prophet is hard to hear. There has been abuse of finances throughout the history of the church and it continues even today in many forms. Salvation and holy living is not a for-profit business. This makes God angry! Second, righteous indignation. Holy anger is sometimes the required response! Later, when a man with a withered hand becomes religious bait to trap Jesus, He looks on His adversaries with anger and grief (Mark 3:5). Third, God's requirement—a clean temple!

Or do you not know that your body is the temple of the Holy Spirit who is in you, whom you have from God, and you are not your own? For you were bought at a price; therefore glorify God in your body and in your spirit, which are God's. (1 Corinthians 6:19-20)

15

Nicodemus Visits Jesus By Night

John 3:1-21

There was a man of the Pharisees named Nicodemus, a ruler of the Jews. This man came to Jesus by night and said to Him, "Rabbi, we know that you are a teacher come from God; for no one can do these signs that You do unless God is with him." Jesus answered and said to him, "Most assuredly, I say to you, unless one is born again, he cannot see the kingdom of God." Nicodemus said to Him, "How can a man be born when he is old? Can he enter a second time into his mother's womb and be born?" . . . Jesus . . . said to him . . . "And as Moses lifted up the serpent in the wilderness, even so must the Son of Man be lifted up, that whoever believes in Him should not perish but have eternal life. For God so loved the world that He game His only begotten Son, that whoever believes in Him should not perish but have everlasting life. For God did not send His Son into the world to condemn the world, but that the world through Him might be saved." (John 3:1-4, 14-17)

Most who observed the cleansing of the temple were impressed, but only superficially. Jesus knew this and would not entrust additional revelation to them. But there was a happy exception—a ruler of the Jews, a member of the Sanhedrin, named Nicodemus. He was afraid of the religious system of which he was a part, so he came to Jesus by night under the cover of darkness. He would not come out of the shadows of veiled belief until he met Joseph of Arimathea at the foot of the cross.

The first statement of Nicodemus shows genuine sincerity and acceptance of the person and work of Jesus.

> *"Rabbi, we know you are a teacher come from God; for no one can do these signs that you do unless God is with him." (John 3:2)*

He had accepted the first light of special revelation in the deeds and teachings of Jesus, and he came in darkness to get additional light. And Jesus entrusted Himself to Nicodemus. We enter a dialogue that includes what is, no doubt, the most famous verse of Scripture:

For God so loved the world that He gave His only begotten Son, that whoever believes in Him should not perish but have everlasting life. (John 3:16)

Additional light? Here we observe evidence of God's desire to communicate to fallen man. God is there and He is not silent. He has spoken often and in many ways.

God, who at various times and in various ways spoke in time past to the fathers by the prophets, has in these last day spoken to us by His Son. (Hebrews 1:1-2)

The Son, who is the Word, speaks a single sentence, and the brightness of the glory of God blazes forth in the salvation message. God in His being executes great deeds of love. He is love and His nature is love. God in His will is motivated out of this love. God in His actions executes great deeds of love. He is love—in being, in will, and in hand! But coming to faith and salvation provided by the love of God is a process. Now, to the rest of the dialogue.

Jesus introduces the subject of being "born again"—a common concept to *our* ears, but not to Nicodemus's. He thinks of physical birth and asks an amusing but serious question. Jesus distinguishes between physical birth and spiritual birth—born of water and born of Spirit. But He speaks more of being born of the Spirit. Perhaps Nicodemus found Jesus sitting on the flat rooftop of an eastern home, enjoying a cool evening breeze. The wind will serve as an excellent illustration of the way divine Wind blows. The Holy Spirit, like the wind, blows where He will in bringing conviction. The Holy Spirit is the Sovereign Evangelist. That is why Nicodemus is with Jesus, and the others who witnessed the temple cleansing are not!

Nicodemus asks Jesus a second question: "How can this be?" Jesus responds with an Old Testament story of redemption of the defeat of the serpent that brought death to Israel. Of the evil serpent, the devil, who brought death to all of mankind. By looking up to the intervention of God—then, a bronze serpent on a pole; soon, the Savior on the cross—deliverance from sin and death and the devil is available.

"And as Moses lifted up the serpent in the wilderness, even so must the Son of Man be lifted up." (John 3:14)

Nicodemus, of all people, would understand the fullness of this statement when he and Joseph of Arimathea removed the body of Jesus from the cross.

As a teacher in Israel, he should have known about the "born again" concept in the New Covenant.

"But this is the covenant that I will make with house of Israel after those days," says the LORD: "I will put My law in their minds, and write it on their hearts; and I will be their God, and they shall be My people." (Jeremiah 31:33)

There are a number of covenants recorded in the Old Testament that relate to God and the nation of Israel.

> ➤ The Abrahamic Covenant, which promises a land (Palestine), people (the Jews), and a Seed (Christ)
>
> ➤ The Mosaic Covenant, which gives the law for Israel (moral, ceremonial, and civil)
>
> ➤ The Davidic Covenant, which promises an eternal house, throne, and kingdom to David and the nation of Israel
>
> ➤ The New Covenant, which will be in effect when the King/Priest, the Lord Jesus Christ, the Messiah, rules over Israel and the world in the coming millennium

The details of the New Covenant describe the reality of the new birth, or being born again—that new beginning sought by Nicodemus.

"Behold, the days are coming," says the LORD, "when I will make a New Covenant with the house of Israel and with the house of Judah—not according to the covenant that I made with their fathers in the day that I took them by the hand to lead them out of the land of Egypt, My covenant which they broke, through I was a husband to them," says the LORD. "But this is the covenant that I will make with the house of Israel after those days," says the LORD: "I will put My law in their minds, and write it on their hearts; and I will be their God, and they shall be My people. No more shall every man teach his neighbor, and every man his brother, saying, 'Know the LORD,' for they all shall know Me, from the least of them to the greatest of them," says the LORD. "For I will forgive their iniquity, and their sin I will remember no more." (Jeremiah 31:31-34)

This is new birth, being born again! These are the spiritual blessings of the New Covenant which the church and future believing Israel share in common. This is Paul's concept of a new creation:

"Therefore, if anyone is in Christ, he is a new creation; old things have passed away; behold all things have become new." (2 Corinthians 5:17)

Yes, a man can be born again, be delivered from sin, and be a new creation in Christ. You must be born again!

16

John Is Imprisoned, and Jesus
Withdraws through Samaria

**John 3:22-36; Luke 3:19, 20; Matthew 4:12;
Mark 1:14; Luke 4:14; John 4:1-42**

*After these things Jesus and His disciples came into the land of
Judea, and there He remained with them and baptized. Now John
also was baptizing in Aenon near Salim, because there was much
water there. And they came and were baptized. For John had not yet
been thrown into prison. (John 3:22-24)*

*But Herod the tetrarch, being rebuked by him [John] concerning
Herodias, his brother Philip's wife, and for all the evils which Herod
had done, also added this, above all, that he shut John up in prison.
(Luke 3:19-20)*

*Therefore, when the Lord knew that the Pharisees had heard that
Jesus made and baptized more disciples than John (though Jesus
Himself did not baptize, but His disciples), He left Judea and
departed again to Galilee. But He needed to go through Samaria. So
He came to a city of Samaria which is called Sychar, near the plot of
ground that Jacob gave to his son Joseph. . . . A woman of Samaria
came to draw water. Jesus said to her, "Give Me a drink." Then the
woman of Samaria said to Him, "How is it that You, being a Jew, ask
a drink from me, a Samaritan woman?" For Jews have no dealings
with Samaritans. . . . The woman said to Him, "Sir, You have nothing
to draw with, and the well is deep. Where then do You get that living
water?" . . . Jesus answered and said to her, "Whoever drinks of
this water will thirst again, but whoever drinks of the water that I
shall give him will never thirst. But the water that I shall give him
will become in him a fountain of water springing up into everlasting
life." . . . The woman said to Him, "Sir, give me this water, that I
may not thirst, nor come here to draw." . . . The woman said to Him,
"Sir, I perceive that You are a prophet." . . . The woman said to Him,
"I know that Messiah is coming" (who is called Christ). "When He
comes, He will tell us all things." . . . Then they [the townspeople]
said to the woman, "Now we believe, not because of what you said,
for we ourselves have heard Him and we know that this is indeed the
Christ, the Savior of the world." (John 4:1-5, 7-9, 11, 13-15, 19, 25, 42)*

T wo groups of disciples are baptizing the repentant in the province of Judea: Jesus and His disciples, and John and his disciples. John's disciples approach him with an observation that arises out of spiritual competition.

> *"Rabbi, He who was with you beyond the Jordan, to whom you have testified—behold, He is baptizing, and all are coming to Him!"*
> *(John 3:26)*

John the Baptist reiterates the principle he understood and accepted as the Messiah's forerunner.

> *"You yourselves bear me witness that I said, 'I am not the Christ,' but, 'I have been sent before Him.' He who has the bride is the bridegroom; but the friend of the bridegroom, who stands and hears him, rejoices greatly because of the bridegroom's voice. Therefore this joy of mine is fulfilled. He must increase, but I must decrease."*
> *(John 3:28-30)*

Soon this decline of influence will be imposed on John as Herod Antipas is angered over John's denunciation of his continued immorality. He imprisons John, a more evil deed than all the rest of his evil deeds.

Because of the imagined competition with John over baptism, and because of the arrest of John the Baptist, Jesus withdraws from Judea and goes to Galilee. He takes the less traveled route through Samaria. Although Jews had no dealings with Samaritans, the woman of Samaria would be a glorious exception. The fact that Samaritans practiced a corrupted form of Judaism (which grew out of the captivities of Israel [2 Kings 17:24ff]) will become part of the dialogue between Jesus and the Samaritan woman.

It is noon. Jesus is weary from His travels. His disciples have gone to town for provisions. He sits down right next to the well; He's thirsty! A Samaritan woman appears at the noon hour—a convenient time of rest when most of the women would not come. But Jesus has come, and He requests a drink of cool water, at which point she initiates a dialogue concerning ethnic discrimination.

Jesus enters the dialogue and elevates the subject as He speaks of His gift of eternal life—living water—and of His deity. She responds with respect but is still thinking of the water in the well and the Lord's lack of a vessel with which to draw the water. Later she mixes physical water with the spiritual water of salvation. The subject of discussion is being focused by Jesus, but she is not there yet.

One more statement from Jesus will cut to the heart of her spiritual poverty. "Go call your husband, and come here." Jesus in His grace gives her opportunity to escape an embarrassing confrontation. She could have disappeared into the haze of the heat of high noon. But she stays and responds in truth, "I have no husband." Because she chooses to stay, Jesus speaks on and tells her of her great sins, and she acknowledges Him as a prophet. This stranger has to be from God—how else could He know of the five husbands and the present immorality?

Since He is from God, the question of true worship is a logical topic for debate.

"Our fathers worshiped on this mountain, and you Jews say that in Jerusalem is the place where one ought to worship." (John 4:20)

A dialogue that began with a request for water now involves the chief end of man (which is to glorify God and enjoy Him forever, according to the Westminster Shorter Catechism!). And with that the conclusion of their conversation is reached:

"I know that Messiah is coming" (who is called Christ). "When He comes, He will tell us all things." Jesus said to her, "I who speak to you am He." (John 4:25-26)

The woman leaves and the disciples return, astonished that Jesus is refreshed without physical nourishment. Spiritual refreshment overcomes physical weakness, then and now! I wonder if Jesus ever got a drink! Later, the woman returns with the entire village, and their response is,

"Now we believe, for we ourselves have heard Him and we know that this is indeed the Christ, the Savior of the world." (John 4:42)

This exceptional evangelization gives us the model of Jesus for evangelism:

> ➢ Start where the person is and establish common ground.
> ➢ Introduce the spiritual component.
> ➢ Allow for freedom to continue or close the discussion.
> ➢ Pursue the spiritual need.
> ➢ Introduce the Savior.

This evangelism is exceptional for another reason. Jesus will later say, "Go only to the lost sheep of the house of Israel." After His resurrection, Samaria and all the world will be His focus. Now, as with the Syrophoenician woman later, this Samaritan woman is an exception of evangelism.

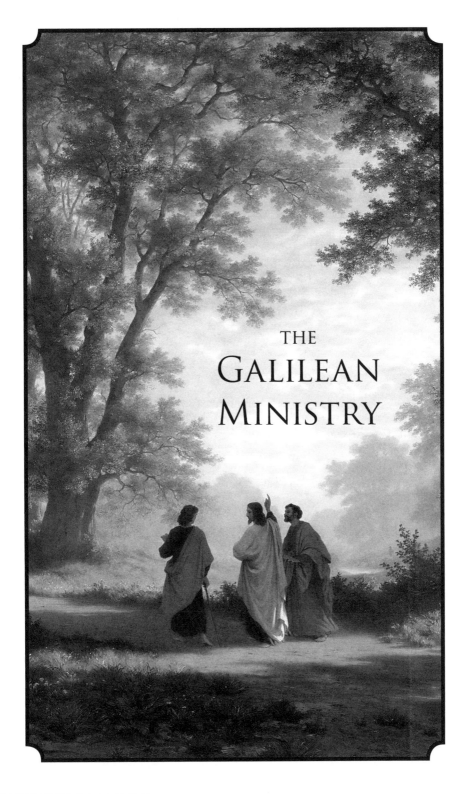

THE
GALILEAN
MINISTRY

17

Jesus Heals the Nobleman's Son
and Is Rejected at Nazareth

John 4:43-54; Luke 4:14-30

So Jesus came again to Cana of Galilee where He had made the water wine. And there was a certain nobleman whose son was sick at Capernaum. When he heard that Jesus had come out of Judea into Galilee, he went to Him and implored Him to come down and heal his son, for he was at the point of death. . . . The nobleman said to Him, "Sir, come down before my child dies!" Jesus said to him, "Go your way; your son lives." So the man believed the word that Jesus spoke to him, and he went his way. And as he was now going down, his servants met him and told him, saying, "Your son lives!" Then he inquired of them the hour when he got better. And they said to him, "Yesterday at the seventh hour the fever left him." (John 4:46-47, 49-52)

So He came to Nazareth, where He had been brought up. And as His custom was, He went into the synagogue on the Sabbath day, and stood up to read. And He was handed the book of the prophet Isaiah. And when He had opened the book, He found the place where it was written: "The Spirit of the LORD is upon Me . . . to proclaim the acceptable year of the LORD." . . . So all those in the synagogue, when they heard these things, were filled with wrath, and rose up and thrust Him out of the city; and they led Him to the brow of the hill on which their city was built, that they might throw Him down over the cliff. Then passing through the midst of them, He went His way. (Luke 4:16-19, 28-30)

Two days after the interlude in Samaria Jesus returns to Judaism in the province of Galilee. He begins a ministry of visiting the synagogues with the message of repentance. He does not expect a positive response, as "a prophet has no honor in his own country."

At Cana, where He had turned the water into wine, Jesus is met by a royal official of Capernaum serving under Herod Antipas. The man is desperate: his son is at the point of death. He had left his son in Capernaum upon hearing that Jesus was in the province and traveled those thirty miles or so to Cana as quickly as possible to get help from Jesus. He finds Jesus and begs Him to "come down before my son dies." He receives a rebuke from Jesus: "Unless you people see signs and wonders, you will by no means believe" (John 4:48). Again the nobleman begs for help, and this time he hears those great words of compassion from Jesus, "Go, your son will live!" The royal official believed! But he did not see the miracle. That is the point of this story—he believed without seeing a miracle. That is the kind of faith Jesus desires: faith in His word *alone*. That's why Jesus did it this way!

But did the miracle take place? Upon returning home to Capernaum the nobleman is met by his servants with the anticipated good news—his son lives! In response to the nobleman's question, the time when the fever broke is identified: an hour after noon, one o'clock. That was when Jesus said, "Your son will live." He is the Lord of space and distance. He can heal from Cana to Capernaum—no challenge!

But there is another lesson here about faith in the words of God—it brings peace. When asked about the timing of the miracle, the servants say, "Yesterday at one o'clock in the afternoon." Notice, *yesterday.* There had been time for a hasty return trip from Cana to Capernaum before nightfall. I doubt the royal official walked! He could have easily returned *the previous day* for visual confirmation of the miracle. But his faith did not need that! He believed. Somewhere, he stayed overnight in some Holyland Inn, and returned in peace—the peace of faith in the words of Jesus. His faith is deepened and the whole household believes, an outcome of eternal value from a temporal dilemma. God often works that way!

Resuming His synagogue ministry, Jesus travels the short distance from Cana to Nazareth and to the synagogue of His youth. The rest of the family would have been in the habit of attending that synagogue. Jesus is given opportunity to read the lesson for the day, and He reads:

> *"The Spirit of the Lord is upon Me, because He has anointed Me to preach the gospel to the poor; He has sent Me to heal the brokenhearted, to proclaim liberty to the captives, and recovery of sight to the blind, to set at liberty those who are oppressed; to proclaim the acceptable year of the Lord." (Luke 4:18-19)*

He stops in the middle of a verse:

> *And the day of vengeance of our God; to comfort all who mourn. (Isaiah 61:1-2)*

This was the day of His grace, His invitation to repentance, His offer of the kingdom—not vengeance yet! And the response? "Is not this Joseph's son?" Jesus was right when He said that no prophet is acceptable in his own country. Elijah brought blessings to the widow of Zarephath and to Naaman, the leper of Syria, while Israel languished. This statement of Jesus arouses great hostility. The reference made to what Jesus did in Capernaum may be an allusion to the healing of the royal official's son, since he would have been a Gentile. The members of the Nazareth synagogue that Jesus attended by custom all His life are filled with wrath. They lead him out to the cliff and try to cast Him down headlong. In a passive miracle, Jesus eludes their anger and a premature death by passing through their midst.

Each movement in the life of Christ ends with rejection. The Period of Preparation begins this pattern. With the close of the Preparation Period, Galilee becomes the focus of God's grace in the coming months with numerous miracles and repeated calls to repentance by Jesus and His disciples. How will the Galilean ministry end? That will be the next segment of the life of Christ.

The grace of God is demonstrated in the healing of the official's son and in the offer of repentance to Israel prior to the execution of God's vengeance. The lesson learned in the household of the royal official is *the* lesson of life— how to be saved and thus escape the wrath of God. A near-death experience focused attention on the reality of life and death with salvation as the result. We should be thankful for crises! On the other hand, grace rejected, as with the members of the synagogue, will guarantee the judgment of God, which is waiting but certain.

18

.
.
.

Jesus Settles at Capernaum and Calls the Disciples

Matthew 4:13-22; Mark 1:14-20; Luke 4:31-5:11

And leaving Nazareth, He came and dwelt in Capernaum, which is by the sea, in the regions of Zebulun and Naphtali, that it might be fulfilled which was spoken by Isaiah the prophet, saying: "The land of Zebulun and the land of Naphtali, by the way of the sea, beyond the Jordan, Galilee of the Gentiles: The people who sat in darkness have seen a great light, and upon those who sat in the region and shadow of death Light has dawned." From that time Jesus began to preach and to say, "Repent, for the kingdom of heaven is at hand." (Matthew 4:13-17)

And as He walked by the Sea of Galilee, He saw Simon and Andrew his brother casting a net into the sea; for they were fishermen. (Mark 1:16)

So it was, as the multitude pressed about Him to hear the word of God, that He stood by the Lake of Gennesaret, and saw two boats standing by the lake; but the fishermen had gone from them and were washing their nets. Then He got into one of the boats, which was Simon's, and asked him to put out a little from the land. And He sat down and taught the multitudes from the boat. When He had stopped speaking, He said to Simon, "Launch out into the deep and let down your nets for a catch." But Simon answered and said to Him, "Master, we have toiled all night and caught nothing; nevertheless at Your word I will let down the net." And when they had done this, they caught a great number of fish, and their net was breaking. So they signaled to their partners in the other boat to come and help them. And they came and filled both the boats, so that they began to sink. When Simon Peter saw it, he fell down at Jesus' knees, saying, "Depart from me, for I am a sinful man, O Lord!" For he and all who were with him were astonished at the catch of fish which they had taken; and so also were James and John, the sons of Zebedee, who were partners with Simon. And Jesus said to Simon, "Do not be afraid. From now on you will catch men." So when they had brought their boats to land, they forsook all and followed Him. (Luke 5:1-11)

Then Jesus said to them, "Follow Me, and I will make you become fishers of men." They immediately left their nets and followed Him. When He had gone a little farther from there, He saw James the son of Zebedee, and John his brother, who also were in the boat mending their nets. And immediately He called them, and they left their father Zebedee in the boat with the hired servants, and went after Him. (Mark 1:17-20)

Having been rejected in Nazareth, Jesus comes to Capernaum, the main city of the province of Galilee located on the northeast shore of the Sea of Galilee. He had come earlier with His family and disciples for a few days to arrange for housing. Capernaum will be their base of operation for the entire Galilean ministry. It would be "home" for about a year and a half. Galilee bordered on Gentile territory and occupied the region of the northern-most tribes of Israel. It was to be the location where light would dawn, where the Light of the World would commence His ministry to Israel.

Notice the time designation: "*From that time* Jesus began to preach and to say. . ." (Matthew 4:17). This marks the beginning of the extensive ministry in Galilee, which would include numerous miracles and extensive teaching—the Sabbath debates, the Sermon on the Mount, the feeding of the five thousand, and the Bread of Life Discourse. Indeed, Galilee *will* see a great light as the dawn of Israel's redemption dispels the darkness of the shadow of death. So great and bright will be that light that Jesus will say later,

"And you, Capernaum, who are exalted to heaven, will be brought down to Hades; for if the mighty works which were done in you had been done in Sodom, it would have remained until this day." (Matthew 11:23)

Notice the message of Jesus: "Repent, for the kingdom of heaven is at hand." Mark records His words a bit differently: "The kingdom of God is at hand. . . . Repent . . ." Apparently the terms can be used interchangeably—of heaven, and of God. Once again, it is important to remember the nature of the offer of the kingdom. As in the annunciations of His birth and the kingdom teaching in the Preparation Period, so here—the kingdom is being offered to the nation of Israel to repent and to have the Son of David, Jesus Christ, rule as king over the nation from the Holy City, Jerusalem. The King is offering the kingdom to Israel—it is at hand!

The evangelization of Galilee will require a team of helpers. John, Andrew, Peter, Nathanael, and Philip had already become disciples. Others will follow. Now comes the call to action. Jesus had used Peter's boat as a floating pulpit to teach the crowds. When He ended his teaching, Jesus told Peter to go out into the deep, to lower the nets, and to catch fish—and Peter objected. How wonderful that Peter felt free to object to Jesus! His objection was based on his fisherman's logic—he had fished all night and caught nothing. It was not based on faith in the One who spoke. But he obeyed, and the result was a massive catch. The result was greater than a catch of fish, however. Peter confessed the sinfulness of doubt—his lack of faith—and as a result his faith was strengthened. His partners in business, James and John, shared Peter's experience. And Jesus calls them to join Him in the evangelization of Galilee.

"Don't be afraid. Follow Me. I will make you become . . . ." Blessed assurance!

They forsook all and followed Him. They were successful fisherman in partnership—Peter, perhaps brother Andrew as well, brothers James and John and their father Zebedee. They had hired servants. But they forsook all to follow Jesus and to become His disciples. Their great step of faith would take them into all the world. Their great catch of men would include millions; it includes each of us. "One small step for man. One giant step for mankind." Their first steps would take them into every town and village of Galilee, and later, the whole world. Tradition puts Peter in Gaul, Britain, and then Rome; Andrew in Scythia and Greece; John in Ephesus and Patmos; Philip in Hierapolis; Matthew in Egypt; Thomas in India; Bartholomew in Armenia; James in Syria; Thaddaeus in Edessa; and Simon the Zealot perhaps in Egypt and Carthage—to say nothing of the lands visited by that "late" apostle, Paul.

Three gospels include the call of these disciples to service. They all conclude with a common statement, that they followed Him. As disciples of the original disciples, their response to follow Jesus should find resonance in *our* commitment to the Savior.

19

The Beginning Burst of Miracles

Mark 1:21-34; Luke 4:31-41; Matthew 8:14-17

Then they went into Capernaum, and immediately on the Sabbath He entered the synagogue and taught. And they were astonished at His teaching, for He taught them as one having authority, and not as the scribes. Now there was a man in their synagogue with an unclean spirit. And he cried out, saying, "Let us alone! What have we to do with You, Jesus of Nazareth? Did You come to destroy us? I know who You are—the Holy One of God!" But Jesus rebuked him, saying, "Be quiet, and come out of him!" And when the unclean spirit had convulsed him and cried out with a loud voice, he came out of him. Then they were all amazed, so that they questioned among themselves, saying, "What is this? What new doctrine is this? For with authority He commands even the unclean spirits, and they obey Him." And immediately His fame spread throughout all the region around Galilee. (Mark 1:21-28)

Now when Jesus had come into Peter's house, He saw his wife's mother lying sick with a fever. So He touched her hand, and the fever left her. And she arose and served them. When evening had come, they brought to Him many who were demon-possessed. And He cast out the spirits with a word, and healed all who were sick, that it might be fulfilled which was spoken by Isaiah the prophet, saying: "He Himself took our infirmities and bore our sicknesses." (Matthew 8:14-17)

The Galilean ministry began with a burst of miracles, a Sabbath day full of miraculous works by the Great Miracle Worker. Clusters of miracles are scattered throughout Scripture to confirm new revelation from God. The beginning of the Galilean ministry was no exception, and it all happened on that first Sabbath—a non-work day!

Jesus enters the synagogue on the Sabbath and begins teaching as an itinerate rabbi. But He is different from other rabbis—He teaches with authority—He is the God-Man! An immediate confrontation occurs between Jesus and a demoniac. Demons understand the truth, but they reject it. Jesus is the Holy One of God—that's what Gabriel told Mary, and the demons know it! Jesus is selective in receiving worshipful statements—they must be in spirit and in truth. He therefore silences the demon and commands his exodus from the possessed man. The congregation is amazed. Jesus manifests divine power over the spirit world in this first miracle in the ministry of Galilee. Not only that, but it takes place in a religious setting—the synagogue. But the Sabbath day is just beginning. There's much more work to do on this non-work day!

The second movement of this passage relates to the healing of Peter's mother-in-law. This states something obvious about Peter—that he was a married man. The men leave the synagogue and enter the house of Peter and Andrew. James and John are with them. They find Peter's mother-in-law cast down, severely ill with a high fever. Another miracle is performed—this time, it is a private miracle and followed by immediate service to the Lord and the company of disciples. It must have been a wonderful time of fellowship around that Sabbath dinner table.

The third movement in the Sabbath day of miracles brings crowds from the whole region. The whole city gathers at the door of His home in Capernaum, and He turns no one away.

> *At evening, when the sun had set, they brought to Him all who were sick and those who were demon-possessed. And the whole city was gathered together at the door. Then He healed many who were sick with various diseases, and cast out many demons; and He did not allow the demons to speak, because they knew Him. (Mark 1:32-34)*

Again, Christ does not allow the demons to speak, even though they know Him. These numerous miracles were performed in a public setting. This one Sabbath day is full of mighty miracles—in a religious setting, in a private home, and in public view. The attention of the population of Galilee is now focused on Him. Debate over the Sabbath miracles will arise soon. It is time now to go into all the villages of Galilee. Jesus has their attention!

This section concludes with a quotation from Isaiah 53 that was fulfilled in these events.

> *Surely He has borne our griefs and carried our sorrows; yet we esteemed Him stricken, smitten by God, and afflicted. But He was wounded for our transgressions, He was bruised for our iniquities; the chastisement for our peace was upon Him, and by His stripes we are healed. (Isaiah 53:4-5)*

It is clear in the events of the narrative that physical healing is the subject. The quotation from Isaiah speaks primarily of spiritual healing—of forgiveness. But there is healing in Christ's atoning work at Calvary. The multiplied healings were of many individuals with varied diseases. All who came were healed of their physical diseases, and those possessed of demons were delivered. Not all came to faith, but all were healed and delivered.

Thus the Isaiah passage is interpreted in the life of Christ: there is spiritual healing from sin and there is physical healing for the believer in Christ's atoning for sin. In the kingdom message, it would be consistent to view the coming condition of the millennial kingdom as a time of health and long length of days apart from the curse on the earth. Those resurrected saints from of old and of the church will have glorified bodies here on earth in those kingdom days and will enjoy physical as well as spiritual healing through the redemptive work of our Savior. This will be but a precursor to eternity. But it is not yet with us! Rather,

> . . . I consider that the sufferings of this present time are not worthy to be compared with the glory which shall be revealed in us. . . . For we know that the whole creation groans and labors with birth pangs together until now. Not only that, but we also who have the firstfruits of the Spirit, even we ourselves groan within ourselves, eagerly waiting for the adoption, the redemption of our body. . . . Likewise the Spirit also helps in our weaknesses. For we do not know what we should pray for as we ought, but the Spirit Himself makes intercession for us with groanings which cannot be uttered. . . . And we know that all things work together for good to those who love God, to those who are the called according to His purpose. . . . [nothing] shall be able to separate us from the love of God which is in Christ Jesus our Lord. (Romans 8:18, 22-23, 26, 28, 39)

20

The Beginning of the Evangelistic
Campaign in Galilee

Mark 1:35-45; Luke 4:42-44; 5:12-16; Matthew 4:23-24; 8:2-4

Now in the morning, having risen a long while before daylight, He went out and departed to a solitary place; and there He prayed. And Simon and those who were with Him searched for Him. When they found Him, they said to Him, "Everyone is looking for You." But He said to them, "Let us go into the next towns, that I may preach there also, because for this purpose I have come forth." (Mark 1:35-38)

And Jesus went about all Galilee, teaching in their synagogues, preaching the gospel of the kingdom, and healing all kinds of sickness and all kinds of disease among the people. Then His fame went throughout all Syria; and they brought to Him all sick people who were afflicted with various diseases and torments, and those who were demon-possessed, epileptics, and paralytics; and He healed them. (Matthew 4:23-24)

Now a leper came to Him, imploring Him, kneeling down to Him and saying to Him, "If You are willing, You can make me clean." Then Jesus, moved with compassion, stretched out His hand and touched him, and said to him, "I am willing; be cleansed." As soon as He had spoken, immediately the leprosy left him, and he was cleansed. And He strictly warned him and sent him away at once, and said to him, "See that you say nothing to anyone; but go your way, show yourself to the priest, and offer for your cleansing those things which Moses commanded, as a testimony to them." However, he went out and began to proclaim it freely, and to spread the matter, so that Jesus could no longer openly enter the city, but was outside in deserted places; and they came to Him from every direction. (Mark 1:40-45)

So He Himself withdrew into the wilderness and prayed. (Luke 5:16)

The Galilean Campaign had three movements—Jesus prays at the beginning, He preaches in all of the synagogues of Galilee, and He prays at its conclusion. The lesson is clear: ministry is to be bathed in prayer. That's what Jesus would do!

Jesus got up very early for prayer this day. It was not normal for Him to do this; His disciples didn't know where He had gone and they were searching for Him. This was not His normal habit—it was exceptional for a reason. He states the reason: He is about to begin an extensive preaching tour reaching every corner of the province of Galilee. He needed to pray for special strength to preach the gospel of the kingdom in every village of the province. Great tasks for God demand much prayer—even for Jesus!

A very succinct summary statement is made about Jesus' province-wide preaching:

> *And Jesus went about all Galilee, teaching in their synagogues, preaching the gospel of the kingdom, and healing all kinds of sickness and all kinds of disease among the people. (Matthew 4:23)*

A sample of the ministry is given in the healing of the leper. The leper approaches Jesus with both the desire to be cleansed and faith that Jesus was capable of performing that miracle. The leper has heard of other miracles of Jesus, so he comes in faith to be cleansed. *Cleansed* is more specific than *healed*. It is one thing to be healed of a normal malady, but leprosy made its victim unclean and put him "outside the camp," ostracized from society and cut off from normal life. The leper needs to not only be healed, but cleansed.

And Jesus *touches* the man! To touch a leper would render one unclean. But when Jesus touches the leper, the leper is made clean! Moved with pity and compassion for this outcast, Jesus performs a miracle of mercy. It is not without stern instructions, however. The law prescribed regulations for reinstatement into society, and Jesus reiterated the law—"See that you say nothing to anyone; but go your way, show yourself to the priest, and offer for your cleansing those things which Moses commanded, as a testimony to them" (Mark 1:44). The instruction was not obeyed. The leper's joy is understandable, and his failure to obey, forgivable. But two consequences followed. First, the priest in Jerusalem did not get the message—the testimony—that a leper healer was on the scene. Such a message may have reminded him of the teaching of Jesus in Nazareth about Naaman (2 Kings 5). They tried to kill Jesus at home for what He had said. Second, the crowds increased to such a degree as a result of the zeal of the newly cleansed leper that Jesus could not continue His ministry in an orderly way.

"So He Himself withdrew into the wilderness and prayed." The opening verse of the next lesson shows us that Jesus returned to Capernaum after some days. This is another summary statement of our Lord's devotional life—an extended time of prayer at the conclusion of His first evangelistic campaign.

What can we learn about the prayer life of Jesus from this beginning of His Galilean ministry?

First, Jesus was a man of prayer—He regularly prayed to His Father throughout His lifetime. The God-Man prayed! The author of Hebrews lifts a line out of the future testimony of a restored Israel and ascribes it to Jesus: "I will put My trust in Him" (Hebrews 2:13). Jesus entrusted Himself to God in prayer for divine help in His ministry. He did this so often that His disciples would later ask Him, "Lord, teach us to pray." He teaches us the necessity of frequent prayer through His life practice.

Second, Jesus intensified His prayer time for specific endeavors. The evangelistic campaign into Galilee was a massive undertaking for Him. Special spiritual activities require even more prayer, both before and after: before, to guide, and after, to preserve the efforts. Extended, focused times of prayer for special ministry or crisis happenings are marks of being a disciple of Jesus.

Third, focused prayer requires suitable conditions: a great while before day, a quiet place, an extended time, away from the crowds—in secret, as He will teach later. Serious prayer requires planning. In addition to "special exercise" prayer, there is the "pray without ceasing" concept that addresses the unpredictable, oncoming events of daily activities. This prayer is less easily scheduled, of necessity.

Finally, the prayer life of Jesus is flexible: sometimes early in the morning; sometimes all night; sometimes at the hour of prayer in the temple; sometimes alone; sometimes in the presence of others. *Lord, teach us to pray!*

21

Healing and Forgiving a Paralytic, and Offending the Pharisees

Matthew 9:2-8; Mark 2:3-12; Luke 5:17-26

And again He entered Capernaum after some days, and it was heard that He was in the house. Immediately many gathered together, so that there was no longer room to receive them, not even near the door. And He preached the word to them. (Mark 2:1-2)

Now it happened on a certain day, as He was teaching, that there were Pharisees and teachers of the law sitting by, who had come out of every town of Galilee, Judea, and Jerusalem. And the power of the Lord was present to heal them. (Luke 5:17)

Then they came to Him, bringing a paralytic who was carried by four men. And when they could not come near Him because of the crowd, they uncovered the roof where He was. So when they had broken through, they let down the bed on which the paralytic was lying. When Jesus saw their faith, He said to the paralytic, "Son, your sins are forgiven you." And some of the scribes were sitting there and reasoning in their hearts, "Why does this Man speak blasphemies like this? Who can forgive sins but God alone?" But immediately, when Jesus perceived in His spirit that they reasoned thus within themselves, He said to them, "Why do you reason about these things in your hearts? Which is easier, to say to the paralytic, 'Your sins are forgiven you,' or to say, 'Arise, take up your bed and walk'? But that you may know that the Son of Man has power on earth to forgive sins"—He said to the paralytic, "I say to you, arise, take up your bed, and go to your house." Immediately he arose, took up the bed, and went out in the presence of them all, so that all were amazed and glorified God, saying, "We never saw anything like this!" (Mark 2:3-12)

After some days in prayer in the wilderness, Jesus returns home to Capernaum and the crowds gather. Even Pharisees and teachers of the law have come from Jerusalem to observe.

A group of five men of faith approach the home of Jesus. Four of them are carrying the fifth—a paralytic—on a stretcher. When they realize that they can't get near because of the crowd, they take the outside stairs to the flat roof and lower their friend into the Lord's presence. Seeing the faith of the five, Jesus makes a certain gracious and amazing statement for the first time: "My son, your sins are forgiven you." Let's pause, rejoice, and worship at these first words of forgiveness from the Savior to both the paralytic and all paralyzed by sin who come to Jesus in faith!

But the Pharisees and teachers of the law were not amazed at the gracious words of Jesus. They were good theologians—"Who can forgive sins but God alone?" They did not have the faith of the paralytic. Their theology was correct on forgiveness but incorrect on the incarnation—"God with us"— the greatest of miracles. "And without controversy great is the mystery of godliness: God was manifested in the flesh" (1 Timothy 3:16). Without the incarnation there can be no forgiveness of sin, no justification, no redemption, no reconciliation, no propitiation, no heaven—only judgment! The gracious words of Jesus are rejected and called blasphemy by the misdirected orthodox theology of the Pharisees and the teachers of the law.

The clever argument of Jesus silences the opponents! It's easier to say "Your sins are forgiven" than to say "Rise, take up your bed, and walk." Anybody can say the former. Thousands have said it with no visible proof or results, because "only God can forgive sins." Forgiveness of sins can only be seen by God and accepted by the sinner. "Rise, take up your bed, and walk" gives the visible confirmation of the truthfulness of both statements. Faith gives place to sight.

Two great objections to the Person and work of Christ grow out of the burst of miracles that opened the Galilean ministry (previous lesson) and the forgiving of the paralytic. The Pharisees seize on these—breaking the Sabbath and forgiving sin—and mount a campaign of opposition. They do not believe what Jesus says, nor will they be convinced by what He does. Jesus will say later:

> "If I bear witness of Myself, My witness is not true. There is another who bears witness of Me, and I know that the witness which He witnesses of Me is true. You have sent to John, and he has borne witness to the truth. Yet I do not receive testimony from man, but I say these things that you may be saved. He was the burning and shining lamp, and you were willing for a time to rejoice in his light. But I have a greater witness than John's; for the works which the Father has given Me to finish—the very works that I do—bear

witness of Me, that the Father has sent Me. And the Father Himself, who sent Me, has testified of Me. You have neither heard His voice at any time, nor seen His form. But you do not have His word abiding in you, because whom He sent, Him you do not believe. You search the Scriptures, for in them you think you have eternal life; and these are they which testify of Me. But you are not willing to come to Me that you may have life." (John 5:31-40)

The deity debate will continue throughout the ministry of Jesus, and He will address it finally on Tuesday of Passion Week.

While the Pharisees were gathered together, Jesus asked them, saying, "What do you think about the Christ? Whose Son is He?" They said to Him, "The Son of David." He said to them, "How then does David in the Spirit call Him 'Lord,' saying: 'The LORD said to my Lord, "Sit at My right hand, Till I make Your enemies Your footstool"'? If David then calls Him 'Lord,' how is He his Son?" And no one was able to answer Him a word, nor from that day on did anyone dare question Him anymore. (Matthew 22:41-46)

The debate relating to miracles finds a more immediate decision on the part of the Pharisees. Soon they will say, "He has Beelzebub," and "By the ruler of the demons He casts out demons" (Mark 3:22). This becomes the standard answer of the Pharisees to the miracles of Jesus. These two issues will be ongoing subjects of confrontation.

Those five men with faith found the healing they pursued. The response of the crowds was fear and amazement and giving glory to God. They soon will turn away, following their leaders. The self-righteous leaders become indignant and confirm themselves in the unbelief of misdirected orthodoxy. As always, there are differing responses to the message of God, but all have eternal consequences. As Jesus will later say, "Better that you would have been born blind than to remain in your self-righteousness."

22

New Disciples of Jesus, and Old Disciples of John

Matthew 9:9-17; Mark 2:13-22; Luke 5:27-39

As Jesus passed on from there, He saw a man named Matthew sitting at the tax office. And He said to him, "Follow Me." So he arose and followed Him. Now it happened, as Jesus sat at the table in the house, that behold, many tax collectors and sinners came and sat down with Him and His disciples. And when the Pharisees saw it, they said to His disciples, "Why does your Teacher eat with tax collectors and sinners?" When Jesus heard that, He said to them, "Those who are well have no need of a physician, but those who are sick. But go and learn what this means: 'I desire mercy and not sacrifice.' For I did not come to call the righteous, but sinners, to repentance." Then the disciples of John came to Him, saying, "Why do we and the Pharisees fast often, but Your disciples do not fast?" And Jesus said to them, "Can the friends of the bridegroom mourn as long as the bridegroom is with them? But the days will come when the bridegroom will be taken away from them, and then they will fast. No one puts a piece of unshrunk cloth on an old garment; for the patch pulls away from the garment, and the tear is made worse. Nor do they put new wine into old wineskins, or else the wineskins break, the wine is spilled, and the wineskins are ruined. But they put new wine into new wineskins, and both are preserved." (Matthew 9:9-17)

Two groups of disciples are before us: a new man for the team, Matthew, along with his evangelistic zeal for his tax collectors' friends, and John's disciples, who had questions about the disciples of Jesus and their practices. The disciples of Jesus are about to begin an extensive ministry throughout Israel. Soon Jesus will name the Twelve and deliver to them the Sermon on the Mount, the guidelines for their kingdom evangelism. The disciples of John see their leader declining in importance. He was already in prison, and things would get worse! It is easier to be excited at the beginning of a ministry than at the close of a ministry! John's disciples were asking questions, even identifying with the practices of the Pharisees. They were discouraged. Soon John would be asking the same kind of questions out of his own discouragement.

First, Matthew and his friends. Matthew was a tax collector for the Roman empire. The Jewish tax collectors would make a living by placing a surcharge on the taxes required by the empire. They were hated by their fellow Jews and considered traitors. Matthew the tax collector would have known about Jesus. He would have known the nobleman, the Roman official whose son was healed. Roman officials knew the tax collectors, you can be sure of that! He would have known the stir caused by the many miracles Jesus performed throughout all of Galilee. As he sat at the tax booth located by the commercial route through Capernaum, he would tap into the latest news of the province. That news was about Jesus!

Matthew's knowledge about Jesus would now become very personal. Jesus approaches Matthew in his tax booth and issues an invitation and command, "Follow me"—and Matthew responds.

Full of zeal and enthusiasm, Matthew reaches out to introduce Jesus to his circle of friends—tax collectors and sinners. This prototype of friendship/hospitality evangelism remains a valid model of outreach for all who would introduce Jesus, the Savior, to friends and sinners. But the Pharisees in their self-righteousness rejected such contact with that sort of people. Jesus addresses them:

> "Those who are well have no need of a physician, but those who are sick. But go and learn what this means: 'I desire mercy and not sacrifice.' For I did not come to call the righteous, but sinners, to repentance." (Matthew 9:12-13)

John's discouraged disciples side with the complaining Pharisees!

> Then the disciples of John came to Him, saying, "Why do we and the Pharisees fast often, but Your disciples do not fast?" (Matthew 9:14)

A question of fasting was now raised—a surface issue. The real issue was how to handle change. A great change was taking place, as the ministry of John was declining; the focus was being redirected to the ministry of Jesus. The Pharisees fasted for ritual reasons and the prestige received from it; it made them look righteous. The fasting of John's disciples was spiritually oriented. Their leader was imprisoned, and it was appropriate and fitting to be given to fasting and prayer in this time of crisis for John.

But it was not fitting for Jesus and His disciples to fast at the outset of the Galilean ministry. The message of the gospel of the kingdom was good news that was confirmed by miracles of healings and casting out of demons—no cause to fast! Rejection would come and Jesus would be taken away, and then fasting would be appropriate. But there was no cause for fasting while the Bridegroom was present.

Jesus presents two illustrations for clarity, of patches and wineskins. Change is coming with Christ's kingdom: from the Mosaic Covenant to the New Covenant, from ritualism to reality, from shadow to substance, from being a subservient nation to ruling the world in righteousness and holiness. This is not a patched-up version of the previous order; stretched wineskins would not contain the new order of kingdom joy and celebration. The rigors of the condemning Mosaic Covenant are replaced by the nature-changing power of the New Covenant! But some will be opposed to change—most, in fact! They will say as in the illustration of Jesus:

> *"And no one, having drunk old wine, immediately desires new; for he says, 'The old is better.'"* (Luke 5:39)

"The old is better." Change is always a threat. It disturbs habits and traditions and customs—it makes us uncomfortable! But when habits and traditions and customs are taught as doctrine, they must come under the scrutiny of the doctrine they claim to support. Jesus will speak to that failure later. Appropriate response to change is the heart of this passage. Yes, the disciples of Jesus should celebrate, and the disciples of John should fast—but neither group should be taken up with the empty practice of the Pharisees. Nor should we, in our application of Christian living. Form and function should be complementary, not competitive, in our service for God and our worship of God.

23

·
·
·

Healing the Crippled Man on the Sabbath, and the Controversy

John 5:1-47

After this there was a feast of the Jews, and Jesus went up to Jerusalem. Now there is in Jerusalem by the Sheep Gate a pool, which is called in Hebrew, Bethesda, having five porches. In these lay a great multitude of sick people, blind, lame, paralyzed, waiting for the moving of the water. For an angel went down at a certain time into the pool and stirred up the water; then whoever stepped in first, after the stirring of the water, was made well of whatever disease he had. Now a certain man was there who had an infirmity thirty-eight years. When Jesus saw him lying there, and knew that he already had been in that condition a long time, He said to him, "Do you want to be made well?" The sick man answered Him, "Sir, I have no man to put me into the pool when the water is stirred up; but while I am coming, another steps down before me." Jesus said to him, "Rise, take up your bed and walk." And immediately the man was made well, took up his bed, and walked. And that day was the Sabbath. The Jews therefore said to him who was cured, "It is the Sabbath; it is not lawful for you to carry your bed." He answered them, "He who made me well said to me, 'Take up your bed and walk.'" Then they asked him, "Who is the Man who said to you, 'Take up your bed and walk'?" But the one who was healed did not know who it was, for Jesus had withdrawn, a multitude being in that place. Afterward Jesus found him in the temple, and said to him, "See, you have been made well. Sin no more, lest a worse thing come upon you." The man departed and told the Jews that it was Jesus who had made him well. For this reason the Jews persecuted Jesus, and sought to kill Him, because He had done these things on the Sabbath. But Jesus answered them, "My Father has been working until now, and I have been working." Therefore the Jews sought all the more to kill Him, because He not only broke the Sabbath, but also said that God was His Father, making Himself equal with God. (John 5:1-18)

*"If I bear witness of Myself, My witness is not true. . . . You have
sent to John, and he has borne witness to the truth. . . . But I have
a greater witness than John's; for the works which the Father has
given Me to finish—the very works that I do—bear witness of Me,
that the Father has sent Me. . . . You search the Scriptures, for in
them you think you have eternal life; and these are they which testify
of Me." (John 5:31, 33, 36, 39)*

The controversy over working on the Sabbath was intensifying. The
event was the healing of a man handicapped for thirty-eight years. He
was carried regularly to the pool of Bethesda for miraculous healing, yet
remained in his helpless condition without that wished-for miracle.

Then Jesus came to the feast of the Jews, through the Sheep Gate, to the
pool of Bethesda. The Savior comes through the Sheep Gate to the House of
Mercy where a multitude of invalids, blind, lame, and paralyzed were looking
for one solitary miracle. The spiritual picture is clear!

The interpretation of this passage revolves around verses 4 and 7.

*For an angel went down at a certain time into the pool and stirred
up the water; then whoever stepped in first, after the stirring of the
water, was made well of whatever disease he had. . . . The sick man
answered Him, "Sir, I have no man to put me into the pool when
the water is stirred up; but while I am coming, another steps down
before me." (John 5:4, 7)*

Verse 4 is not included in most translations of the Bible due to questionable
manuscript support, whereas verse 7 is included in all translations. The Jews
had a tradition that an angel came down from heaven and stirred the water
which resulted in subsequent healing for the first one into the pool. A strange
miracle indeed! What height of wave was high enough to be the miracle
wave? The person least needing a miracle would be cured due to his ability
to move faster, while the more seriously ill (like the man in question) would
be left in his wake. It was a tradition with results. Imagined sicknesses were
cured, and the genuine ones remained—witness the man's response:

". . . while I am coming, another steps down before me." (John 5:7)

Getting beyond the empty tradition, Jesus heals the man. The crowds were
looking to tradition with Reality in their midst! Jesus said to him, "Rise, take
up your bed and walk." And he was really healed! But it was the Sabbath, and
keeping Sabbath traditions was more important to Judaism than the healing
of a man limited for thirty-eight years. A confrontation of tradition with
Reality follows.

Therefore the Jews sought all the more to kill Him, because He not only broke the Sabbath, but also said that God was His Father, making Himself equal with God. (John 5:18)

Jesus said that God was His Father! He supports this claim with a flood of statements concerning His deity—His equality with God as God.

> Whatever the Father does, the Son does
> The Father raises the dead and the Son gives life to whom He will
> The Son has all judgment of all of mankind
> The Father and the Son are worthy of honor
> The Father has life in Himself and the Son has life in Himself
> The Father has borne witness to the Son

Jesus then speaks of the fourfold witness to His person:

> His own personal witness was not acceptable in court but still true
> The witness of John the Baptist
> The works that He does from the Father
> The testimony of Scriptures—that Scripture might be fulfilled

Yes, He does call God His Father, making Himself equal with God. Yes, Jesus is equal to God because He *is* God. The attributes of deity are shared equally by the Father, the Son, and the Spirit, each Person in the Godhead being the same in essence but distinct in substance—the Holy Trinity! That Jesus is Lord of the Sabbath will be the subject of the next great debate with the Jewish opposition.

24

Jesus Is Lord of the Sabbath

Matthew 12:1-12; Mark 2:23-3:6; Luke 6:1-10

At that time Jesus went through the grain fields on the Sabbath. And His disciples were hungry, and began to pluck heads of grain and to eat. And when the Pharisees saw it, they said to Him, "Look, Your disciples are doing what is not lawful to do on the Sabbath!" But He said to them, "Have you not read what David did when he was hungry, he and those who were with him: how he entered the house of God and ate the showbread which was not lawful for him to eat, nor for those who were with him, but only for the priests? Or have you not read in the law that on the Sabbath the priests in the temple profane the Sabbath, and are blameless? Yet I say to you that in this place there is One greater than the temple. But if you had known what this means, 'I desire mercy and not sacrifice,' you would not have condemned the guiltless. For the Son of Man is Lord even of the Sabbath." Now when He had departed from there, He went into their synagogue. And behold, there was a man who had a withered hand. And they asked Him, saying, "Is it lawful to heal on the Sabbath?"—that they might accuse Him. Then He said to them, "What man is there among you who has one sheep, and if it falls into a pit on the Sabbath, will not lay hold of it and lift it out? Of how much more value then is a man than a sheep? Therefore it is lawful to do good on the Sabbath." Then He said to the man, "Stretch out your hand." And he stretched it out, and it was restored as whole as the other. Then the Pharisees went out and plotted against Him, how they might destroy Him. (Matthew 12:1-14)

The first debate with the Pharisees was over the question of Christ forgiving sins, which only God can do. Jesus answered that question, demonstrating His deity and His relationship with His Father. This second debate was over His mighty miracles performed on the Sabbath. Jesus will demonstrate from the Old Testament and from daily practice that His actions on the Sabbath were totally justified.

There are three movements to this section—the disciples breaking a Sabbath custom, the strong argument of Jesus justifying His Sabbath actions, and a bold Sabbath healing with His opposition as the audience.

It was an innocent thing that the disciples did as they were walking along through the grain fields. To pluck a few sheaths of grain and to rub the sheaths to release the grain for a small meal did not really amount to reaping and threshing. But in the tradition of the Pharisees, in their expanded law, the disciples had broken the Sabbath and Jesus was viewed as the culprit.

"Have you not read . . . ?" With a veiled insult to the proud students of the law, Jesus in rapid fire order gives five reasons justifying both the actions of His disciples and His own actions on the Sabbath.

> David violated the law legally when he and his men ate the Bread of the Presence, establishing historical precedent.

> Priests were breaking the law regularly and legally when they carried the weight of sacrifices in the Levitical system of worship.

> The desire for mercy to be shown to others overrode the law as a manifestation of the priorities of God.

> The Sabbath was made for the benefit of man, not to be a burden to man (Mark 2:27).

> Jesus is Lord of the Sabbath; He made the rules and He can change the rules if He desires.

The verbal warfare continued in the next synagogue. A conspiracy was afoot. The Pharisees had arranged for a man with a withered right hand to be a conspicuous member of the congregation.

So the scribes and Pharisees watched Him closely, whether He would heal on the Sabbath, that they might find an accusation against Him. (Luke 6:7)

They asked Him, "Is it lawful to heal on the Sabbath?" Jesus called the man with the withered hand to come forward and He said to them, "Is it lawful to heal on the Sabbath, to do good or to do harm, to save life or to kill?" He then introduced "the sheep in the ditch" argument for the first time. It would be repeated often!

Then He said to them, "What man is there among you who has one sheep, and if it falls into a pit on the Sabbath, will not lay hold of it and lift it out? Of how much more value then is a man than a sheep? Therefore it is lawful to do good on the Sabbath." (Matthew 12:11-12)

The responses of Jesus and the Pharisees are to be noted. Before He performs this miracle of grace on this manipulated cripple He looks around at the insensitive Pharisees with anger, being grieved at their hardness and lack of compassion. Not only would they perpetuate the crippled condition of this man, but they would use him as a trap in their conspiracy against Jesus, who could bring healing. Jesus is angry! Jesus is grieved! At His command, the man's hand is healed. The trap the Pharisees set entrapped the Pharisees and freed the crippled man!

The synagogue emptied in a rage. The Pharisees were furious and held counsel with a rival party, the Herodians, to plot the death of Jesus. For religious reasons and political reasons these opposing parties found a common threat in the message of Jesus. Jesus forgave sins making Himself equal to God, calling God His Father. Jesus worked on the Sabbath. Both of these were unforgivable sins to the orthodox—sins worthy of death. The Lamb of God who would bear away the sin of the world was counted a sinner worthy of death by the orthodox of Judaism.

Orthodoxy that eliminates compassion for sinners cannot find its origin in God. Orthodoxy that produces a continual judgmental attitude cannot find its origin in God. Orthodoxy that is unfriendly to sinners and tax collectors cannot find its origin in God. The lessons of that day find fresh application to the present world of Christian orthodoxy and evangelism.

The Appointment of the Twelve Apostles

Mark 3:13-19; Luke 6:12-16

And He went up on the mountain and called to Him those He Himself wanted. And they came to Him. Then He appointed twelve, that they might be with Him and that He might send them out to preach, and to have power to heal sicknesses and to cast out demons. (Mark 3:13-15)

Now it came to pass in those days that He went out to the mountain to pray, and continued all night in prayer to God. And when it was day, He called His disciples to Himself; and from them He chose twelve whom He also named apostles: Simon, whom He also named Peter, and Andrew his brother; James and John; Philip and Bartholomew; Matthew and Thomas; James the son of Alphaeus, and Simon called the Zealot; Judas the son of James, and Judas Iscariot who also became a traitor. (Luke 6:12-16)

Choosing the apostles! This was a momentous event with long-lasting results. The apostles would receive special authority to perform numerous miracles during the offer of the kingdom to Israel. They were going to become the foundation of the coming church. They would take the good news of salvation through faith in Christ into all the world. They were going to author much of the New Testament. They would suffer persecution and death for their faithfulness, yet in the coming millennial kingdom the apostles will rule over the twelve tribes of Israel. And one of them was going to betray the Lord—Jesus knew this from the beginning.

We come to know many of the disciples from the pages of the Gospels and the book of Acts.

Andrew introduced his brother Simon (Peter) to the Messiah. Philip and Nathanael (Bartholomew) were early disciples. James and John, fishing partners with Peter and Andrew, we know, were nicknamed "Sons of Thunder." Matthew the tax collector we know, and Thomas the cautious we know. But the rest we do not know except for their inclusion in group actions. Yes, we know Judas who will betray the Lord! Close relationships developed within the group of twelve. Peter, Andrew, James, and John are always grouped in the listings. Peter is always mentioned first. Peter, James, and John were close to the Lord; only they were at the transfiguration. John was the beloved apostle, the closest to the Lord. Human friendships differ in intensity, even with the apostles, even with Jesus!

History has more to say about the apostles—at least, the *traditions* of history. Peter may have visited Britain and Gaul; he was crucified under Nero in Rome. A similar end came to Andrew, who was crucified at Patras in Achaia after preaching in Asia Minor and Greece. James, of course, was executed by Herod Agrippa I, as recorded in Acts. John was exiled to Patmos and died a natural death in old age at Ephesus. Philip, according to tradition, was crucified in Hierapolis. Matthew is connected with Ethiopia, Thomas with India. Bartholomew was martyred in Armenia. James son of Alphaeus is connected with Syria, Judas with Edessa, and Simon the Zealot with Persia and Egypt.

Having chosen and appointed the twelve apostles, Jesus will deliver to them the first discourse of His ministry: the Sermon on the Mount. The subject of this sermon is discipleship:

> ➤ the blessings of being a disciple of Jesus
> ➤ the characteristics of a disciple or Jesus which exceed the demands of the law
> ➤ the practice of personal piety of the disciples of Jesus
> ➤ the relationship of disciples of Jesus to others
> ➤ the wisdom of being a disciple of Jesus

The Sermon on the Mount will be discussed in the next three chapters.

In determining the interpretation of the Sermon on the Mount, a number of basic approaches have surfaced over the years. Some view the sermon as evangelistic, with the criteria for salvation being the two golden rules of "Do to others as you would have them do to you" and "Judge not, that you be not judged." While these are popular verses in the secular/religious world, these principles are not the means of salvation; rather, they are a product of salvation.

Others view the sermon as the rule of life for the church or the rule of life during the millennial kingdom. The details of the sermon do not coincide with the life experience in either of these periods of time.

It is best to view the sermon as an interim ethic, a way of life when the gospel of the kingdom is being preached to the nation of Israel and prior to the establishment of that kingdom. That was what Jesus and the disciples were doing. In this sermon Jesus teaches the disciples the conduct of life required of His disciples during the proclamation to Israel to "repent, for the kingdom of God is at hand." The following verses from Tuesday of Passion Week indicate the withdrawal of that offer and subsequent re-offering of the gospel of the kingdom in the tribulation:

> *"Therefore I say to you, the kingdom of God will be taken from you and given to a nation bearing the fruits of it." (Matthew 21:43)*

> *"And this gospel of the kingdom will be preached in all the world as a witness to all the nations, and then the end will come." (Matthew 24:14)*

Thus, there are two times when the Sermon on the Mount finds direct application: during the life of the Lord, and during the tribulation period, both times when the proclamation is, "Repent, the kingdom of God is at hand." The *principles* of discipleship found in the Sermon on the Mount are applicable for any follower of Jesus at any time, as are principles of life recorded throughout the Old Testament.

The summary statements of the three main sections of the body of the Sermon on the Mount are illustrations of universal application to followers of Christ:

> *"Therefore you shall be perfect, just as your Father in heaven is perfect." (Matthew 5:48)*

> *"But seek first the kingdom of God and His righteousness, and all these things shall be added to you. Therefore do not worry about tomorrow, for tomorrow will worry about its own things. Sufficient for the day is its own trouble." (Matthew 6:33-34)*

> *"Therefore, whatever you want men to do to you, do also to them, for this is the Law and the Prophets." (Matthew 7:12)*

26

The Blessings of Being
a Disciple of Jesus

Matthew 5:1-15; Luke 7:20-26

*And seeing the multitudes, He went up on a mountain, and when He
was seated His disciples came to Him. Then He opened His mouth
and taught them, saying:*
"Blessed are the poor in spirit, for theirs is the kingdom of heaven.
Blessed are those who mourn, for they shall be comforted.
Blessed are the meek, for they shall inherit the earth.
*Blessed are those who hunger and thirst for righteousness, for they
shall be filled.*
Blessed are the merciful, for they shall obtain mercy.
Blessed are the pure in heart, for they shall see God.
Blessed are the peacemakers, for they shall be called sons of God.
*Blessed are those who are persecuted for righteousness' sake, for
theirs is the kingdom of heaven.*
*Blessed are you when they revile and persecute you, and say all
kinds of evil against you falsely for My sake.*
*Rejoice and be exceedingly glad, for great is your reward in
heaven, for so they persecuted the prophets who were before
you. You are the salt of the earth; but if the salt loses its flavor,
how shall it be seasoned? It is then good for nothing but to be
thrown out and trampled underfoot by men. You are the light of
the world. A city that is set on a hill cannot be hidden. Nor do
they light a lamp and put it under a basket, but on a lampstand,
and it gives light to all who are in the house." (Matthew 5:1-15)*

While the apostles were offering the kingdom to Israel it would be
of great encouragement to understand what it will be like for them
when the kingdom does come. In the Beatitudes, Jesus looks into the future
and tells them what it will be like when He reigns in His kingdom here on
earth. We can enter into the disciples' joy as we look forward to that same
kingdom.

And they sang a new song, saying: "You are worthy to take the scroll, and to open its seals; for You were slain, and have redeemed us to God by Your blood out of every tribe and tongue and people and nation, and have made us a kingdom of priests to our God; and we shall reign on the earth." (Revelation 5:9-10)

Blessed are the poor in spirit—those who have turned to Jesus out of their personal spiritual poverty—for these believers will be citizens of the kingdom!

Blessed are those who mourn—those who have acknowledged and confessed their own sins—for God will comfort them, turning mourning into joy in His kingdom.

Blessed are the meek—those who do not assert their rights—for they will inherit the earth and rule with Christ in His coming kingdom.

Blessed are those who hunger and thirst for righteousness—those who are disappointed in the unjust practice of religious and political government—for they will be satisfied when the Priest/King rules in His kingdom.

Blessed are the merciful—those who are compassionate and caring—for they will be twice blessed, both now and in the coming kingdom.

Blessed are the pure in heart—those who love the Lord their God as a single priority of life—for they will see God manifested in His transfiguration glory in the coming kingdom.

Blessed are the peacemakers—those who proclaim the message of peace with God and of the coming rule of the Prince of Peace—for they will be acknowledged as the sons of God in His peaceful kingdom.

Blessed are those who are persecuted for righteousness' sake—those whose message of reconciliation brings retaliation—for they will be honored citizens of the kingdom where righteousness rules.

Blessed are those whom people revile and persecute and utter all kinds of evil against falsely for Christ's sake—those whose message of reconciliation brings open hatred and vicious personal attacks—for they will join the faithful prophets who were so treated before them. In the kingdom where righteousness rules, they will receive an even greater reward proportional to their suffering.

Following the encouraging Beatitudes, Jesus sets forth the well-known illustration of salt and light.

Salt had two uses—to flavor food and to preserve food. Jesus seems to be emphasizing the former when He speaks of taste. Salt is pervasive in seasoning, and the testimony of the apostles is to be pervasive in the world. That was true in the day of the offer of the kingdom, and it is true of disciples of Jesus in the present day. Salt is of no use if it is not used for its designated purpose. Disciples must function according to the purpose of the Savior.

Light dispels darkness, and Jesus identifies His apostles as the light of the world. The light is to be placed high on a hill and not to be placed under a bushel (a basket). The light is to be visible and easily seen. The light is identified as the good works done by the disciples of the Lord which are observable in a world of darkness. The end product of the good works is glory for God.

The blessings of being a disciple of Jesus and the evangelistic purpose of their mission introduce the Sermon on the Mount—the body of the sermon will follow. The introduction anticipates the great blessing when the offer of the kingdom is realized and the kingdom is established. That will be a time of great joy!

27

The Sermon on the Mount —Fulfilling the Law

Matthew 5:17-48; Luke 6:27-33

"You have heard that it was said to those of old, 'You shall not murder, and whoever murders will be in danger of the judgment.' But I say to you that whoever is angry with his brother without a cause shall be in danger of the judgment. . . . You have heard that it was said to those of old, 'You shall not commit adultery.' But I say to you that whoever looks at a woman to lust for her has already committed adultery with her in his heart. . . . Furthermore it has been said, 'Whoever divorces his wife, let him give her a certificate of divorce.' But I say to you that whoever divorces his wife for any reason except sexual immorality causes her to commit adultery; and whoever marries a woman who is divorced commits adultery. . . . Again you have heard that it was said to those of old, 'You shall not swear falsely, but shall perform your oaths to the Lord. . . . But let your 'Yes' be 'Yes,' and your 'No,' 'No.' For whatever is more than these is from the evil one. You have heard that it was said, 'An eye for an eye and a tooth for a tooth.' But I tell you not to resist an evil person. But whoever slaps you on your right cheek, turn the other to him also. . . . You have heard that it was said, 'You shall love your neighbor and hate your enemy.' But I say to you, love your enemies, bless those who curse you, do good to those who hate you, and pray for those who spitefully use you and persecute you. . . . Therefore you shall be perfect, just as your Father in heaven is perfect." (Matthew 5:21-22, 27-28, 31-33, 37-39, 43-44, 48)

Six times over Jesus introduces His discussion of the law of Moses by the words, "You have heard that it was said . . ." They are followed by a recurring clause—"But I say to you . . ."—by which He exposes the real and deeper meaning of the law—its very heart. By doing this He is challenging His disciples, then and now, to habitually live according to the reality of the law as it relates to character, not merely avoiding the final, external violation of the law.

Anger is at the heart of murder. Few people commit murder, but the vast majority of humanity has been angry, even very angry, with someone. Anger, insult, defamation of character—these form the progressive growth that, if unchecked, will lead to murder.

The disciple of Jesus is to be on the other end of the anger spectrum. If a disciple of Jesus is in the act of worship and recalls that a brother has something against him, he is to be first reconciled to his brother, and then worship God. Similarly, immediate reconciliation is to be made with an accuser. The appeal is clear—anger is to be cut off as soon as possible and reconciliation secured. Remember, a disciple of Jesus is a peacemaker; He said that in the Beatitudes!

Lust is at the heart of adultery. More commit adultery than murder, but adultery is still exceptional and viewed as a deviation from acceptable behavior. A lustful look, however, is a pervasive practice, mostly private, and rationalised by the deceitful human heart as acceptable. But it leads to a corrupted imagination that, if unchecked, will result in an overt illicit action.

The disciple of Jesus is to be ruthless in controlling what he sees and what he does so that temptation to lust is not accessible. Literal application of the words of Jesus in Matthew 5:29-30 as to removing an eye or a hand would not solve the problem of the mind and the imagination—it is an expression of severity of action as a safeguard against sin. Remember, a disciple of Jesus is pure in heart; He said that in the Beatitudes!

Divorce is unacceptable. God hates divorce. He granted it through Moses due to their hardness of heart. It was not so from the beginning. He made them male and female—the institution of marriage was monogamous between man and woman—by definition of God!

> *Therefore a man shall leave his father and mother and be joined to his wife, and they shall become one flesh. (Genesis 2:24)*

There are two elements in marriage as seen in the original defining statement recorded in Genesis. The first element is *leaving and cleaving.* A new entity is established when a man leaves his family structure of father and mother. This is reflected in the traditional question in the marriage ceremony, "Who gives this woman to this man?" The second element of marriage is the physical relationship described in the clause, "*and they shall become one flesh.*" Only the physical union is in question in this statement, not a mystical spiritual union of one-mindedness, as supported in the following:

> *Or do you not know that he who is joined to a harlot is one body with her? For "the two," He says, "shall become one flesh."*
> *(1 Corinthians 6:16)*

Jesus allows divorce only on the grounds of unfaithfulness, which violates the unique *one flesh* element of marriage. Paul allows for desertion as grounds for divorce, which violates the *leaving and cleaving* element of marriage as supported in the following:

> But if the unbeliever departs, let him depart; a brother or a sister is not under bondage in such cases. But God has called us to peace. (1 Corinthians 7:15)

A disciple of Jesus views marriage as a life-long relationship as with Christ and His church. Remember, a disciple of Jesus loves righteousness; He said that in the Beatitudes!

Oaths should be unnecessary. The truthfulness of character established by consistent performance negates the need for swearing under oath. Consistency of action is required of the disciple of Jesus so that his word is received as truth. A consistent walk speaks louder than an isolated oath, which never changes reality. The taking of oaths in a court setting is allowed in Scripture; the Lord was put under oath by Caiaphas in His Jewish trial, and God swore to Abraham at the institution of the Abrahamic Covenant. But the desire of a life of consistency validating the spoken word is reinforced by the brother of Jesus in his epistle:

> But above all, my brethren, do not swear, either by heaven or by earth or with any other oath. But let your "Yes," be "Yes," and your "No," "No," lest you fall into judgment. (James 5:12)

Remember, a disciple of Jesus will be called a son of God, the God who swears by His holy character, the God who cannot lie. Jesus said that in the Beatitudes!

Kindness should replace retaliation. Jesus quotes a passage from the law that was a series of limitations of judgment:

> "But if any harm follows, then you shall give life for life, 'eye for eye, tooth for tooth, hand for hand, foot for foot, burn for burn, wound for wound, stripe for stripe.'" (Exodus 21:23-25)

These limitations were in place to restrain undue punishment. But retaliation of any kind is not to be part of the character of a person forgiven by God—rather, mercy, kindness, and gentleness. Remember, when a disciple of Jesus is merciful, he will receive mercy. Jesus said that in the Beatitudes!

Love should be manifested to enemies and neighbors. The law did say, "Love your neighbor," but it did not say, "Hate your enemies." This was a traditional addition and reflected the attitude of the Pharisees. The context teaches the opposite.

"And if a stranger dwells with you in your land, you shall not mistreat him. The stranger who dwells among you shall be to you as one born among you, and you shall love him as yourself; for you were strangers in the land of Egypt: I am the LORD your God." (Leviticus 19:33-34)

Jesus exhorts His disciple to love as God loves, as He who sends the rain on the just and the unjust. Remember—a disciple of Jesus does not hate, he makes peace; Jesus said that in the Beatitudes!

28

The Sermon on the Mount
—Piety and Personal Life

Matthew 6:1-34

"Beware of practicing your piety before men in order to be seen by them; for then you will have no reward from your Father who is in heaven. . . . But when you give alms, do not let your left hand know what your right hand is doing, so that your alms may be in secret; and your Father who sees in secret will reward you. . . . But when you pray, go into your room and shut the door and pray to your Father who is in secret; and your Father who sees in secret will reward you. . . . But when you fast, anoint your head and wash your face, that your fasting may not be seen by men but by your Father who is in secret; and your Father who sees in secret will reward you. Do not lay up for yourselves treasures on earth, where moth and rust consume and where thieves break in and steal, but lay up for yourselves treasures in heaven, where neither moth nor rust consumes and where thieves do not break in and steal. For where your treasure is, there will your heart be also. . . . Therefore do not be anxious, saying, 'What shall we eat?' or 'What shall we drink?' or 'What shall we wear?' For the Gentiles seek all these things; and your heavenly Father knows that you need them all. But seek first his kingdom and his righteousness, and all these things shall be yours as well. Therefore do not be anxious about tomorrow, for tomorrow will be anxious for itself. Let the day's own trouble be sufficient for the day." (Matthew 6:1, 3-4, 6, 17-21, 31-34)

Giving, praying, fasting, and finances—how does a disciple of Jesus translate these acts of piety into truly godly actions according to the will of God? The answers of Jesus are clear and go to the heart of the matter. This is the same approach He uses in filling up the law of Moses in the previous segment of the sermon.

Jesus introduces the presentation with an insightful warning: "Beware of practicing your piety before men to be seen by them." The measure of reality of any given act is the motivation. When the motivation produces an act for God's observation alone it is true piety.

Giving. The Pharisees deposited their shekels into the trumpet-shaped receptacles with a flourish, and the echoing sound would draw attention from all in the temple courtyard. That attention was their reward—a short-lived reward! Jesus teaches that giving should by anonymous even to the giver; the left hand is not to know what the right hand is doing. That's impossible, but it does convey the emphasis of giving for the glory of God alone and not glory for the giver. The real motivation of giving is demonstrated if only God knows. Of course, pure motivation can be in place even when giving is not anonymous. In either case, with right motivation, there will be reward for the giver from the Father, who sees in secret.

Praying. The Pharisees loved public prayer. They prayed in the synagogues and on the street corners to be seen of men. That attention was their reward—a short-lived reward! Jesus again goes to the heart of the matter. Go into a private room, shut the door, and pray privately. Motivation again is tested by the private nature of the act, where its authenticity is tested. God responds openly to private prayer! Regular public prayer without regular private prayer resembles the hypocrisy of the Pharisees.

In this section of the Sermon on the Mount the Lord gives a model prayer known as "The Lord's Prayer." It is not meant to be endlessly repeated—He warns about that—but it is a model. There is an introduction: "Our Father in heaven, hallowed be Your name." There is a conclusion: "For Yours is the kingdom and the power and the glory forever. Amen." There are four requests that relate to the four areas in which we need help as a result of sin coming into the world: Help from God is needed to get along with Him, to get along with our environment, to get along with one another, and to get along with ourselves. Hence,

> ➢ Your will be done on earth as it is in heaven. *The Will of God*
> ➢ Give us this day our daily bread. *The Environment*
> ➢ And forgive us our debts, as we forgive our debtors. *Relationships*
> ➢ And do not lead us into temptation. *Personal Practice*

All of our petitions fall into these categories of prayer. It is a model prayer!

Fasting. The Pharisees fasted for public recognition; their misshapen faces of misery asked for sympathy and adulation. That attention was their reward—a short-lived reward! Jesus approved of *appropriate* fasting, as in the case of John's disciples upon John's imprisonment. Fasting would be appropriate as well for His disciples in His coming absence. But fasting should never be for show. It is always for spiritual concentration, for mourning, for self discipline—never for show. It is private in nature, with normal public appearance, thus insuring the reality of the reason for fasting.

Finances. The use of money is a litmus test of true spirituality. Jesus is very direct—treasure is laid up either on earth or in heaven. A person either serves God or mammon, and both are jealous masters. Having stated this competition so clearly, Jesus addresses the resultant questions relating to life on the earth: the necessities of life, of food, shelter, and clothing. To the question "If I don't take care of myself, who will?" Jesus gives an eloquent answer: "Your heavenly Father will."

> *"Look at the birds of the air, for they neither sow nor reap nor gather into barns; yet your heavenly Father feeds them. Are you not of more value than they? Which of you by worrying can add one cubit to his stature? So why do you worry about clothing? Consider the lilies of the field, how they grow: they neither toil nor spin; and yet I say to you that even Solomon in all his glory was not arrayed like one of these. Now if God so clothes the grass of the field, which today is, and tomorrow is thrown into the oven, will He not much more clothe you, O you of little faith? Therefore do not worry, saying, 'What shall we eat?' or 'What shall we drink?' or 'What shall we wear?' For after all these things the Gentiles seek. For your heavenly Father knows that you need all these things." (Matthew 6:26-32)*

His promise is equally clear.

> *"But seek first the kingdom of God and His righteousness, and all these things shall be added to you. Therefore do not be anxious about tomorrow, for tomorrow will be anxious for itself. Let the day's own trouble be sufficient for the day." (Matthew 6:33-34)*

29

The Sermon on the Mount
—Judging and Judgment

Matthew 7:1-29; Luke 6:37-49

"Judge not, that you be not judged. For with what judgment you judge, you will be judged; and with the measure you use, it will be measured back to you. And why do you look at the speck in your brother's eye, but do not consider the plank in your own eye? Or how can you say to your brother, 'Let me remove the speck from your eye'; and look, a plank is in your own eye? Hypocrite! First remove the plank from your own eye, and then you will see clearly to remove the speck from your brother's eye." (Matthew 7:1-6)

"Judge not, and you shall not be judged. Condemn not, and you shall not be condemned. Forgive, and you will be forgiven." (Luke 6:37)

"Therefore, whatever you want men to do to you, do also to them, for this is the Law and the Prophets. Enter by the narrow gate; for wide is the gate and broad is the way that leads to destruction, and there are many who go in by it. Because narrow is the gate and difficult is the way which leads to life, and there are few who find it. Therefore whoever hears these sayings of Mine, and does them, I will liken him to a wise man who built his house on the rock: and the rain descended, the floods came, and the winds blew and beat on that house; and it did not fall, for it was founded on the rock. But everyone who hears these sayings of Mine, and does not do them, will be like a foolish man who built his house on the sand: and the rain descended, the floods came, and the winds blew and beat on that house; and it fell. And great was its fall." (Matthew 7:12-14, 24-27)

In the opening segment of the Sermon on the Mount, Jesus explained the core meaning of the Mosaic law. In the second segment He addressed the reality of personal piety. In the final segment He instructed His disciples on how to relate to others.

Two of the most well-known verses in the Bible are in this section.

> ➢ "Judge not, that you be not judged."
> ➢ "Therefore, whatever you want men to do to you, do also to them, for this is the Law and the Prophets."

These verses are normally quoted without any connection to the context—the first, to justify non-involvement in identifying sin in another person; and the second, as a works-based method of salvation.

In reality, the passage teaches that a loving person *does* judge sinning people—with a view to removing the "speck in the eye" for the benefit of restoration to a holy life and a fulfilling existence. This is not to be done, however, without self-judgment first, the removing of "the log in the eye." What Jesus is speaking against is a perpetual judgmental attitude—the professional "speck in the eye" evaluator of others!

The corollary to confrontation is forgiveness. Here again Jesus identifies an attitude of life—this time a commendable one. A disciple of Jesus is to be a forgiving person by nature since he has been forgiven himself. A person characterized as a forgiving person will himself be forgiven when he falls into sin—always by God, usually by men. Remember, Jesus taught us to pray that way earlier in the sermon.

"For if you forgive men their trespasses, your heavenly Father will also forgive you. But if you do not forgive men their trespasses, neither will your Father forgive your trespasses." (Matthew 6:14-15)

The "Golden Rule" finds fulfillment in this consistent interpretation of this passage. Loving confrontation out of a consistent life, followed by forgiveness and restoration of fellowship, is treatment all should desire!

Jesus also gives a warning about confrontation: it is not always accepted, even when it arises out of a consistent life with honorable motivation. If the person repents, a brother will be gained; if he does not, a friendship will be lost. Jesus warns about this possibility.

"Do not give what is holy to the dogs; nor cast your pearls before swine, lest they trample them under their feet, and turn and tear you in pieces." (Matthew 7:6)

There is always the danger of rejected counsel. Jesus warns against spending spiritual energies on unwilling adversaries. A person has limited spiritual energies and they should be used efficiently. Rejected counsel should not be often repeated—this is a waste of time that could be used in more beneficial ways. The apostle Paul emphasizes this when he gives words of instruction and encouragement to Timothy:

> *And the things that you have heard from me among many witnesses,* <u>*commit these to faithful men*</u> *who will be able to teach others also. (2 Timothy 2:2)*

Counsel and encouragement is to be directed to "faithful" men who will multiply the effectiveness of what is taught. This is wise use of time!

Jesus concludes the sermon with a twofold invitation. First, He invites the hearers to enter by the gate that leads to life, a narrow gate through Him and His message that leads to the kingdom He was offering. He warns against the wide and spacious gate populated by the Pharisees and their followers that leads to destruction. Few find the first; many find the second. The majority is seldom right spiritually.

The second analogy correlates to the first in that it illustrates the minority who choose the narrow gate and the majority who choose the wide gate. The wise man builds his house of life on the solid rock of the teachings of Jesus. The foolish man rejects His teaching and builds his life on the shifting sands of human wisdom. The first produces a stable life; the second, a disaster!

Thus concludes the classic Sermon on the Mount.

> ➤ Introduction: the blessings of the Beatitudes for the disciples of Jesus
> ➤ Point 1: the fulfilling of the heart of the law in the life of the disciples of Jesus
> ➤ Point 2: the reality of personal piety in the life of the disciples of Jesus
> ➤ Point 3: the purity of relating to others by the disciples of Jesus
> ➤ Conclusion: the narrow gate and the wise builder seen in the disciples of Jesus

30

A Servant Is Healed, and a Widow's Son Is Restored to Life

Matthew 8:5-13; Luke 7:1-17

Now when Jesus had entered Capernaum, a centurion came to Him, pleading with Him, saying, "Lord, my servant is lying at home paralyzed, dreadfully tormented." And Jesus said to him, "I will come and heal him." The centurion answered and said, "Lord, I am not worthy that You should come under my roof. But only speak a word, and my servant will be healed. For I also am a man under authority, having soldiers under me. And I say to this one, 'Go,' and he goes; and to another, 'Come,' and he comes; and to my servant, 'Do this,' and he does it." When Jesus heard it, He marveled, and said to those who followed, "Assuredly, I say to you, I have not found such great faith, not even in Israel! And I say to you that many will come from east and west, and sit down with Abraham, Isaac, and Jacob in the kingdom of heaven. But the sons of the kingdom will be cast out into outer darkness. There will be weeping and gnashing of teeth." Then Jesus said to the centurion, "Go your way; and as you have believed, so let it be done for you." And his servant was healed that same hour. (Matthew 8:5-13)

Now it happened, the day after, that He went into a city called Nain; and many of His disciples went with Him, and a large crowd. And when He came near the gate of the city, behold, a dead man was being carried out, the only son of his mother; and she was a widow. And a large crowd from the city was with her. When the Lord saw her, He had compassion on her and said to her, "Do not weep." Then He came and touched the open coffin, and those who carried him stood still. And He said, "Young man, I say to you, arise." So he who was dead sat up and began to speak. And He presented him to his mother. Then fear came upon all, and they glorified God, saying, "A great prophet has risen up among us"; and, "God has visited His people." And this report about Him went throughout all Judea and all the surrounding region. (Luke 7:11-17)

Two miracles are in view here: the healing of a centurion's servant and the raising from the dead of a widow's son. Two cities of Galilee receive powerful testimony from the Messiah: Capernaum and Nain. Recall, Capernaum was the center and home of Jesus during the Galilean ministry. The Roman nobleman who lived in Capernaum had his son delivered from near death through the Lord's miraculous intervention. He and his household became believers. Matthew, now one of the apostles, had been the tax official in that area. And now a Roman a centurion, a military man, comes to Jesus. It is interesting to note that all centurions recorded in Scripture were of noble character. This centurion had a servant that he was fond of and regarded highly, but this servant had become paralyzed. The elders of the synagogue of Capernaum are sent to Jesus to intercede on behalf of the centurion (Luke 7), and then the man himself comes. On hearing of the man's condition, Jesus responds by saying He would come and heal the servant.

The centurion's response based is based on his knowledge of the miracle of the nobleman's son who was healed from a distance (see chapter 17).

> The centurion answered and said, "Lord, I am not worthy that You should come under my roof. But only speak a word, and my servant will be healed." (Matthew 8:8)

The centurion's logic for his faith was based on the concept of authority. The centurion was under authority in the Roman army and he exercised authority over those soldiers in his command. Now he is face to face with the ultimate authority—Jesus, the Son of God! The healing of his servant was a matter of authority.

Jesus commends this faith as the highest form of faith—that which submits to the authority of God, the ultimate authority; faith that accepts the spoken word of God as true and certain. Not in all of Israel had Jesus found this kind of faith. The centurion was a precursor to those Gentiles who would take their place in the coming kingdom.

The second miracle also demonstrates that the authority of Jesus reaches even to power over death.

It was a sad scene: the funeral procession of the only son of a widow. There were two great crowds—the one following Jesus from Capernaum, and the other following the widow in the funeral procession from Nain. These crowds would witness the authority of Jesus over death, hell, and the grave.

Notice the pathos of the scene—Jesus did! The widow had already lost her husband, and now her son. And he was a young man. The open coffin revealed the youthfulness of the deceased. The widow was weeping, and the mourners mirrored her distraught condition. What will she do now without husband or son to care for her? But Jesus cared! And Jesus had compassion. He came and touched the coffin. The procession stopped. Jesus spoke. "Young man, I say to you, arise." The young man sits up in the coffin and speaks. Jesus presents him alive to his mother!

The response of the crowds is fear. A miracle that defies death will normally produce fear. There is little practice in dealing with death! God is glorified as a result of the miracle. But as good as the verbal response is, it is not enough.

> *Then fear came upon all, and they glorified God, saying, "A great prophet has risen up among us"; and, "God has visited His people." (Luke 7:16)*

It is true that a great prophet had arisen among them. And it is also true that God had come to help His people. But Jesus was more than just a great prophet. He was the Son of God—fully God and perfectly Man! It is true that He had come to help them. But the help was more than healing and raising people from the dead. It comprised the blessings of forgiveness of sin, eternal life, and the promised kingdom.

The faith of the centurion accepted and understood the authority of Jesus. The witnesses to the restoration of life to the widow's son came close, but not close enough! They saw Christ's work but missed His message. Faith has three aspects: *cognitive faith*, which recognizes the facts; *emotional faith*, which responds with appropriate feelings; and *volitional faith*, which acts according to the content of the message. The third is "saving faith" in that it builds on the other two dimensions of faith. The centurion believed and acted upon his belief. The crowds only observed and rejoiced!

31

John the Baptist,
Discouraged and Praised

Matthew 11:2-19; Luke 7:18-35

And when John had heard in prison about the works of Christ, he sent two of his disciples and said to Him, "Are You the Coming One, or do we look for another?" Jesus answered and said to them, "Go and tell John the things which you hear and see: The blind see and the lame walk; the lepers are cleansed and the deaf hear; the dead are raised up and the poor have the gospel preached to them. And blessed is he who is not offended because of Me. . . . For this is he of whom it is written: 'Behold, I send My messenger before Your face, who will prepare Your way before You.' Assuredly, I say to you, among those born of women there has not risen one greater than John the Baptist; but he who is least in the kingdom of heaven is greater than he. And from the days of John the Baptist until now the kingdom of heaven suffers violence, and the violent take it by force. For all the prophets and the law prophesied until John. And if you are willing to receive it, he is Elijah who is to come. He who has ears to hear, let him hear!" (Matthew 11:2-6, 10-15)

The ministry of a forerunner has a built-in termination factor; John had always known that. And now the Messiah for whom he had sought to prepare the Jews was here!

He confessed, and did not deny, but confessed, "I am not the Christ." And they asked him, "What then? Are you Elijah?" He said, "I am not." "Are you the Prophet?" And he answered, "No." Then they said to him, "Who are you, that we may give an answer to those who sent us? What do you say about yourself?" He said: "I am 'the voice of one crying in the wilderness: Make straight the way of the LORD,' as the prophet Isaiah said." (John 1:20-23)

"You yourselves bear me witness that I said, 'I am not the Christ,' but, 'I have been sent before Him.' . . . He must increase, but I must decrease." (John 3:28, 30)

Now that John was imprisoned, however, he was doubting his own ministry and purpose in life. Worse than that, he was doubting the One he had baptized—doubting that He was, in fact, "the Lamb of God that bears away the sin of the world." John sends two of his disciples with the disappointing question, "Are You the Coming One, or do we look for another?"

Yes, faithful disciples do get discouraged, doubting, and questioning. Jesus does not respond with a message immediately; rather, He performs many miracles. He then gives the disciples of John the message, "Go and tell John the things which you hear and see." This is followed by a gentle rebuke, "Blessed is he who is not offended because of Me." It is of great encouragement to see that the giants of the faith, like John, share in the weaknesses of humanity common to all believers.

The disciples of John return to their imprisoned leader and Jesus testifies of John the Baptist to the crowds:

> *"For this is he of whom it is written: 'Behold, I send My messenger before Your face, Who will prepare Your way before You.' Assuredly, I say to you, among those born of women there has not risen one greater than John the Baptist; but he who is least in the kingdom of heaven is greater than he." (Matthew 11:10-11)*

Highest praise for a discouraged, doubtful, and questioning forerunner! A gracious evaluation of a life lived and finally given for the glory of God.

It should be noticed that the high praise given of John the Baptist was delivered to the crowds after John's disciples had left to return to him. Would it not have been of benefit to John to hear the positive words of Jesus concerning him? It would not be very long before John would be executed in a violent way, yet it appears that the gentle rebuke is the last communication of Jesus to John. But John's faith was yet developing through discouragement. High praise comes when the task is completed, and soon it would be!

It is important to understand the role of John the Baptist. In his ministry he was the potential fulfillment of the Malachi prophecy.

> *"Behold, I will send you Elijah the prophet before the coming of the great and dreadful day of the LORD. And he will turn the hearts of the fathers to the children, and the hearts of the children to their fathers, lest I come and strike the earth with a curse." (Malachi 4:5-6)*

> *[Jesus said,] "And if you are willing to receive it, he is Elijah who is to come." (Matthew 11:14)*

> *Jesus answered and said to them, "Indeed, Elijah is coming first and will restore all things. But I say to you that Elijah has come already,*

*and they did not know him but did to him whatever they wished.
Likewise the Son of Man is also about to suffer at their hands." Then
the disciples understood that He spoke to them of John the Baptist.
(Matthew 17:11-13)*

In short, Jesus is teaching that John the Baptist could have been the fulfillment of the Malachi prophecy if the Jews had responded positively to his message. But they did not accept his message, and therefore the prophecy was not fulfilled. So also was the offer of the kingdom by Jesus, another indication of the sovereign plan of God in bringing salvation through the rejection of both the Messiah and His forerunner.

A word about prophecy and its fulfillment: one of the amazing aspects of the Bible is its numerous prophetic statements. Some of them have been historically fulfilled, some remain to be fulfilled, and not one word will pass away until all *is* fulfilled. A phrase that is often repeated throughout the biblical record of the life of Christ is, "that the Scripture might be fulfilled." God was deliberately and precisely working out His plan of salvation, fulfilling prophecy according to scriptural statements made hundreds of years earlier. Yet He was doing this through humans who were unaware of their participation in the sovereign plan of God! The apostles' corporate prayer in Acts 4 shows they came to discern this truth:

*"For truly against Your holy Servant Jesus, whom You anointed,
both Herod and Pontius Pilate, with the Gentiles and the people of
Israel, were gathered together to do whatever Your hand and Your
purpose determined before to be done . . ." (Acts 4:27-28)*

This providential will of God working behind the scenes to accomplish His purposes is personalized to each believer when Jesus says,

*"Are not two sparrows sold for a copper coin? And not one of
them falls to the ground apart from your Father's will. Do not fear
therefore; you are of more value than many sparrows." (Matthew
10:29, 31)*

The multifaceted will of God is carried out according to His sovereign plan, often without the awareness of the participants involved—whether Herod, or Pilate, or the sparrow, or even you and me—with respect to both our coming to salvation and our being guided in the details of our lives.

32

A Sinful Woman, and Women Helpers

Luke 7:36-8:3

Then one of the Pharisees asked Him to eat with him. And He went to the Pharisee's house, and sat down to eat. And behold, a woman in the city who was a sinner, when she knew that Jesus sat at the table in the Pharisee's house, brought an alabaster flask of fragrant oil, and stood at His feet behind Him weeping; and she began to wash His feet with her tears, and wiped them with the hair of her head; and she kissed His feet and anointed them with the fragrant oil. Now when the Pharisee who had invited Him saw this, he spoke to himself, saying, "This man, if He were a prophet, would know who and what manner of woman this is who is touching Him, for she is a sinner." And Jesus answered and said to him, "Simon, I have something to say to you." So he said, "Teacher, say it." "There was a certain creditor who had two debtors. One owed five hundred denarii, and the other fifty. And when they had nothing with which to repay, he freely forgave them both. Tell Me, therefore, which of them will love him more?" Simon answered and said, "I suppose the one whom he forgave more." And He said to him, "You have rightly judged." Then He turned to the woman and said to Simon, "Do you see this woman? I entered your house; you gave Me no water for My feet, but she has washed My feet with her tears and wiped them with the hair of her head. You gave Me no kiss, but this woman has not ceased to kiss My feet since the time I came in. You did not anoint My head with oil, but this woman has anointed My feet with fragrant oil. Therefore I say to you, her sins, which are many, are forgiven, for she loved much. But to whom little is forgiven, the same loves little." Then He said to her, "Your sins are forgiven." And those who sat at the table with Him began to say to themselves, "Who is this who even forgives sins?" Then He said to the woman, "Your faith has saved you. Go in peace."

Now it came to pass, afterward, that He went through every city and village, preaching and bringing the glad tidings of the kingdom of God. And the twelve were with Him, and certain women who had been healed of evil spirits and infirmities—Mary called Magdalene, out of whom had come seven demons, and Joanna the wife of Chuza,

Herod's steward, and Susanna, and many others who provided for Him from their substance. (Luke 7:36-8:3)

There are four segments in the life of Christ where women find particular attention—Elizabeth and Mary at His incarnation; the ones in the passage now under consideration; the woman with the issue of blood and the daughter of Jairus; and the many women at resurrection time.

It was customary for Jesus to eat with tax collectors and sinners, but now He received an invitation from a Pharisee. This Pharisee, Simon, was like the rest of his Pharisee friends—he did not eat with sinners because he did not consider himself to be a sinner, though he could recognize others who *were* sinners! His response reveals his mindset.

Now when the Pharisee who had invited Him saw this, he spoke to himself, saying, "This man, if He were a prophet, would know who and what manner of woman this is who is touching Him, for she is a sinner." (Luke 7:39)

But give Simon credit—he did invite Jesus to eat with him, something no other Pharisee is recorded doing. And Jesus responded to the invitation. This was a teaching moment, with many observing the semi-private occasion. The narrative is significant in detail. Every movement of the unexpected woman is noted. It was an astonishing series of actions.

She was a woman of the city, a sinner who had sinned many times according to Jesus, a sinner well recognized by reputation and appearance according to Simon. She was a sinner of some means, having accumulated five years of wages in a bottle. *This woman!*

"Do you see this woman? I entered your house; you gave Me no water for My feet, but she has washed My feet with her tears and wiped them with the hair of her head. You gave Me no kiss, but this woman has not ceased to kiss My feet since the time I came in. You did not anoint My head with oil, but this woman has anointed My feet with fragrant oil. Therefore I say to you, her sins, which are many, are forgiven, for she loved much. But to whom little is forgiven, the same loves little." (Luke 7:44-47)

Anyone who comes to salvation must recognize his spiritual poverty—that he's a lost sinner who needs forgiveness. This woman did; this Pharisee did not! Simon, being "righteous," loved little—he issued an invitation to dinner, but rejected the invitation to salvation. She, however, demonstrated her great love by her acts of love: washing Christ's feet with her tears, drying them with her hair, kissing His feet in worship, anointing His head with costly myrrh with all of its symbolism. Her faith saved her!

Luke now mentions a number of women who functioned behind the scenes of Christ's ministry. Three are mentioned by name—Mary, Joanna, and Susanna. There were many others who are not identified specifically. This group is described as having been healed of evil spirits and infirmities. Mary, called Magdalene, who had seven demons cast out, is identified. She is not the woman of the earlier passage, nor is she the Mary of Bethany. But she is the Mary who went to the tomb to anoint the body of Christ, who told Peter and John that the tomb was empty, who returned to the garden and was the first person to see the resurrected Jesus. This Mary was a consistent provider for the ministry of Christ and the disciples until His death and resurrection.

Joanna, wife of the steward of Herod Antipas, Chuza, also provided for the ministry of Jesus and the disciples. The message of Christ reached to the high levels of government, even to one whose husband served Herod Antipas, the governor who would execute John the Baptist and hold trial over Jesus in Passion Week. The third woman is Susanna, of whom we know nothing except that she provided for the ministry. Many other women also served in this way.

Jesus did not work personal miracles for every meal needed by the Twelve! Clothing and sandals in need of replacement or repair were not the objects of omnipotence. Expenses of travel and lodging were not normally supplied by shekels found in the mouths of fish! These ladies provided for the ministry throughout those three short years and are here honored on the pages of the inspired text. God keeps track of even the anonymous and behind-the-scenes ministries!

There is a common thread to both of these settings. It focuses on the response of love by these godly women to their Savior's delivering them. The unnamed woman of sin worshipped the Lord in appreciation by washing and kissing His feet, anointing His head, and accepting His forgiveness. The healed women displayed their love as they provided for the material needs of the traveling disciples and their Lord.

33

Opposition of Friends, Foes, and Family

Mark 3:19-21; Matthew 12:22-50; Mark 3:22-35; Luke 8:19-21

... And they went into a house. Then the crowd came together again, so that they could not so much as eat bread. But when his own people heard about this, they went out to lay hold of Him, for they said, "He is out of His mind." (Mark 3:19-21)

Then one was brought to Him who was demon-possessed, blind and mute; and He healed him, so that the blind and mute man both spoke and saw. And all the multitudes were amazed and said, "Could this be the Son of David?" Now when the Pharisees heard it they said, "This fellow does not cast out demons except by Beelzebub, the ruler of the demons." But Jesus knew their thoughts, and said to them: "Every kingdom divided against itself is brought to desolation, and every city or house divided against itself will not stand. If Satan casts out Satan, he is divided against himself. How then will his kingdom stand?" (Matthew 12:22-26)

Then His brothers and His mother came, and standing outside they sent to Him, calling Him. And a multitude was sitting around Him; and they said to Him, "Look, Your mother and Your brothers are outside seeking You." But He answered them, saying, "Who is My mother, or My brothers?" And He looked around in a circle at those who sat about Him, and said, "Here are My mother and My brothers! For whoever does the will of God is My brother and My sister and mother." (Mark 3:31-35)

Opposition to the ministry of Jesus was growing! He had angered official Judaism by breaking the Sabbath, by forgiving sin and claiming equality with God, and by exposing their love for legalistic aspects of the Mosaic law and their hypocrisy of life in relationship to the law. Now from friend, foe, and family comes discouragement.

Jesus returns to His home in Capernaum and the gathering crowds demand His time and energies. The demands continue so long that they cannot even eat. At this time the friends, those who were around Him, conclude that He has lost His senses—that He is beside himself. Zeal is one thing; being out of touch with reality is another.

The Pharisees' attack is more direct. Their verdict has been long in coming, but they finally concoct an explanation for the supernatural, miraculous works of Jesus. They cannot deny the accumulating weight of numerous miracles—the blind receiving their sight, the lame walking, lepers being cleansed, hearing of deaf people being restored, and the dead being raised up. The good news was being preached to them, as well! That was the summary Jesus sent to doubting John—an accurate summary that the disbelieving Sanhedrin must refute on theological grounds. And refute it they do: the miracles are being performed by another supernatural being—Beelzebub, the prince of demons.

Jesus responds with cutting logic.

> *"How can Satan cast out Satan? If a kingdom is divided against itself, that kingdom cannot stand." (Mark 3:23-24)*

He then goes on to give a damning sentence of judgment.

> *"Therefore I say to you, every sin and blasphemy will be forgiven men, but the blasphemy against the Spirit will not be forgiven men. Anyone who speaks a word against the Son of Man, it will be forgiven him; but whoever speaks against the Holy Spirit, it will not be forgiven him, either in this age or in the age to come." (Matthew 12:31-32)*

This is not unlike the judgment of the apostate in the book of Hebrews:

> *Of how much worse punishment, do you suppose, will he be thought worthy who has trampled the Son of God underfoot, counted the blood of the covenant by which he was sanctified a common thing, and insulted the Spirit of grace? (Hebrews 10:29)*

> *And the LORD said, "My Spirit shall not strive with man forever, for he is indeed flesh." (Genesis 6:3)*

This verdict of the Sanhedrin will be repeated throughout the remaining ministry of Christ. And they will suffer the promised consequence of their rebellious unbelief against the light they were given.

Friend and foe—and now, family. The crowds were still at His home in Capernaum, so when His mother and brothers came to see Him, they could not get near Him. They stood outside asking to see Him. A messenger was sent by the family asking Him to come to them. If the messenger could get through the crowd, certainly the honored mother and His brothers could find a path through the crowd. They would surely have yielded their place to the mother of Jesus.

The stern response of Jesus indicates that His family did not understand the zeal of the Lord—just like His friends! Jesus was all about doing the will of His heavenly Father. And those who share that zeal are His real family. It is clear that two of His half-brothers, James and John, were not yet believers. Mary, in the characteristic way of all mothers, was concerned with the physical and emotional well-being of her Son. He was pushing Himself very hard in being the obedient Son. He had been like that from the beginning. She remembered the temple incident when He was twelve. "Don't you want Me to be about My Father's business?" Mary probably would not say He was beside Himself, but she thought He was approaching it. Hence, the mild rebuke from Jesus.

Opposition to the ministry of Jesus was growing: violent opposition from official Judaism; the discouragement of a disappointed forerunner; the misunderstanding of friends and family. All of this opposition, and the first phase of the ministry was not even completed—there was still much to do in the province of Galilee. Remaining were the provinces of Judea and Perea. An unyielding zeal for doing the Father's will motivated the entire life of Jesus, concluding with "Your will be done!" uttered in Gethsemane.

The application to our daily life from this section is obvious. There are numerous threats from friends, foes, family, the world system, and Satan that threaten to overcome our personal commitment to live for the glory of God. Christ-like zeal is needed for endurance—to continue to be a faithful member of the church, to pray, to witness, to study the Bible, to serve—to be about our Father's business!

> *Therefore we also, since we are surrounded by so great a cloud of witnesses, let us lay aside every weight, and the sin which so easily ensnares us, and let us run with endurance the race that is set before us, looking unto Jesus, the author and finisher of our faith, who for the joy that was set before Him endured the cross, despising the shame, and has sat down at the right hand of the throne of God. (Hebrews 12:1-2)*

34

.
.
.

"Why do You speak to them in parables?"

Matthew 13:1-53; Mark 4:1-34; Luke 8:4-18

"Behold, a sower went out to sow. And as he sowed, some seed fell by the wayside; and the birds came and devoured them. Some fell on stony places, where they did not have much earth; and they immediately sprang up because they had no depth of earth. But when the sun was up they were scorched, and because they had no root they withered away. And some fell among thorns, and the thorns sprang up and choked them. But others fell on good ground and yielded a crop: some a hundredfold, some sixty, some thirty." . . . Another parable He put forth to them, saying: "The kingdom of heaven is like a man who sowed good seed in his field; but while men slept, his enemy came and sowed tares among the wheat and went his way. But when the grain had sprouted and produced a crop, then the tares also appeared." . . . Another parable He put forth to them, saying: "The kingdom of heaven is like a mustard seed, which a man took and sowed in his field, which indeed is the least of all the seeds; but when it is grown it is greater than the herbs and becomes a tree, so that the birds of the air come and nest in its branches." Another parable He spoke to them: "The kingdom of heaven is like leaven, which a woman took and hid in three measures of meal till it was all leavened." . . . "Again, the kingdom of heaven is like treasure hidden in a field, which a man found and hid; and for joy over it he goes and sells all that he has and buys that field. Again, the kingdom of heaven is like a merchant seeking beautiful pearls, who, when he had found one pearl of great price, went and sold all that he had and bought it. Again, the kingdom of heaven is like a dragnet that was cast into the sea and gathered some of every kind, which, when it was full, they drew to shore; and they sat down and gathered the good into vessels, but threw the bad away." (Matthew 13:3-8, 24-26, 31-33, 44-48)

T he answer of the Lord to His disciples is striking.

> *"Therefore I speak to them in parables, because seeing they do not see, and hearing they do not hear, nor do they understand. And in them the prophecy of Isaiah is fulfilled, which says: 'Hearing you will hear and shall not understand, and seeing you will see and not perceive; for the hearts of this people have grown dull. Their ears are hard of hearing, and their eyes they have closed, lest they should see with their eyes and hear with their ears, lest they should understand with their hearts and turn, so that I should heal them.'"* (Matthew 13:13-15)

Israel's rejection of her Messiah was prophesied by Isaiah. Its fulfillment was certain, as all biblical prophecy is, and the Sanhedrin unknowingly but willingly exercised their individual and collective will to reject the teachings of Christ. The final line of rejection had been crossed, and now Jesus spoke in a veiled way so that His true disciples could understand, and His detractors could not. Hence, the parables.

All of the parables speak of the progress of the spread of the kingdom message and its reception.

The parable of the sower of seed. There would be varying response to the presentation of the message of the gospel of the kingdom.

The parable of the wheat and the tares. The true message of the kingdom will find a counterfeit, and the true and false followers will be divided at the end.

The parable of the mustard seed. Beginning with a small start, the gospel of the kingdom will be proclaimed and multitudes will believe before the kingdom comes.

The parable of the leaven. The message of the kingdom will be all-pervasive.

The parable of the hidden treasure. The redeemed are hidden in the field of the world and purchased at a great cost.

The parable of the pearl of great worth. The valuable pearl of the redeemed is purchased at a great cost.

The parable of the dragnet. The righteous will be separated from the unrighteous at the beginning of the kingdom.

While speaking in parables was a judgment against the Jews and their rejection of the teachings of Jesus, it also aroused the curiosity and interest of the apostles. Jesus speaks to them and us of the blessed position of the believer.

"It has been given to you to know the mysteries of the kingdom of heaven, but to them it has not been given. . . . But blessed are your eyes for they see, and your ears for they hear; for assuredly, I say to you that many prophets and righteous men desired to see what you see, and did not see it, and to hear what you hear, and did not hear it." (Matthew 13:11, 16-17)

"It has been given to you to know . . ." Jesus reveals to His disciples that their understanding of spiritual and eternal truths is due to the grace of God. The revelation to Jesus' disciples was greater than the revelation given to the faithful of previous generations. That principle applies to each of us as part of the continuing revelation of God to His people. From this point in the life of Christ until the present time there has been a great burst of spiritual enlightenment. The full development of the redemptive purposes of God through the death and resurrection of His Son, the coming of the Holy Spirit, the church, the full range of prophecy including the rapture, tribulation, and the millennium—all of this has been given to us to know. This understanding is not a result of human cleverness. As the apostle Paul will later say:

For you see your calling, brethren, that not many wise according to the flesh, not many mighty, not many noble, are called. But God has chosen the foolish things of the world to put to shame the wise, and God has chosen the weak things of the world to put to shame the things which are mighty; and the base things of the world and the things which are despised God has chosen, and the things which are not, to bring to nothing the things that are, that no flesh should glory in His presence. But of Him you are in Christ Jesus, who became for us wisdom from God—and righteousness and sanctification and redemption—that, as it is written, "He who glories, let him glory in the LORD." (1 Corinthians 1:26-31)

"It has been given to you to know . . ."! Blessed be the God and Father of our Lord Jesus Christ who has blessed us with all spiritual blessings in the heavenlies . . . to the praise of the glory of His grace.

35
.
.
.
.

Galilee and Gadara: A Storm on the Sea, and a Storm on Land

Matthew 8:18-34; Mark 4:35-5:20; Luke 8:22-39

And when Jesus saw great multitudes about Him, He gave a command to depart to the other side. . . . Now when He got into a boat, His disciples followed Him. And suddenly a great tempest arose on the sea, so that the boat was covered with the waves. But He was asleep. Then His disciples came to Him and awoke Him, saying, "Lord, save us! We are perishing!" But He said to them, "Why are you fearful, O you of little faith?" Then He arose and rebuked the winds and the sea, and there was a great calm. So the men marveled, saying, "Who can this be, that even the winds and the sea obey Him?" (Matthew 8:18, 23-27)

Then they sailed to the country of the Gadarenes, which is opposite Galilee. And when He stepped out on the land, there met Him a certain man from the city who had demons for a long time. And he wore no clothes, nor did he live in a house but in the tombs. When he saw Jesus, he cried out, fell down before Him, and with a loud voice said, "What have I to do with You, Jesus, Son of the Most High God? I beg You, do not torment me!" For He had commanded the unclean spirit to come out of the man. For it had often seized him, and he was kept under guard, bound with chains and shackles; and he broke the bonds and was driven by the demon into the wilderness. Jesus asked him, saying, "What is your name?" And he said, "Legion," because many demons had entered him. And they begged Him that He would not command them to go out into the abyss. Now a herd of many swine was feeding there on the mountain. So they begged Him that He would permit them to enter them. And He permitted them. Then the demons went out of the man and entered the swine, and the herd ran violently down the steep place into the lake and drowned. When those who fed them saw what had happened, they fled and told it in the city and in the country. Then they went out to see what had happened, and came to Jesus, and found the man from whom the demons had departed, sitting at the feet of Jesus, clothed and in his right mind. And they were afraid. They also who had seen it told them by what means he who had been demon-possessed was healed. (Luke 8:26-36)

R emember, friends and family were telling Jesus to take a break—they thought He was beside Himself. His zeal for serving His Father had overtaken Him! But instead of stopping, He taught the multitudes the intricate parables of the kingdom, telling stories so some could understand and others could not. Now He would take a break.

> And when Jesus saw great multitudes about Him, He gave a command to depart to the other side. (Matthew 8:18)

The King gave a command to go to the other side, entered the boat, went to the stern, and fell asleep on a cushion. He needed rest! But a great storm arose—not an uncommon occurrence, due to the mountainous topography to the north of the lake.

This was really a great storm. The seasoned fishermen, experts on the Sea of Galilee, were frightened.

> And they awoke Him and said to Him, "Teacher, do You not care that we are perishing?" (Mark 4:38)

Jesus arose from His sleep, rebuked the disciples, and then rebuked the winds and the sea. Immediately there was calm, and amazement that even the winds and the waves obeyed Him. But why did He rebuke the disciples? Is it not an exercise of faith in God to cry out for help in time of danger? Are we not taught to do that? Not when the Lord has given a command, an order, to go to the other side. This event is the *unneeded miracle*. The King had given orders. What should the disciples have done? They should have rowed harder and baled more water.

The storm on the sea was over; now comes the storm on the land. This was Gentile territory, a center for the swine industry supplying the Gentiles and the occupying Roman legions. Upon coming to shore the demoniac of Gadera greets Jesus and the disciples. There were two demoniacs, but just one is the focus of the gospel accounts. What a scene!

> And when He stepped out on the land, there met Him a certain man from the city who had demons for a long time. And he wore no clothes, nor did he live in a house but in the tombs . . . and no one could bind him, not even with chains, because he had often been bound with shackles and chains. And the chains had been pulled apart by him, and the shackles broken in pieces; neither could anyone tame him. And always, night and day, he was in the mountains and in the tombs, crying out and cutting himself with stones. (Luke 8:27; Mark 5:3-5)

The demoniac approached Jesus in a confused state of worship, fear, and accusation arising out of the turmoil of Jesus' command for the demons to leave the man. The man spoke, the demons spoke, and Jesus spoke. "Come out of the man, you unclean spirit!" It turns out that there were many demons. Legion was their name. They were demons who understood prophecy. They begged not to be imprisoned before the time—the time of the coming of the kingdom. They also knew of the previously imprisoned demons of Genesis 6. Demons love to possess, so they begged to possess the nearby herd of swine. "And He permitted them." The Lord controls the world of the demons. The possessed pigs plunged into the Sea of Galilee and the demons again were dispossessed.

The results?

> *Then they went out to see what had happened, and came to Jesus, and found the man from whom the demons had departed, sitting at the feet of Jesus, clothed and in his right mind. (Luke 8:35)*

> *Then they began to plead with Him to depart from their region (Mark 5:17)*

> *Now the man from whom the demons had departed begged Him that he might be with Him. But Jesus sent him away, saying, "Return to your own house, and tell what great things God has done for you." And he went his way and proclaimed throughout the whole city what great things Jesus had done for him. (Luke 8:38-39)*

The demoniac was clothed and in his right mind. The population asked Jesus to depart; their lifestyle had been disturbed by the grace of Jesus. The demoniac desired to join the disciples with Jesus, but he was instructed to witness to his own city.

There is a world of demonic opposition to Jesus and His purposes. There is a world of human beings more interested in their possessions and comfortable life than their neighbors. And there are few in the world who are committed to tell the rest ". . . what great things the Lord has done for you, and how He has had compassion on you" (Mark 5:19).

Rest had not come to Jesus. Awakened by faithless disciples in the storm, He could not rest. Coming on shore He met the demoniacs, and He had no rest. Now He would return to His home in Capernaum across the lake. It seems as though He got some rest on the boat in His return trip across Galilee. He needed that rest, because the crowds were waiting for Him at home!

36

Jesus Heals a Dying Girl and a Suffering Woman

Matthew 9:18-26; Mark 5:21-43; Luke 8:40-56

So it was, when Jesus returned, that the multitude welcomed Him, for they were all waiting for Him. And behold, there came a man named Jairus, and he was a ruler of the synagogue. And he fell down at Jesus' feet and begged Him to come to his house, for he had an only daughter about twelve years of age, and she was dying. But as He went, the multitudes thronged Him. Now a woman, having a flow of blood for twelve years, who had spent all her livelihood on physicians and could not be healed by any, came from behind and touched the border of His garment. And immediately her flow of blood stopped. And Jesus said, "Who touched Me?" When all denied it, Peter and those with him said, "Master, the multitudes throng and press You, and You say, 'Who touched Me?'" But Jesus said, "Somebody touched Me, for I perceived power going out from Me." Now when the woman saw that she was not hidden, she came trembling; and falling down before Him, she declared to Him in the presence of all the people the reason she had touched Him and how she was healed immediately. And He said to her, "Daughter, be of good cheer; your faith has made you well. Go in peace." While He was still speaking, someone came from the ruler of the synagogue's house, saying to him, "Your daughter is dead. Do not trouble the Teacher." But when Jesus heard it, He answered him, saying, "Do not be afraid; only believe, and she will be made well." When He came into the house, He permitted no one to go in except Peter, James, and John, and the father and mother of the girl. Now all wept and mourned for her; but He said, "Do not weep; she is not dead, but sleeping." And they ridiculed Him, knowing that she was dead. But He put them all outside, took her by the hand and called, saying, "Little girl, arise." Then her spirit returned, and she arose immediately. And He commanded that she be given something to eat. And her parents were astonished, but He charged them to tell no one what had happened. (Luke 8:49-56)

A young girl about to enter womanhood was dying. She was twelve years of age. A woman had suffered for twelve years from a malfunction of womanhood. It left her ceremonially disqualified as well as perpetually burdened with distraught emotions. Jesus would touch them both! The God who had created the wonderfully complex woman to be a perfect complement for man would now meet the deepest needs of womanhood for these two in their time of need.

First, the daughter of Jairus. Jesus had returned to His home in Capernaum from across the Sea of Galilee. The ruler of the synagogue, Jairus, came to seek the miracle help of Jesus. Remember, the nobleman of Capernaum had a son who had been near death and was healed. There was the centurion of great faith whose servant was healed. There was Matthew, the tax collector, now a disciple. And the fisherman brothers, James and John, sons of well known Zebedee. Jairus knew where to go to get help—he went to Jesus. There is always help from Jesus! He begged Jesus to come to the aid of his daughter, and Jesus began to return with him to his home.

The journey to the home of Jairus was interrupted. In the great crowd that followed was a certain woman.

> Now a certain woman had a flow of blood for twelve years, and had suffered many things from many physicians. She had spent all that she had and was no better, but rather grew worse. (Mark 5:25-26)

Dr. Luke adds, "She could not be healed by anyone." She made a faith-based conclusion: to simply touch the hem of Jesus' garment would bring healing. This embarrassing disease could be cured privately. And the touch did bring healing! But it was noticed. Jesus noticed that power had gone from Him—a strange comment to make. He then asked who touched Him—a strange question. Many people were touching Him, but not with the touch of faith. It was a teaching moment, and Jesus taught both the woman and the crowds. She went public and told the whole truth—and Jesus was glorified. Having gone public, Jesus addressed the woman with tenderness and encouragement.

> But Jesus turned around, and when He saw her He said, "Be of good cheer, daughter; your faith has made you well." And the woman was made well from that hour. (Matthew 9:22)

> And He said to her, "Daughter, your faith has made you well. Go in peace, and be healed of your affliction." (Mark 5:34)

The woman was miraculously healed, a result of her faith and the power of Jesus. The Lord was glorified, and the multitudes heard the public testimony of the private healing by the joyful woman. But the daughter of Jairus had died! The message came from home:

"Your daughter is dead. Why trouble the Teacher any further?" (Mark 5:35)

Jesus responded by saying, "Do not fear, only believe." Taking Peter, James, John, and the parents He went where the child was. He excluded those who laughed at Him in disbelief. With a tender touch and in terms of endearment Jesus acts.

Then He took the child by the hand, and said to her, "Talitha, cumi," which is translated, "Little girl, I say to you, arise." Immediately the girl arose and walked, for she was twelve years of age. And they were overcome with great amazement. (Mark 5:41-42)

Not only did Jesus raise her from the dead, He also prescribed nourishment to restore her strength. A miracle coupled with normative health care!

Amazement followed, but Jesus charged them to tell no one. That was impossible, and the report went throughout the whole area. Two miracles follow (Jesus gives sight to two blind men, and delivers a demoniac) and the instruction to tell no one is repeated. People were following Jesus for the miracles but not in faith. Soon that fact would be obvious, after the feeding of the five thousand. Some followed the official verdict of the Pharisees—that He did the miracles through Beelzebub. The ministry of Galilee was coming to a close—with a negative response.

But a dying girl of twelve and a woman suffering for twelve years had come into contact with the Savior, and the result for both was deliverance. Their lives were changed for time and eternity.

37

Final Visits to Nazareth and Galilee, and the Death of John

Matthew 13:54-58; Mark 6:1-13; Matthew 9:35-38, 10:5-42, 11:1

And when He had come to His own country, He taught them in their synagogue, so that they were astonished and said, "Where did this Man get this wisdom and these mighty works? Is this not the carpenter's son? Is not His mother called Mary? And His brothers James, Joses, Simon, and Judas? And His sisters, are they not all with us? Where then did this Man get all these things?" So they were offended at Him. But Jesus said to them, "A prophet is not without honor except in his own country and in his own house." Now He did not do many mighty works there because of their unbelief. (Matthew 13:54-58)

And when He had called His twelve disciples to Him, He gave them power over unclean spirits, to cast them out, and to heal all kinds of sickness and all kinds of disease. . . . These twelve Jesus sent out and commanded them, saying: "Do not go into the way of the Gentiles, and do not enter a city of the Samaritans. But go rather to the lost sheep of the house of Israel. And as you go, preach, saying, 'The kingdom of heaven is at hand.' Heal the sick, cleanse the lepers, raise the dead, cast out demons. Freely you have received, freely give. Provide neither gold nor silver nor copper in your money belts, nor bag for your journey, nor two tunics, nor sandals, nor staffs; for a worker is worthy of his food. Now whatever city or town you enter, inquire who in it is worthy, and stay there till you go out. And when you go into a household, greet it. If the household is worthy, let your peace come upon it. But if it is not worthy, let your peace return to you. And whoever will not receive you nor hear your words, when you depart from that house or city, shake off the dust from your feet." (Matthew 10:1, 5-14)

Now Herod the tetrarch heard of all that was done by Him; and he was perplexed, because it was said by some that John had risen from the dead, and by some that Elijah had appeared, and by others that one of the old prophets had risen again. Herod said, "John I have beheaded, but who is this of whom I hear such things?" So he sought to see Him. (Luke 9:7-9)

The end of the Galilean ministry is close. Jesus will be finally rejected at Nazareth, His boyhood home. There will be one last evangelistic tour throughout all of Galilee. He will feed the five thousand and deliver a penetrating message, and then the masses will forsake Him. During this period the news of the execution of John the Baptist will reach the disciples.

First, the last visit to Nazareth. While He, the Messiah, teaches in their synagogue for the final time, the people of Nazareth see only a carpenter's son and His brothers and sisters. Nobody from Nazareth could possibly know this much and do this much. They are astonished and do not believe. Jesus responds:

> *"A prophet is not without honor except in his own country, among his own relatives, and in his own house." (Mark 6:4)*

Imagine having Joseph, Mary, and Jesus as neighbors for thirty years (Joseph may have died earlier), and the amount of "light" they were rejecting all that time. Imagine going to synagogue together week by week. Imagine hearing the teachings of Jesus on several occasions. Imagine a final rejection.

> *"Woe to you, Chorazin! Woe to you, Bethsaida! For if the mighty works which were done in you had been done in Tyre and Sidon, they would have repented long ago in sackcloth and ashes. But I say to you, it will be more tolerable for Tyre and Sidon in the day of judgment than for you. And you, Capernaum, who are exalted to heaven, will be brought down to Hades; for if the mighty works which were done in you had been done in Sodom, it would have remained until this day. But I say to you that it shall be more tolerable for the land of Sodom in the day of judgment than for you." (Matthew 11:21-24)*

One could add, "Woe to you, Nazareth!"

Now, on the last tour through Galilee, Jesus gives specific directions to His disciples. The *audience* is limited to those of Israel—only the lost sheep of the house of Israel. The *message* is targeted—"The kingdom of God is at hand!" The *reaction to the response* is twofold—either bless with peace or shake off the dust of the sandals as a judgment against them. The *expected response* is negative—they will use the Beelzebub argument to explain the supernatural.

So they went out and preached that people should repent. And they cast out many demons, and anointed with oil many who were sick, and healed them. (Mark 6:12-13)

Galilee experienced an extended opportunity to respond to many invitations to receive the kingdom of God. In this last tour the response will be the same in every town and village. The anticipated negative response will be confirmed following the last great miracle of the Galilean ministry—the feeding of the five thousand.

During this last tour of Galilee, the news of the execution of John the Baptist reaches the group of disciples. The account of his death is recorded at this point in the gospel because the fame of Jesus has reached the ears of Herod Antipas. Herod becomes troubled by the rumors that John the Baptist has been raised from the dead.

Included here is a brief chronological review of the ministry of John.

[The angel Gabriel speaking] "And he will turn many of the children of Israel to the Lord their God. He will also go before Him in the spirit and power of Elijah, 'to turn the hearts of the fathers to the children,' and the disobedient to the wisdom of the just, to make ready a people prepared for the Lord." . . . . [His father Zacharias speaking] "And you, child, will be called the prophet of the Highest; for you will go before the face of the Lord to prepare His ways, to give knowledge of salvation to His people by the remission of their sins, through the tender mercy of our God, with which the Dayspring from on high has visited us; to give light to those who sit in darkness and the shadow of death, to guide our feet into the way of peace." So the child grew and became strong in spirit, and was in the deserts till the day of his manifestation to Israel. (Luke 1:16-17, 76-80)

In those days John the Baptist came preaching in the wilderness of Judea, and saying, "Repent, for the kingdom of heaven is at hand!" (Matthew 3:1-2)

[John speaking] "You yourselves bear me witness, that I said, 'I am not the Christ,' but, 'I have been sent before Him.' He who has the bride is the bridegroom; but the friend of the bridegroom, who stands and hears him, rejoices greatly because of the bridegroom's voice. Therefore this joy of mine is fulfilled. He must increase, but I must decrease." (John 3:28-30)

But Herod the tetrarch, being rebuked by him concerning Herodias, his brother Philip's wife, and for all the evils which Herod had done, also added this, above all, that he shut John up in prison. (Luke 3:19-20)

Then the disciples of John reported to him concerning all these things. And John, calling two of his disciples to him, sent them to Jesus, saying, "Are You the Coming One, or do we look for another?" When the men had come to Him, they said, "John the Baptist has sent us to You, saying, 'Are You the Coming One, or do we look for another?'" And that very hour He cured many of infirmities, afflictions, and evil spirits; and to many blind He gave sight. Jesus answered and said to them, "Go and tell John the things you have seen and heard: that the blind see, the lame walk, the lepers are cleansed, the deaf hear, the dead are raised, the poor have the gospel preached to them. And blessed is he who is not offended because of Me." (Luke 7:18-23)

[Jesus speaking] "For all the prophets and the law prophesied until John. And if you are willing to receive it, he is Elijah who is to come." (Matthew 11:13-14)

In the next segment of the life of Christ, Jesus will say,

And His disciples asked Him, saying, "Why then do the scribes say that Elijah must come first?" Jesus answered and said to them, "Indeed, Elijah is coming first and will restore all things. But I say to you that Elijah has come already, and they did not know him but did to him whatever they wished. Likewise the Son of Man is also about to suffer at their hands." Then the disciples understood that He spoke to them of John the Baptist. (Matthew 17:10-13)

The forerunner has been executed, and Jesus states that His own death is to follow. The close of Galilean ministry is but the first phase of rejection—so it will be until the clear, massive response of Good Friday, "We will not have this man to rule over us!" But God's plan is precisely on schedule: "For this hour came I into the world."

38

The Feeding of the Five Thousand

Matthew 14:13-36; Mark 6:31-56; Luke 9:11-17; John 6:1-71

When Jesus heard it [the beheading of John the Baptist], He departed from there by boat to a deserted place by Himself. But when the multitudes heard it, they followed Him on foot from the cities. And when Jesus went out He saw a great multitude; and He was moved with compassion for them, and healed their sick. When it was evening, His disciples came to Him, saying, "This is a deserted place, and the hour is already late. Send the multitudes away, that they may go into the villages and buy themselves food." But Jesus said to them, "They do not need to go away. You give them something to eat." And they said to Him, "We have here only five loaves and two fish." He said, "Bring them here to Me." Then He commanded the multitudes to sit down on the grass. And He took the five loaves and the two fish, and looking up to heaven, He blessed and broke and gave the loaves to the disciples; and the disciples gave to the multitudes. So they all ate and were filled, and they took up twelve baskets full of the fragments that remained. Now those who had eaten were about five thousand men, besides women and children (Matthew 14:13-21)

Then Jesus said to them, "Most assuredly, I say to you, Moses did not give you the bread from heaven, but My Father gives you the true bread from heaven. For the bread of God is He who comes down from heaven and gives life to the world." Then they said to Him, "Lord, give us this bread always." And Jesus said to them, "I am the bread of life. He who comes to Me shall never hunger, and he who believes in Me shall never thirst. . . . Most assuredly, I say to you, he who believes in Me has everlasting life. I am the bread of life. Your fathers ate the manna in the wilderness, and are dead. This is the bread which comes down from heaven, that one may eat of it and not die. I am the living bread which came down from heaven. If anyone eats of this bread, he will live forever; and the bread that I shall give is My flesh, which I shall give for the life of the world." The Jews therefore quarreled among themselves, saying, "How can this Man give us His flesh to eat?" Then Jesus said to them, "Most assuredly, I say to you, unless you eat the flesh of the Son of Man and drink His blood, you have no life in you. Whoever eats My flesh and drinks My blood has eternal life, and I will raise him up at the last day. For My flesh is food indeed, and My blood is drink indeed. He who eats My flesh and drinks My blood abides in Me, and I in him. As the living Father sent Me, and I live because of the Father, so he who feeds on Me will live because of Me. This is the bread which came down from heaven—not as your fathers ate the manna, and are dead. He who eats this bread will live forever." (John 6:32-35, 47-58)

Jesus knew that His disciples needed a break. They had just traveled throughout Galilee in their final visit to that province. The response was not good. They also learned about the death of John. Some of them had been his disciples. So Jesus prepared for a bit of leisure.

And He said to them, "Come aside by yourselves to a deserted place and rest a while." For there were many coming and going, and they did not even have time to eat. So they departed to a deserted place in the boat by themselves. (Mark 6:31-32)

But leisure did not come, since many knew where they were going and ran there on foot. As soon as Jesus and the disciples came on shore, the great throng caught up with them. Jesus looked on the crowds with compassion because they were like sheep without a shepherd. Later He would develop the theme of good shepherding versus bad shepherding. Now He would heal, teach about the kingdom of God, and feed the "sheep."

Feeding the sheep was a challenge, however. There were about five thousand men plus the women and children—more like ten thousand. It was a teaching moment. The disciples would learn about the God of provision as they distributed the fish and bread miraculously created by Jesus. The young lad would learn about sharing what little you have to spread blessing. As for the crowds—there was much they *could* have learned. The crowds could have learned of the care of Jesus as He seated them in a pleasant grassy hillside overlooking the Sea of Galilee. They could have learned of His administrative ability as He seated them in groups of fifties and hundreds. They could have learned of His dependence on His Father as He lifted His head to heaven. They could have learned that He was the Creator-God as He multiplied the fish and bread. They could have learned of His generosity as they ate their fill. They could have learned of His frugality as He collected the leftovers. They could have learned these things, but after His discourse it seems as if they did not learn very much at all—but they did have a good meal!

After the meal, the crowds were dismissed to go home, the disciples boarded the boat to return to Bethsaida, and Jesus went up into the hills to pray by

Himself. A great storm arose, Jesus walked to them on the water, Peter joined Jesus for a few steps, Peter and Jesus got in the boat, and the boat was immediately at the place they were going—a series of amazing miracles that were witnessed only by the disciples. They worshiped with the great confession, "Truly, You are the Son of God."

The next day the people found Him.

> On the following day, when the people who were standing on the other side of the sea saw that there was no other boat there, except that one which His disciples had entered, and that Jesus had not entered the boat with His disciples, but His disciples had gone away alone— however, other boats came from Tiberias, near the place where they ate bread after the Lord had given thanks— when the people therefore saw that Jesus was not there, nor His disciples, they also got into boats and came to Capernaum, seeking Jesus. And when they found Him on the other side of the sea, they said to Him, "Rabbi, when did You come here?" (John 6:22-25)

Jesus could have said, "I walked over on the lake." I doubt they would have believed Him. They seldom believed Him. The answer to their question is an extended one—the Bread of Life Discourse. This is the second of five great discourses in the life of Christ:

> ➤ The Sermon on the Mount in the Galilean Ministry
> ➤ The Bread of Life Discourse in the Galilean Ministry
> ➤ The Good Shepherd Discourse in the Judean Ministry
> ➤ The Olivet Discourse in Passion Week
> ➤ The Upper Room Discourse in Passion Week

The first discourse was on the subject of discipleship. The second is on the subject of salvation—Christ's final invitation to salvation in Galilee.

The introduction to the discourse is abrupt.

> "Most assuredly, I say to you, you seek Me, not because you saw the signs, but because you ate of the loaves and were filled. Do not labor for the food which perishes, but for the food which endures to everlasting life, which the Son of Man will give you, because God the Father has set His seal on Him." Then they said to Him, "What shall we do, that we may work the works of God?" Jesus answered and said to them, "This is the work of God, that you believe in Him whom He sent." (John 6:26-29)

The work required by God is not a work—it is belief. Those who had received the fish and bread in the feeding of the five thousand asked for a sign just like the sign their ancestors asked for in Moses' day. Had they not just received bread from the hand of God—the Son of God, Jesus? Jesus moved on in the discourse to introduce the bread of God that satisfies spiritual hunger forever. Like the woman of Samaria, they were only thinking of physical sustenance, and they say, "Give us this bread always." But Jesus says:

> *"I am the bread of life. He who comes to Me shall never hunger, and he who believes in Me shall never thirst. . . . I am the bread which came down from heaven. . . . I am the living bread which came down from heaven. If anyone eats of this bread, he will live forever; and the bread that I shall give is My flesh, which I shall give for the life of the world." (John 6:35, 41, 51)*

> *"Most assuredly, I say to you, unless you eat the flesh of the Son of Man and drink His blood, you have no life in you. Whoever eats My flesh and drinks My blood has eternal life, and I will raise him up at the last day." (John 6:53-54)*

The Jews took what He said as literal cannibalism, and they were offended by this. If their interpretation was correct, they *should* have been offended. But they missed the point. To "eat" His flesh and to "drink" His blood is to receive Him, assimilate Him into one's life—to *believe* Him. Belief is the sole condition for salvation.

> *"Most assuredly, I say to you, he who believes in Me has everlasting life." (John 6:47)*

It was a discouraging time, this close of the Galilean ministry. The thousands just fed by Jesus would not take the Bread of Life come down from heaven. They withdrew from following Jesus. And Jesus said to the Twelve, "Will you go away also?" But Peter speaks.

> *"Lord, to whom shall we go? You have the words of eternal life. Also we have come to believe and know that You are the Christ, the Son of the living God." (John 6:68-69)*

The first phase of the Lord's public ministry concludes with rejection.

Remaining are the provinces of Judea and Perea. But before visiting them, Christ will take His twelve disciples out of the country for private instruction and encouragement for what is known as the Teaching of the Twelve.

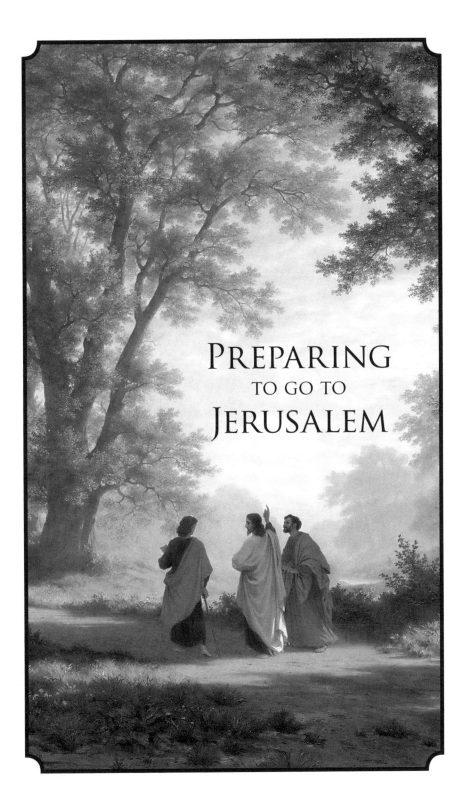

PREPARING
TO GO TO
JERUSALEM

39

Opposition Follows Jesus to Phoenicia

Matthew 15:1-20; Mark 7:1-23

Then the Pharisees and some of the scribes came together to Him, having come from Jerusalem. Now when they saw some of His disciples eat bread with defiled, that is, with unwashed hands, they found fault. For the Pharisees and all the Jews do not eat unless they wash their hands in a special way, holding the tradition of the elders. When they come from the marketplace, they do not eat unless they wash. And there are many other things which they have received and hold, like the washing of cups, pitchers, copper vessels, and couches. Then the Pharisees and scribes asked Him, "Why do Your disciples not walk according to the tradition of the elders, but eat bread with unwashed hands?" He answered and said to them, "Well did Isaiah prophesy of you hypocrites, as it is written: 'This people honors Me with their lips, but their heart is far from Me. And in vain they worship Me, teaching as doctrines the commandments of men.' For laying aside the commandment of God, you hold the tradition of men—the washing of pitchers and cups, and many other such things you do." He said to them, "All too well you reject the commandment of God, that you may keep your tradition. . . ." When He had entered a house away from the crowd, His disciples asked Him concerning the parable. So He said to them, "Are you thus without understanding also? Do you not perceive that whatever enters a man from outside cannot defile him, because it does not enter his heart but his stomach, and is eliminated, thus purifying all foods?" And He said, "What comes out of a man, that defiles a man. For from within, out of the heart of men, proceed evil thoughts, adulteries, fornications, murders, thefts, covetousness, wickedness, deceit, lewdness, an evil eye, blasphemy, pride, foolishness. All these evil things come from within and defile a man." (Mark 7:1-9, 17-23)

The Galilean ministry came to a close with rejection. Jesus now leads His disciples out of Israel into the land of Phoenicia and other Gentile areas where He will minister to the Twelve privately. But before that, there is another confrontation with the Pharisees who had come to Capernaum from Jerusalem. There are three movements to the confrontation: the challenge by the Pharisees, Jesus' responses, and the explanation of those responses to His disciples.

First, the challenge by the Pharisees to Jesus.

> *Then the Pharisees and scribes asked Him, "Why do Your disciples not walk according to the tradition of the elders, but eat bread with unwashed hands?" (Mark 7:5)*

It was an old argument. From the very beginning of the ministry of Jesus, the Pharisees objected to the actions of Jesus and His disciples. "We never did it that way." The keeping of the law, the traditions of the elders, the interpretation of Old Testament Scriptures, the customs and practices of Judaism—all were challenged by the actions and teachings of Jesus and His disciples. The challenge here addresses the ritual custom of cleansing after a shopping venture into the marketplace. The Pharisees would not think of eating without washing their hands; it was not a practice of hygiene but of ceremonial cleansing from spiritual defilement. Washing with soap and water is a good practice to remove germs, but it will never remove sin or spiritual uncleanness—water can't do that. There were other such practices relating to cleansing utensils for eating, and even the cleansing of the dining couch. There were no quick meals in the homes of the Pharisees!

Second, the response of Jesus to the Jews.

> *He answered and said to them, "Well did Isaiah prophesy of you hypocrites, as it is written: 'This people honors Me with their lips, but their heart is far from Me. And in vain they worship Me, teaching as doctrines the commandments of men.' For laying aside the commandment of God, you hold the tradition of men—the washing of pitchers and cups, and many other such things you do." He said to them, "All too well you reject the commandment of God that you may keep your tradition . . . making the word of God of no effect through your tradition which you have handed down. And many such things you do." (Mark 7:6-9, 13)*

Teaching the commandments of men as doctrine is an ever-present danger! Notice the possibility that the traditions of men can nullify the teachings in the Word of God. There are many extra-biblical traditions and customs which do not interfere with the teaching of the Word of God; some even enhance its teaching. But it is true that some traditions can negate Holy Scripture—for instancce, a simple thing like ceremonial washing of hands could negate the biblical command of love and hospitality.

Third, the teaching of Jesus to the disciples.

The disciples approach Jesus with an evaluation of Jesus interpersonal relationship with the Pharisees.

Then His disciples came and said to Him, "Do You know that the Pharisees were offended when they heard this saying?" (Matthew 15:12)

They also request explanation of a simple parable that the Lord presented to them which captured the essence of His teaching here:

"Hear Me, everyone, and understand: There is nothing that enters a man from outside which can defile him; but the things which come out of him, those are the things that defile a man." (Mark 7:14-15)

The disciples are gently rebuked, as Jesus assumes that they should have the ability to understand the brief parable. What's so hard about it? What goes into the mouth does not determine the moral validity of a person's character. Food is consumed and digested. The mouth, in the parable, expresses the heart, which is the totality of a person's being. Out of the heart the mouth speaks, revealing the character of a man.

"What comes out of a man, that defiles a man. For from within, out of the heart of men, proceed evil thoughts, adulteries, fornications, murders, thefts, covetousness, wickedness, deceit, lewdness, an evil eye, blasphemy, pride, foolishness. All these evil things come from within and defile a man." (Mark 7:20-23)

The confrontation is over the form of religion versus the reality of character. This is a leftover of the Galilean opposition. No doubt the departure out of Israel to Phoenicia was a relief to Jesus and the disciples.

Then Jesus went out from there and departed to the region of Tyre and Sidon. (Matthew 15:21)

40

A Daughter Is Delivered, 4,000 Are Fed, and a Blind Man Is Healed

Matthew 15:21-16:12; Mark 7:24-8:26

And behold, a woman of Canaan came from that region and cried out to Him, saying, "Have mercy on me, O Lord, Son of David! My daughter is severely demon-possessed." But He answered her not a word. And His disciples came and urged Him, saying, "Send her away, for she cries out after us." But He answered and said, "I was not sent except to the lost sheep of the house of Israel." Then she came and worshiped Him, saying, "Lord, help me!" But He answered and said, "It is not good to take the children's bread and throw it to the little dogs." And she said, "Yes, Lord, yet even the little dogs eat the crumbs which fall from their masters' table." Then Jesus answered and said to her, "O woman, great is your faith! Let it be to you as you desire." And her daughter was healed from that very hour. . . . Now Jesus called His disciples to Himself and said, "I have compassion on the multitude, because they have now continued with Me three days and have nothing to eat. And I do not want to send them away hungry, lest they faint on the way." Then His disciples said to Him, "Where could we get enough bread in the wilderness to fill such a great multitude?" Jesus said to them, "How many loaves do you have?" And they said, "Seven, and a few little fish." So He commanded the multitude to sit down on the ground. And He took the seven loaves and the fish and gave thanks, broke them and gave them to His disciples; and the disciples gave to the multitude. So they all ate and were filled, and they took up seven large baskets full of the fragments that were left. Now those who ate were four thousand men, besides women and children. And He sent away the multitude, got into the boat, and came to the region of Magdala. (Matthew 15:22-28, 32-39)

Then He came to Bethsaida; and they brought a blind man to Him, and begged Him to touch him. So He took the blind man by the hand and led him out of the town. And when He had spit on his eyes and put His hands on him, He asked him if he saw anything. And he looked up and said, "I see men like trees, walking." Then He put His hands on his eyes again and made him look up. And he was restored and saw everyone clearly. Then He sent him away to his house, saying, "Neither go into the town, nor tell anyone in the town." (Mark 8:22-26)

Jesus ignores the woman of Canaan—not even a word. The disciples ask Jesus to send her away. He responds to them, "I was not sent except to the lost sheep of the house of Israel." After all, Jesus had left Galilee and Israel to be alone with the disciples, to encourage them in the face of rejection and the death of John the Baptist, to reveal to them new truth concerning the coming church, and to give some of the disciples a taste of the kingdom on the Mount of Transfiguration. It was not yet Gentile time. He reiterates what He had told them before: "Go only to the lost sheep of the house of Israel."

But think of the poor woman hearing this theological discussion that kept her separated from help for her daughter. She could have been offended. But her need was greater than her pride. So she begs.

The Lord responds to her persistence, opening the door for a humble plea that leads to Jesus performing a miracle for her. Jesus states:

"It is not good to take the children's bread and throw it to the little dogs." (Matthew 15:26)

In a lowly but clever way she assumes the place of a pet dog.

And she said, "Yes, Lord, yet even the little dogs eat the crumbs which fall from their masters' table." (Matthew 15:27)

She only desires a little crumb of a miracle to touch her daughter. Amazed at her faith, the Lord grants her request, and the daughter is freed from the demon. The woman was Greek, a Syrophoenician by race. It was a gracious miracle, outside of the intended purpose for entering into Gentile territory (to spend time with the Twelve), outside of the chronology of the gospel going into the entire world, outside of the renewal of the offer of the kingdom when next returning to Jewish territory. It was a miracle of grace, and the woman returned to her Gentile way of life with her demon-free daughter. And together they glorified the God of Israel.

This isolated miracle led to a flurry of miracles in the Gentile territory, and once again Jesus looks on the hungry masses with compassion. Some of them had traveled a long way and would have fainted without food. This time, there were four thousand men, besides women and children. This time, there were seven loaves and a few fish. They were seated, Jesus gave thanks, He broke seven fish and few loaves into sufficient food to feed the multitude, and they were satisfied. There were seven baskets of leftovers on this occasion.

The third event takes place, indicative of the new teaching that Jesus would deliver to His disciples during the Teaching of the Twelve: a blind man gets his sight in stages. The disciples would understand in stages the revelation concerning the church and the meaning of the transfiguration experience.

A blind man is brought to Jesus for healing. Jesus takes him by the hand and leads him out of the village. Having spit on his eyes, Jesus asks if he sees anything. He sees, but not clearly. Jesus touches him again, he sees clearly, and then he is instructed not to return to the village of his blindness. Clearly the miracle is not for public recognition. It is symbolic of what is going to happen.

> *Then He commanded His disciples that they should tell no one that He was Jesus the Christ. (Matthew 16:20)*

> *Now as they came down from the mountain, Jesus commanded them, saying, "Tell the vision to no one until the Son of Man is risen from the dead." (Matthew 17:9)*

> *So they kept this word to themselves, questioning what the rising from the dead meant. (Mark 9:10)*

> *But they did not understand this saying, and it was hidden from them so that they did not perceive it; and they were afraid to ask Him about this saying. (Luke 9:45)*

The disciples would hear about the church but not understand until later. Some would view the King in His glory, but not understand until later. The stage was now set for the first great revelation of the mystery which from the beginning of ages had been hidden in God. On to the area of the Decapolis— and to Peter's great confession of Christ.

41

Peter's Confession, and the Church

Matthew 16:13-28; Mark 8:27-9:1; Luke 9:18-27

When Jesus came into the region of Caesarea Philippi, He asked His disciples, saying, "Who do men say that I, the Son of Man, am?" So they said, "Some say John the Baptist, some Elijah, and others Jeremiah or one of the prophets." He said to them, "But who do you say that I am?" Simon Peter answered and said, "You are the Christ, the Son of the living God." Jesus answered and said to him, "Blessed are you, Simon Bar-Jonah, for flesh and blood has not revealed this to you, but My Father who is in heaven. And I also say to you that you are Peter, and on this rock I will build My church, and the gates of Hades shall not prevail against it. And I will give you the keys of the kingdom of heaven, and whatever you bind on earth will be bound in heaven, and whatever you loose on earth will be loosed in heaven." Then He commanded His disciples that they should tell no one that He was Jesus the Christ. From that time Jesus began to show to His disciples that He must go to Jerusalem, and suffer many things from the elders and chief priests and scribes, and be killed, and be raised the third day. . . . "For the Son of Man will come in the glory of His Father with His angels, and then He will reward each according to his works. Assuredly, I say to you, there are some standing here who shall not taste death till they see the Son of Man coming in His kingdom." (Matthew 16:13-21, 27-28)

Jesus is alone with the Twelve in the Gentile territory of the Decapolis (the area of the ten cities). Now He has opportunity to reveal some major new truths to the apostles. But before Jesus reveals the great mystery of the church and alludes to the coming transfiguration, He has a question for them: "Who do men say that the Son of Man is?"

The title "Son of Man" originates in the book of Daniel. In Daniel's vision, the prophet sees the following:

"I watched till thrones were put in place, and the Ancient of Days was seated; His garment was white as snow, and the hair of His head was like pure wool. His throne was a fiery flame, its wheels a burning fire; a fiery stream issued and came forth from before

Him. A thousand thousands ministered to Him; ten thousand times ten thousand stood before Him. The court was seated, and the books were opened. . . . I was watching in the night visions, and behold, One like the Son of Man, coming with the clouds of heaven! He came to the Ancient of Days, and they brought Him near before Him. Then to Him was given dominion and glory and a kingdom that all peoples, nations, and languages should serve Him. His dominion is an everlasting dominion, which shall not pass away, And His kingdom the one which shall not be destroyed." (Daniel 7:9-10, 13-14)

The setting is the vision in which five great world empires are revealed—Babylon, Persia, Greece, Rome, and finally the kingdom of God on earth. The Son of Man approaches the Ancient of Days and receives the promise of this kingdom. This is the kingdom that is in view in Psalm 2, quoted several times in Scripture in reference to Jesus:

"I will declare the decree: The LORD has said to Me, 'You are My Son, today I have begotten You. Ask of Me, and I will give You the nations for Your inheritance, and the ends of the earth for Your possession." (Psalm 2:7-8)

Jesus refers to the Daniel passage in His trial before Caiaphas in Passion Week.

But Jesus kept silent. And the high priest answered and said to Him, "I put You under oath by the living God: Tell us if You are the Christ, the Son of God!" Jesus said to him, "It is as you said. Nevertheless, I say to you, hereafter you will see the Son of Man sitting at the right hand of the Power, and coming on the clouds of heaven." (Matthew 26:63-64)

The title "Son of Man" was the title Jesus used the most when referring to Himself. It is His incarnational title connected with the kingdom. It virtually disappears from use in the epistles to the church. And so He asks His disciples, "Who do men say that the Son of Man is?"

There are a number of suggestions made by the people: John the Baptist, Elijah, Jeremiah, one of the prophets. But Peter speaks for the apostles, and he speaks correctly, inspired by the Spirit of God Himself. "You are the Christ, the Son of the living God!"

Upon hearing this confession, Jesus makes a profound prophecy.

"And I also say to you that you are Peter, and on this rock I will build My church, and the gates of Hades shall not prevail against it." (Matthew 16:18)

"This rock"! Is it Peter's confession? The apostles? Christ? All are spoken of as the foundation of the church elsewhere in Scripture.

"My church"! This is the first appearance of the word in the Gospels. It is not the kingdom—it is the church. This new term will be filled with meaning in the epistles. It begins on the day of Pentecost (recorded in Acts 2). It includes Jew and Gentile in one new entity. All members will be priests. All members will have spiritual gifts. Baptism and communion will become regular practices. It will spread all over the earth. It will be concluded with its rapture. The church is not the kingdom. This is a new revelation—a mystery hidden in God, now slightly revealed.

> For this reason I, Paul, the prisoner of Christ Jesus for you Gentiles— if indeed you have heard of the dispensation of the grace of God which was given to me for you, how that by revelation He made known to me the mystery (as I have briefly written already, by which, when you read, you may understand my knowledge in the mystery of Christ), which in other ages was not made known to the sons of men, as it has now been revealed by the Spirit to His holy apostles and prophets: that the Gentiles should be fellow heirs, of the same body, and partakers of His promise in Christ through the gospel. (Ephesians 3:1-6)

The Scriptures do not reveal what the apostles thought concerning this new revelation. We do know what they thought about the *next* new revelation. Notice what Jesus began to declare openly from that time onwards.

> From that time Jesus began to show to His disciples that He must go to Jerusalem, and suffer many things from the elders and chief priests and scribes, and be killed, and be raised the third day. Then Peter took Him aside and began to rebuke Him, saying, "Far be it from You, Lord; this shall not happen to You!" But He turned and said to Peter, "Get behind Me, Satan! You are an offense to Me, for you are not mindful of the things of God, but the things of men." (Matthew 16:21-23)

Having been rejected in Galilee, it was now appropriate for Jesus to reveal the mystery of the church to His disciples and to then tell of His impending death and resurrection. How encouraging it must have been to hear of another phase of God's plan of redemption. But how discouraging to hear of the Lord's death. And how to put together the offer of the kingdom, the crucifixion, this new concept of the church, and the plan to take the kingdom message to Judea and Perea—only God could know. In time, the apostles would also know.

42

The Transfiguration:
A Foretaste of the Kingdom

Matthew 17:1-13; Mark 9:2-13; Luke 9:28-36

Now after six days Jesus took Peter, James, and John his brother, led them up on a high mountain by themselves; and He was transfigured before them. His face shone like the sun, and His clothes became as white as the light. And behold, Moses and Elijah appeared to them, talking with Him. Then Peter answered and said to Jesus, "Lord, it is good for us to be here; if You wish, let us make here three tabernacles: one for You, one for Moses, and one for Elijah." While he was still speaking, behold, a bright cloud overshadowed them; and suddenly a voice came out of the cloud, saying, "This is My beloved Son, in whom I am well pleased. Hear Him!" And when the disciples heard it, they fell on their faces and were greatly afraid. But Jesus came and touched them and said, "Arise, and do not be afraid." When they had lifted up their eyes, they saw no one but Jesus only. Now as they came down from the mountain, Jesus commanded them, saying, "Tell the vision to no one until the Son of Man is risen from the dead." And His disciples asked Him, saying, "Why then do the scribes say that Elijah must come first?" Jesus answered and said to them, "Indeed, Elijah is coming first and will restore all things. But I say to you that Elijah has come already, and they did not know him but did to him whatever they wished. Likewise the Son of Man is also about to suffer at their hands." Then the disciples understood that He spoke to them of John the Baptist. (Matthew 17:1-13)

As the Lord concludes His initial revelation of the church He promises that some will not die before they see His kingdom. Rather,

"Assuredly, I say to you, there are some standing here who shall not taste death till they see the Son of Man coming in His kingdom." (Matthew 16:28)

This is appropriate. They will all die before the kingdom actually comes, as will its King. But to demonstrate to them that it *will* come, and that it will come after the church era, He takes His three closest disciples (Peter, James, and John) up to a high mountain to see a microcosm of the coming kingdom and Jesus in His majestic glory. They would see it briefly, and they would never get over it!

> *For we did not follow cunningly devised fables when we made known to you the power and coming of our Lord Jesus Christ, but were eyewitnesses of His majesty. For He received from God the Father honor and glory when such a voice came to Him from the Excellent Glory: "This is My beloved Son, in whom I am well pleased." And we heard this voice which came from heaven when we were with Him on the holy mountain. (2 Peter 1:16-18)*

While Jesus is praying, His glory is revealed. In His later intercessory prayer (recorded in John 17), Jesus asks the Father to restore to Him the glory that He had from the beginning. Here for a brief period that glory is restored for the onlookers to observe. His glory is as white as light, dazzling white. More! Elijah and Moses appear with Him in glory! More! The disciples could hear them speaking of the Lord's departure in Jerusalem—His death and departure to return to heaven, from whence Moses and Elijah had come to earth for this brief visit with Jesus and Peter and James and John. It is a foretaste of those who would reign in the millenial kingdom—the King, the Old Testament saints, and the apostles, the foundation of the church. Glory!

Peter speaks.

> *"Rabbi, it is good for us to be here; and let us make three tabernacles: one for You, one for Moses, and one for Elijah"—because he did not know what to say, for they were greatly afraid. (Mark 9:5-6)*

What Peter says is somewhat fitting, even though he speaks out of fear. The tents he suggests pitching relate to the Feast of Tabernacles, the feast that celebrated the nation of Israel coming into their promised land following the wilderness wanderings. It was repeated once a year as a reminder. This is the feast that will be repeated for the nations in the millennial kingdom to remind them of the primacy of Israel.

> *And it shall come to pass that everyone who is left of all the nations which came against Jerusalem shall go up from year to year to worship the King, the Lord of hosts, and to keep the Feast of Tabernacles. (Zechariah 14:16)*

The foretaste of the kingdom is temporary. A cloud envelopes them, and the voice of God restates what He said at the baptism of the Lord, focusing on the preeminence and virtue of Christ and the value of His message.

> *"This is My beloved Son, in whom I am well pleased. Hear Him!" (Matthew 17:6)*

The cloud departs. Moses and Elijah depart. And the manifestation of glory departs. Jesus touches them, and they see no one but Him. The transfiguration is over.

While coming down from the mountain, Jesus instructs them not to tell anyone about this until after the resurrection. Having just seen and heard Elijah, the disciples begin to discuss the role of Elijah.

> *And His disciples asked Him, saying, "Why then do the scribes say that Elijah must come first?" Jesus answered and said to them, "Indeed, Elijah is coming first and will restore all things. But I say to you that Elijah has come already, and they did not know him but did to him whatever they wished. Likewise the Son of Man is also about to suffer at their hands." Then the disciples understood that He spoke to them of John the Baptist. (Matthew 17:10-13)*

Earlier, Jesus had referred to the role of John the Baptist and Elijah.

> *"For all the prophets and the law prophesied until John. And if you are willing to receive it, he is Elijah who is to come." (Matthew 11:13-14)*

The conditional "if" was not fulfilled, and the rejection of Israel concerning John and Jesus eliminated the possibility of the fulfillment in that day. It will be fulfilled literally in a future day when "they look on [Him] whom they pierced," and repent of having crucified Him.

Reflecting on the encouragement he received when he witnessed Christ's transfiguration, Peter exhorts us to have confidence in God's revelation to us.

> *And so we have the prophetic word confirmed, which you do well to heed as a light that shines in a dark place, until the day dawns and the morning star rises in your hearts; knowing this first, that no prophecy of Scripture is of any private interpretation, for prophecy never came by the will of man, but holy men of God spoke as they were moved by the Holy Spirit. (2 Peter 1:19-21)*

Peter, James, and John saw "the rest of the story"—the kingdom—and so shall we!

.
.
.
•

Discipline in the Church

Matthew 17:22-18:35; Mark 9:33-50; Luke 9:43-60

Then they departed from there and passed through Galilee, and He did not want anyone to know it. For He taught His disciples and said to them, "The Son of Man is being betrayed into the hands of men, and they will kill Him. And after He is killed, He will rise the third day." But they did not understand this saying, and were afraid to ask Him. (Mark 9:30-32)

Then a dispute arose among them as to which of them would be greatest. And Jesus, perceiving the thought of their heart, took a little child and set him by Him, and said to them, Whoever receives this little child in My name receives Me; and whoever receives Me receives Him who sent Me. For he who is least among you all will be great." (Luke 9:46-48)

"But whoever causes one of these little ones who believe in Me to sin, it would be better for him if a millstone were hung around his neck, and he were drowned in the depth of the sea. Woe to the world because of offenses! For offenses must come, but woe to that man by whom the offense comes! . . . Even so it is not the will of your Father who is in heaven that one of these little ones should perish. Moreover if your brother sins against you, go and tell him his fault between you and him alone. If he hears you, you have gained your brother. But if he will not hear, take with you one or two more, that 'by the mouth of two or three witnesses every word may be established.' And if he refuses to hear them, tell it to the church. But if he refuses even to hear the church, let him be to you like a heathen and a tax collector. Assuredly, I say to you, whatever you bind on earth will be bound in heaven, and whatever you loose on earth will be loosed in heaven. Again I say to you that if two of you agree on earth concerning anything that they ask, it will be done for them by My Father in heaven. For where two or three are gathered together in My name, I am there in the midst of them." Then Peter came to Him and said, "Lord, how often shall my brother sin against me, and I forgive him? Up to seven times?" Jesus said to him, "I do not say to you, up to seven times, but up to seventy times seven." (Matthew 18:6-7, 14-22)

J esus returns to His home in Galilee, Capernaum, packs His belongings, and travels to Jerusalem for the evangelization of Judea. He does not want anyone in Galilee to know it because that ministry is now completed. He continues to speak to His disciples about His coming death and resurrection, but by divine intervention they do not understand the underlying message.

> *But they did not understand this saying, and it was hidden from them so that they did not perceive it; and they were afraid to ask Him about this saying. (Luke 9:45)*

A dispute arises among the disciples. The subject of the dispute is, which of them is the greatest! Jesus understands both the debate and its root—*pride.* This, the original sin of Lucifer, has been visited upon all of mankind. Sin is selfishness, pride. Jesus' response is precise.

> *And He sat down, called the twelve, and said to them, "If anyone desires to be first, he shall be last of all and servant of all." (Mark 9:35)*

He sits down to teach, calls them to gather around Him, and introduces the subject with the basic principle of servanthood, not selfishness. To illustrate, He calls a helpless, humble child; humility is the answer to pride. It is best illustrated by children, who are totally dependent on others for life and well-being.

Since pride is the origin of all sin, Jesus teaches His disciples how to handle the issue of sin among His followers. Jesus again uses the word "church" in discussing the topic. Above all, Jesus desires that the church should have holy members. There is a principle that emerges from His teaching—that the knowledge of sin in a person's life should be kept as limited as possible.

> *"Moreover if your brother sins against you, go and tell him his fault between you and him alone. If he hears you, you have gained your brother." (Matthew 18:15)*

Confront the sinning brother alone. If there is repentance, the matter is settled and over. Forgiveness and restoration takes place, and no one else ever needs to know. If there is no success in the initial confrontation, the level of confrontation is intensified.

> *"But if he will not hear, take with you one or two more, that 'by the mouth of two or three witnesses every word may be established.'" (Matthew 18:16)*

This time the confrontation is with witnesses, a far more threatening situation. Once again, the goal is confession, forgiveness, and restoration of fellowship.

This is always the goal of discipline. If there is repentance, the matter is settled and over. No one else ever needs to know. If there is no success, the level of confrontation is intensified.

> *"And if he refuses to hear them, tell it to the church. But if he refuses even to hear the church, let him be to you like a heathen and a tax collector." (Matthew 18:17)*

This time there are two steps to the discipline with rejection assumed—first to present the situation to the church, and then to excommunicate from the church and deliver to the world. It is assumed that the elders of the church are included in the process, though church government has not yet been addressed in the teachings of Jesus. The teachings of the epistles concerning church government build on this model set forth by Christ, the Head of the church.

The discussion that follows the teaching on discipline in the church centers on forgiveness, which is a corollary to discipline; forgiveness and restoration are always the goals of discipline. When there is repentance, forgiveness follows—or at least it should. Peter raises the question of forgiveness and its frequency. He hints at a low number. It is hard to continually forgive! But Jesus gives a high number—not seven times, but 490 times—in other words, continuously. We have all been forgiven by God more than 490 times, and we are to imitate the forgiveness of God in our lives. Jesus has already taught us that we should pray, "Forgive us our trespasses as we forgive those who trespass against us."

Several principles of holiness arise out of this passage:

> ➤ The knowledge of sin (either personal or in another person) is to be as confined as possible.
> ➤ There are progressive steps in confrontation—one to one, etc.
> ➤ Forgiveness should follow confession.
> ➤ Restoration of fellowship should follow forgiveness.
> ➤ Discipline always has forgiveness and restoration as its goals.
> ➤ Forgiveness is to be repeated continuously upon repentance.

> *"Then his master, after he had called him, said to him, 'You wicked servant! I forgave you all that debt because you begged me. Should you not also have had compassion on your fellow servant, just as I had pity on you?'" (Matthew 18:32-33)*

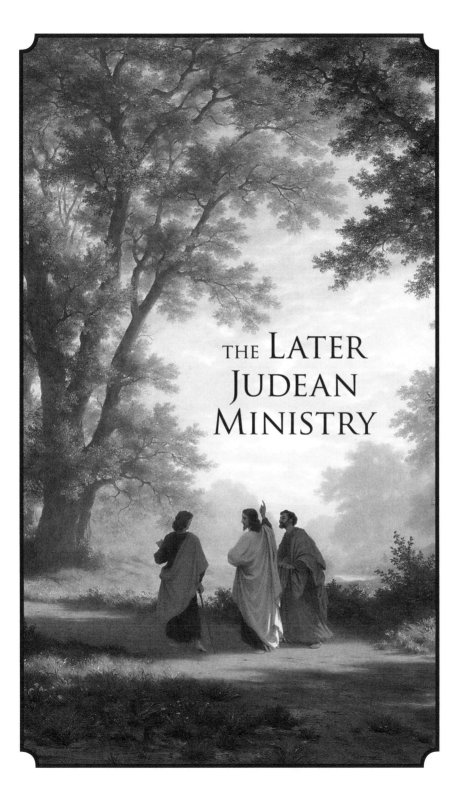

THE LATER
JUDEAN
MINISTRY

44

Setting the Scene
for the Judean Ministry

John 7:1-13; Luke 9:51-62; Matthew 8:19-22

Now it came to pass, when Jesus had finished these sayings that He departed from Galilee and came to the region of Judea beyond the Jordan. (Matthew 19:1)

Now the Jews' Feast of Tabernacles was at hand. His brothers therefore said to Him, "Depart from here and go into Judea, that Your disciples also may see the works that You are doing. For no one does anything in secret while he himself seeks to be known openly. If You do these things, show Yourself to the world." For even His brothers did not believe in Him. Then Jesus said to them, "My time has not yet come, but your time is always ready. The world cannot hate you, but it hates Me because I testify of it that its works are evil. You go up to this feast. I am not yet going up to this feast, for My time has not yet fully come." When He had said these things to them, He remained in Galilee. But when His brothers had gone up, then He also went up to the feast, not openly, but as it were in secret. (John 7:2-10)

Now it came to pass, when the time had come for Him to be received up, that He steadfastly set His face to go to Jerusalem, and sent messengers before His face. And as they went, they entered a village of the Samaritans, to prepare for Him. But they did not receive Him, because His face was set for the journey to Jerusalem. And when His disciples James and John saw this, they said, "Lord, do You want us to command fire to come down from heaven and consume them, just as Elijah did?" But He turned and rebuked them, and said, "You do not know what manner of spirit you are of. For the Son of Man did not come to destroy men's lives but to save them." And they went to another village. Now it happened as they journeyed on the road, that someone said to Him, "Lord, I will follow You wherever You go." And Jesus said to him, "Foxes have holes and birds of the air have nests, but the Son of Man has nowhere to lay His head." Then He said to another, "Follow Me." But he said, "Lord, let me

*first go and bury my father." Jesus said to him, "Let the dead bury
their own dead, but you go and preach the kingdom of God." And
another also said, "Lord, I will follow You, but let me first go and
bid them farewell who are at my house." But Jesus said to him, "No
one, having put his hand to the plow, and looking back, is fit for the
kingdom of God." (Luke 9:51-62)*

The ministry of Jesus in Galilee is completed. Now He moves on to Judea,
the second province to receive the message, "Repent, the kingdom
of God is at hand." Will the result be the same response of rejection? Plus,
how will the disciples preach enthusiastically the gospel of the kingdom for
Israel after being told of the coming church and the predicted death of their
Messiah? The second question is answered in the following statement made
concerning those revelations during the private teaching of the Twelve:

*But they did not understand this saying, and it was hidden from them
so that they did not perceive it; and they were afraid to ask Him
about this saying. (Luke 9:45)*

They will understand later, when the Holy Spirit brings to their remembrance
the teachings of the Lord, just as He promised.

The second question, as to the result in Judea, will be the focus of this section:
the Judean ministry. Leaving Galilee, with its small villages and the agrarian
and fishing sources for the nation, He now comes to the seat of politics and
religion—to the City of David, Jerusalem.

However, He is late for the Feast of Tabernacles. Remember, Peter had the
idea of tents for Jesus, Moses, and Elijah on the Mount of Transfiguration.
The Feast of Tabernacles celebrated the Israelites' arrival in the Promised
Land after forty years of wanderings in the wilderness, and tents reminded
the Jews of that. The Feast of Tabernacles was the next scheduled feast in the
ceremonial calendar that the Lord followed "according to custom."

The brothers of Jesus urged Him to go up to Jerusalem, saying, "Show
Yourself to the world." They did not understand His strategy, nor did they
believe in their Brother. We know some of His family by name.

*"Is this not the carpenter's son? Is not His mother called Mary? And
His brothers James, Joseph, Simon, and Judas? "And His sisters, are
they not all with us? Where then did this Man get all these things?"
(Matthew 13:55-56)*

Amazingly we read, "For even His brothers did not believe in Him." Growing up in the home of Joseph and Mary, with Jesus the oldest in the family, His adult siblings were not yet believers. Even in Jesus' own family circle, salvation comes according to God's schedule. So Jesus says to the urging of His brothers,

> *"You go up to this feast. I am not yet going up to this feast, for My time has not yet fully come" . . . But when His brothers had gone up, then He also went up to the feast, not openly, but as it were in secret. (John 7:8, 10)*

He arrives late for the Feast of Tabernacles by design, going up privately through Samaria and not publicly with the crowds. Unlike the occasion when He stopped at Jacob's Well and was warmly received in Sychar, this time the trip through Samaria was not well received. He was going north then, away from Jerusalem. But now He was going up to a Jewish feast at Jerusalem, and He was on the wrong road. The opposition brought a response from James and John, the Sons of Thunder—a strong statement considering John was later known as the Apostle of Love!

> *And when His disciples James and John saw this, they said, "Lord, do You want us to command fire to come down from heaven and consume them, just as Elijah did?" (Luke 9:54)*

As they continue the trip to Jerusalem, some followers made weak attempts to become disciples. Jesus identifies that He is in transit from Galilee to Judea and has no fixed place to reside. Soon He will be in Bethany, which was His home in Judea. He challenges these would-be disciples to genuine commitment that involves sacrifice.

> *"Foxes have holes and birds of the air have nests, but the Son of Man has nowhere to lay His head." . . . "Lord, I will follow You, but let me first go and bid them farewell who are at my house." But Jesus said to him, "No one, having put his hand to the plow, and looking back, is fit for the kingdom of God." (Luke 9:58, 61-62)*

Meanwhile, what is happening in Jerusalem? Tension is in the air!

> *Then the Jews sought Him at the feast, and said, "Where is He?" And there was much complaining among the people concerning Him. Some said, "He is good"; others said, "No, on the contrary, He deceives the people." However, no one spoke openly of Him for fear of the Jews. (John 7:11-13)*

About the middle of the feast, Jesus comes to the temple and begins to teach. What events are to follow!

- The Living Water and the Water Pouring Ceremony
- The Adulterous Woman
- The Light of the World and the Lamp Lighting Ceremony
- The Debate with the Sanhedrin
- The Man Born Blind
- The Good Shepherd Discourse

What will happen in Judea? Notice the determination of Jesus as He walks into the center of His opposition in Jerusalem. His face had been "set" for the journey there, and now He has arrived. Remember what He had said to the Twelve:

> *From that time Jesus began to show to His disciples that He must go to Jerusalem, and suffer many things from the elders and chief priests and scribes, and be killed, and be raised the third day. (Matthew 16:21)*

45

Jesus, the Fount of Living Water

John 7:11-52

Then the Jews sought Him at the feast, and said, "Where is He?" And there was much complaining among the people concerning Him. Some said, "He is good"; others said, "No, on the contrary, He deceives the people." However, no one spoke openly of Him for fear of the Jews. Now about the middle of the feast Jesus went up into the temple and taught. And the Jews marveled, saying, "How does this Man know letters, having never studied?" . . . Now some of them from Jerusalem said, "Is this not He whom they seek to kill? But look! He speaks boldly, and they say nothing to Him. Do the rulers know indeed that this is truly the Christ?" The Pharisees heard the crowd murmuring these things concerning Him, and the Pharisees and the chief priests sent officers to take Him. . . . On the last day, that great day of the feast, Jesus stood and cried out, saying, "If anyone thirsts, let him come to Me and drink. He who believes in Me, as the Scripture has said, out of his heart will flow rivers of living water." But this He spoke concerning the Spirit, whom those believing in Him would receive; for the Holy Spirit was not yet given, because Jesus was not yet glorified. . . . Then the officers came to the chief priests and Pharisees, who said to them, "Why have you not brought Him?" The officers answered, "No man ever spoke like this Man!" Then the Pharisees answered them, "Are you also deceived? Have any of the rulers or the Pharisees believed in Him? But this crowd that does not know the law is accursed." Nicodemus (he who came to Jesus by night, being one of them) said to them, "Does our law judge a man before it hears him and knows what he is doing?" They answered and said to him, "Are you also from Galilee? Search and look, for no prophet has arisen out of Galilee." (John 7:11-15, 25-26, 32, 37-39, 45-52)

T ension was in the air in Jerusalem. They were looking for Jesus but He wasn't there. They were debating among themselves. "He is good." "No, He deceives the people." But it was a whispered debate because they feared the Jewish authorities who were seeking some way to put Him to death. The authorities had decided on this from the beginning—but how, they wondered, would they achieve this?

Jesus arrived at the middle of the Feast of Tabernacles, and He arrived with boldness. He went up to the temple and taught. What were His topics?

> ➢ The source of His teaching is God, it is not His own.
> ➢ He is speaking by God's authority, not His own.
> ➢ Moses gave the law, but the Jews do not keep it.
> ➢ The Jews are seeking to kill Him.
> ➢ Healing is a legitimate work on the Sabbath.

What was the result of His bold teaching? The Pharisees sent officers to arrest Him.

But Jesus continued to speak with boldness.

On the last day, that great day of the feast, Jesus stood and cried out, saying, "If anyone thirsts, let him come to Me and drink. He who believes in Me, as the Scripture has said, out of his heart will flow rivers of living water." (John 7:37-38)

He was not offering water from a rock, as in the wilderness wanderings. He was offering the same living water He had spoken of with the Samaritan woman. He was the fulfillment of the typology—the permanent satisfaction of spiritual thirst! One could wander through the wilderness of life and never find soul satisfaction; spiritual thirst is never quenched apart from Christ. And so in loud boldness He cried out, "Come to Me and drink."

The temple police sent out by the chief priests and Pharisees returned without a prisoner, and the subsequent exchange is striking.

Then the officers came to the chief priests and Pharisees, who said to them, "Why have you not brought Him?" The officers answered, "No man ever spoke like this Man!" (John 7:45-46)

Both groups insulted one another. The temple police had never heard authoritative teaching like that of Jesus, and certainly not from the chief priests and Pharisees. The Jewish leaders now condemned their civil servants as ignorant and lacking spiritual understanding. As for the masses, "this crowd" that can't possibly understand the law, they were accursed, in their view. What an attitude for the shepherds of Israel to have towards their flock! It is no wonder that Jesus would contrast the good shepherd with the bad shepherds before long.

They asked the question, "Have any of the rulers or the Pharisees believed in Him?" In point of fact, one of them had believed, perhaps two, but they were secret disciples because they feared their colleagues. Nicodemus attempted an answer. Joseph of Arimathea remained silent. When Nicodemus heard the question "Have any of us believed?" surely his private interview with Jesus came to mind.

"And as Moses lifted up the serpent in the wilderness, even so must the Son of Man be lifted up, that whoever believes in Him should not perish but have eternal life. For God so loved the world that He gave His only begotten Son, that whoever believes in Him should not perish but have everlasting life. For God did not send His Son into the world to condemn the world, but that the world through Him might be saved." (John 3:14-17)

Nicodemus was the first ever to hear John 3:16! And he was now a secret disciple. His answer was good, though indirect. It probably was not the immediate answer—"Yes, I have believed"— that flashed through his mind. That answer would have to wait until the time when he and Joseph would take courage and remove the lifeless body of Jesus from the cross. For now the answer would be,

"Does our law judge a man before it hears him and knows what he is doing?" (John 7:51)

The learned chief priests and Pharisees attacked Nicodemus, identifying him with Jesus who was from Galilee, saying,

They answered and said to him, "Are you also from Galilee? Search and look, for no prophet has arisen out of Galilee." (John 7:52)

They were wrong on two counts. First, they evidently did not know that Jesus had actually been born in Bethlehem, where the Messiah was prophesied to be born. And as for prophets from Galilee, they had forgotten Jonah from Gath-hepher in Galilee—that was a "whale" of a mistake. So much for the ignorance of the masses.

What a spectrum of responses to the bold preaching of Jesus. It has always been this way, then and now. Remember the parable of the Sower. The crowds debate, the leadership rejects, the civil servants are amazed, believers are shy or silent—but we will have to wait for the blind man in order to meet a bold believer. The boldness of Jesus in the temple in Jerusalem is not receiving wide acceptance—much like Galilee!

46

A Sinful Woman Is Exposed to the Light of the World

John 7:53-8:20

And everyone went to his own house. But Jesus went to the Mount of Olives. Now early in the morning He came again into the temple, and all the people came to Him; and He sat down and taught them. Then the scribes and Pharisees brought to Him a woman caught in adultery. And when they had set her in the midst, they said to Him, "Teacher, this woman was caught in adultery, in the very act. Now Moses, in the law, commanded us that such should be stoned. But what do You say?" This they said, testing Him, that they might have something of which to accuse Him. But Jesus stooped down and wrote on the ground with His finger, as though He did not hear. So when they continued asking Him, He raised Himself up and said to them, "He who is without sin among you, let him throw a stone at her first." And again He stooped down and wrote on the ground. Then those who heard it, being convicted by their conscience, went out one by one, beginning with the oldest even to the last. And Jesus was left alone, and the woman standing in the midst. When Jesus had raised Himself up and saw no one but the woman, He said to her, "Woman, where are those accusers of yours? Has no one condemned you?" She said, "No one, Lord." And Jesus said to her, "Neither do I condemn you; go and sin no more." Then Jesus spoke to them again, saying, "I am the light of the world. He who follows Me shall not walk in darkness, but have the light of life."

The Pharisees therefore said to Him, "You bear witness of Yourself; Your witness is not true." Jesus answered and said to them, "Even if I bear witness of Myself, My witness is true, for I know where I came from and where I am going; but you do not know where I come from and where I am going. You judge according to the flesh; I judge no one. And yet if I do judge, My judgment is true; for I am not alone, but I am with the Father who sent Me. It is also written in your law that the testimony of two men is true. I am One who bears witness of Myself, and the Father who sent Me bears witness of Me." Then they said to Him, "Where is Your Father?" Jesus answered, "You know neither Me nor My Father. If you had known Me, you would have

*known My Father also." These words Jesus spoke in the treasury, as
He taught in the temple; and no one laid hands on Him, for His hour
had not yet come. (John 7:53-8:20)*

The antagonism between the Jewish authorities and Jesus is reflected in
the incident of the woman taken in adultery. The setting is the Feast of
Tabernacles. Perhaps between the morning water pouring ceremony and the
evening lamp lighting ceremony this woman is cast before the Lord with the
cutting question,

> *"Teacher, this woman was caught in adultery, in the very act. Now
> Moses, in the law, commanded us that such should be stoned. But
> what do You say?" (John 8:4-5)*

They think they have Him trapped—Moses versus Jesus—the Mosaic law
versus Grace. Jesus bends down and begins to write with His finger on the
dust of the ground. He is interrupted by continuous questioning. Standing, He
makes His famous, oft-quoted statement, "He who is without sin among you,
let him throw a stone at her first" (John 8:7).

He stoops again and continues His writing on the ground with His finger. As
He writes, having heard His challenge, they leave one by one, the eldest to
the youngest. What did He write, and why did He write? His words and His
writing convict the accusing, angry, entrapping crowd—they are silenced!
Perhaps He wrote what He had earlier written when He had, via Moses, given
Israel His law.

> *Then the LORD said to Moses, "Come up to Me on the mountain
> and be there; and I will give you tablets of stone, and the law and
> commandments which I have written, that you may teach them."
> (Exodus 24:12)*
>
> *And when He had made an end of speaking with him on Mount Sinai,
> He gave Moses two tablets of the Testimony, tablets of stone, written
> with the finger of God. (Exodus 31:18)*
>
> *"You shall have no other gods before Me.
> You shall not make for yourself a carved image. . .
> You shall not take the name of the LORD your God in vain. . .
> Remember the Sabbath day, to keep it holy. . .
> Honor your father and your mother. . .
> You shall not murder. . .
> You shall not commit adultery. . .
> You shall not steal. . .
> You shall not bear false witness against your neighbor. . .
> You shall not covet." (Exodus 20:3-17)*

They had all committed one, many, or all of these sins; and the longer they had lived, the more they had committed and remembered. Hence they leave in reverse chronological order of age convicted by Christ's one spoken sentence:

> *"He who is without sin among you, let him throw a stone at her first." (John 8:7)*

The adulterous woman stands in the presence of the Light of the World, alone. And Jesus, full of grace and truth, sends her away, forgiven and instructed.

> *"Woman, where are those accusers of yours? Has no one condemned you?" She said, "No one, Lord." And Jesus said to her, "Neither do I condemn you; go and sin no more." (John 8:10-11)*

Grace triumphs over law!

Jesus returns to the ceremony of the Feast of Tabernacles, to the evening lamp lighting ceremony. The lamp-lighting ceremony symbolized the fiery cloud that guided the Israelites through the wilderness to the Promised Land.

> *And the Lord went before them by day in a pillar of cloud to lead the way, and by night in a pillar of fire to give them light, so as to go by day and night. He did not take away the pillar of cloud by day or the pillar of fire by night from before the people. (Exodus 13:21-22)*

> *And the Angel of God, who went before the camp of Israel, moved and went behind them; and the pillar of cloud went from before them and stood behind them. So it came between the camp of the Egyptians and the camp of Israel. Thus it was a cloud and darkness to the one, and it gave light by night to the other, so that the one did not come near the other all that night. (Exodus 14:19-20)*

The Second Person of the Trinity, that Old Testament Divine Guide, now stands before the Jews and cries out,

> *"I am the light of the world. He who follows Me shall not walk in darkness, but have the light of life." (John 8:12)*

The response of the Jews is predictable—they question the truthfulness of the Lord's statement and the legality of personal testimony. Jesus responds to their legal technicality with a legal position from the law.

> *"It is also written in your law that the testimony of two men is true. I am One who bears witness of Myself, and the Father who sent Me bears witness of Me." (John 8:17-18)*

The two witnesses? God the Father and God the Son. The Jewish opposition seize on the identification of the Father, and Jesus responds.

"You know neither Me nor My Father. If you had known Me, you would have known My Father also." These words Jesus spoke in the treasury, as He taught in the temple; and no one laid hands on Him, for His hour had not yet come. (John 8:19-20)

While celebrating the Feast of Tabernacles with the reminders of the water and the light that brought them to the Land, they reject the One who supplied that water and light—the One who is the Living Water and the Light of the World. Tradition rejects Reality!

47

The "Father" Debate

John 8:19-59

Then they said to Him, "Where is Your Father?" Jesus answered, "You know neither Me nor My Father. If you had known Me, you would have known My Father also. . . . "You are from beneath; I am from above. You are of this world; I am not of this world. Therefore I said to you that you will die in your sins; for if you do not believe that I am He, you will die in your sins. . . . And you shall know the truth, and the truth shall make you free." They answered Him, "We are Abraham's descendants, and have never been in bondage to anyone. How can you say, 'You will be made free'?" Jesus answered them, "Most assuredly, I say to you, whoever commits sin is a slave of sin. And a slave does not abide in the house forever, but a son abides forever. Therefore if the Son makes you free, you shall be free indeed. . . . Then they said to Him, "We were not born of fornication; we have one Father—God." Jesus said to them, "If God were your Father, you would love Me, for I proceeded forth and came from God; nor have I come of Myself, but He sent Me. Why do you not understand My speech? Because you are not able to listen to My word. You are of your father the devil, and the desires of your father you want to do. He was a murderer from the beginning, and does not stand in the truth, because there is no truth in him. When he speaks a lie, he speaks from his own resources, for he is a liar and the father of it. But because I tell the truth, you do not believe Me. Which of you convicts Me of sin? And if I tell the truth, why do you not believe Me? He who is of God hears God's words; therefore you do not hear, because you are not of God." . . . Then the Jews said to Him, "Now we know that You have a demon! Abraham is dead, and the prophets; and You say, 'If anyone keeps My word he shall never taste death.' Are You greater than our father Abraham, who is dead? And the prophets are dead. Whom do You make Yourself out to be?" Jesus answered, "If I honor Myself, My honor is nothing. It is My Father who honors Me, of whom you say that He is your God. Yet you have not known Him, but I know Him. And if I say, 'I do not know Him,' I shall be a liar like you; but I do know Him and keep His word. Your father Abraham rejoiced to see My day, and he saw it and was glad." Then the Jews said to Him, "You are not yet fifty years old, and have You seen Abraham?" Jesus said to them, "Most assuredly, I say to you, before Abraham was, I AM." Then they took up stones to throw at Him; but Jesus hid Himself and went out of the temple, going through the midst of them, and so passed by. (John 8:19, 23-24, 32-36, 41-59)

Jesus has just stated that He is going away, returning to heaven, to His Father. This initiates a heated exchange relating to fatherhood. In the section before us the term *father/Father* with pronouns occurs over thirty-five times.

Jesus opens with a bold statement challenging their relationship to God.

"You know neither Me nor My Father. If you had known Me, you would have known My Father also." (John 8:19)

He then identifies the source of their parentage.

"You are from beneath; I am from above. You are of this world; I am not of this world." (John 8:23)

The Jews were proud to claim that they were descendants of Abraham and that they had maintained the distinction throughout their history of being free and never in bondage. Their spirit may have never been broken, but they had frequently been in bondage: at one time in Egypt, now to Rome, and under many other national powers in the years between.

Jesus acknowledges that they were Abraham's descendants ethnically, but not in faith. He then identifies the source of their fatherhood.

"If you were Abraham's children, you would do the works of Abraham. But now you seek to kill Me, a Man who has told you the truth which I heard from God. Abraham did not do this. You do the deeds of your father." (John 8:39-41)

The debate intensifies with a slanderous charge to Jesus.

Then they said to Him, "We were not born of fornication; we have one Father—God." (John 8:41)

Jesus responds.

"If God were your Father, you would love Me, for I proceeded forth and came from God; nor have I come of Myself, but He sent Me. Why do you not understand My speech? Because you are not able to listen to My word. You are of your father the devil, and the desires of your

father you want to do. He was a murderer from the beginning, and does not stand in the truth, because there is no truth in him. When he speaks a lie, he speaks from his own resources, for he is a liar and the father of it." (John 8:42-44)

"You are of your father, the devil." That statement catches their attention and they respond in angry frustration. It is never wise to get into a debate with the Lord, then or now. They react with their accepted explanation of the works of Jesus.

"Do we not say rightly that You are a Samaritan and have a demon?" (John 8:48)

Earlier in the feast the Jews had said,

"You have a demon. Who is seeking to kill You?" (John 7:19-20)

Even earlier in the Lord's ministry the Sanhedrin had a theological explanation of His many miracles.

"This fellow does not cast out demons except by Beelzebub, the ruler of the demons." (Matthew 12:24)

Jesus again rejects their false demon connection and advances the thought of eternal life for those who keep His word. The Jews counter with the obvious, that Abraham is dead.

"Most assuredly, I say to you, if anyone keeps My word he shall never see death." Then the Jews said to Him, "Now we know that You have a demon! Abraham is dead, and the prophets; and You say, 'If anyone keeps My word he shall never taste death.'" (John 8:51-52)

Abraham, the father of the faithful, died—an obvious contradiction to the Lord's statement, so they thought. But this is exactly where Jesus is taking them in the debate that He is about to conclude.

"Your father Abraham rejoiced to see My day, and he saw it and was glad." Then the Jews said to Him, "You are not yet fifty years old, and have You seen Abraham?" (John 8:56-57)

"Have you seen Abraham?" Jesus could have answered in a number of ways.

Then the LORD appeared to him [Abraham] by the terebinth trees of Mamre, as he was sitting in the tent door in the heat of the day. So he lifted his eyes and looked, and behold, three men were standing by him; and when he saw them, he ran from the tent door to meet them, and bowed himself to the ground, and said, "My Lord, if I have now found favor in Your sight, do not pass on by Your servant. Please let a little water be brought, and wash your feet, and rest yourselves

*under the tree. And I will bring a morsel of bread, that you may
refresh your hearts." . . . Abraham ran to the herd, took a tender
and good calf, gave it to a young man, and he hastened to prepare it.
So he took butter and milk and the calf which he had prepared, and
set it before them; and he stood by them under the tree as they ate.
(Genesis 18:1-4, 7-8)*

Jesus could have said, "I had dinner with Abraham." But He says more!

*"Most assuredly, I say to you, before Abraham was, I AM." (John
8:58)*

This is an explicit claim to deity—the name of God!

*And God said to Moses, "I AM WHO I AM." And He said, "Thus
you shall say to the children of Israel, 'I AM has sent me to you.'"
(Exodus 3:14)*

The debate concludes with the Jews attempting to stone Jesus. But He
miraculously passes through their midst.

48

Healing a Man Born Blind

John 9:1-41

Now as Jesus passed by, He saw a man who was blind from birth. And His disciples asked Him, saying, "Rabbi, who sinned, this man or his parents, that he was born blind?" Jesus answered, "Neither this man nor his parents sinned, but that the works of God should be revealed in him. I must work the works of Him who sent Me while it is day; the night is coming when no one can work. As long as I am in the world, I am the light of the world." When He had said these things, He spat on the ground and made clay with the saliva; and He anointed the eyes of the blind man with the clay. And He said to him, "Go, wash in the pool of Siloam" (which is translated, Sent). So he went and washed, and came back seeing. Therefore the neighbors and those who previously had seen that he was blind said, "Is not this he who sat and begged?" Some said, "This is he." Others said, "He is like him." He said, "I am he." Therefore they said to him, "How were your eyes opened?" (John 9:1-10)

They brought him who formerly was blind to the Pharisees. Now it was a Sabbath when Jesus made the clay and opened his eyes. Then the Pharisees also asked him again how he had received his sight. He said to them, "He put clay on my eyes, and I washed, and I see." . . . But the Jews did not believe concerning him, that he had been blind and received his sight, until they called the parents of him who had received his sight. And they asked them, saying, "Is this your son, who you say was born blind? How then does he now see?" . . . So they again called the man who was blind, and said to him, "Give God the glory! We know that this Man is a sinner." He answered and said, "Whether He is a sinner or not I do not know. One thing I know: that though I was blind, now I see." . . . Jesus heard that they had cast him out [of the synagogue]; and when He had found him, He said to him, "Do you believe in the Son of God?" He answered and said, "Who is He, Lord, that I may believe in Him?" (John 9:13-15, 18-19, 24-25, 35-36)

Having escaped the attempted stoning, Jesus reappears to meet a man who had been born blind, to heal him, and to demonstrate that He is the Light of the World. There are six movements to this amazing event.

The Miracle. The man born blind was the object of a theological question. "Who sinned, this man or his parents?" It was a faulty presupposition—that a handicap is a direct result of sin. All maladies indirectly trace a path to the garden of Eden and the original sin, but immediate cause and effect arises from a different source. The disciples gained insight from this miraculous event—the man was there with his lifetime blindness by divine appointment.

> *Jesus answered, "Neither this man nor his parents sinned, but that the works of God should be revealed in him. I must work the works of Him who sent Me while it is day; the night is coming when no one can work. As long as I am in the world, I am the light of the world." (John 9:3-5)*

The man's condition was a product of the Divine Planner, executed with precision for the glory of God. This was not a new concept—Moses heard about it long before when he was chosen to be God's spokesman.

> *Then Moses said to the LORD, "O my Lord, I am not eloquent, neither before nor since You have spoken to Your servant; but I am slow of speech and slow of tongue." So the LORD said to him, "Who has made man's mouth? Or who makes the mute, the deaf, the seeing, or the blind? Have not I, the LORD?" (Exodus 4:10-11)*

For all who will ever experience a so-called human tragedy, this event serves as a bedrock lesson of God's involvement in our lives for His glory. But it was still hard for the blind man and his parents, even though it was for the glory of God.

Having corrected the faulty doctrine, Jesus, who made the blind, now initiates the steps that will bring sight, both physical and spiritual, to this particular man who had been born blind. It was an act of faith to go to an unseen pool to wash the clay off of his unseeing eyes in obedience to an unknown man. The blind man will see Him soon. The words of victory were serenely simple: "So he went and washed, and came back seeing."

The Questioning of the Neighbors. The neighbors and those who saw the blind man could not positively identify him. They had only ever observed him as an object of pity, a fixture in the temple courtyard, sitting hunched over his begging bag. All they had ever done was look down on him, both physically and spiritually. They would drop in a coin or two, but they did not know what he looked like—they had never looked into his face. But now he was standing and seeing. They had never seen him this way, so they could not recognize him.

The formerly blind man spoke in his bold and simple style.

> *Some said, "This is he." Others said, "He is like him." He said, "I am he. A Man called Jesus made clay and anointed my eyes and said to me, 'Go to the pool of Siloam and wash.' So I went and washed, and I received sight." (John 9:9-11)*

The blind man had not yet seen Jesus, but he would see Him soon.

The Interview with the Pharisees. It was the Sabbath when the healing took place, resulting in an inquisition by the Pharisees, the keepers of the Sabbath.

> *Therefore some of the Pharisees said, "This Man is not from God, because He does not keep the Sabbath." Others said, "How can a man who is a sinner do such signs?" And there was a division among them. (John 9:16)*

The educated Pharisees fell into a trap when they reframed their question to the blind man.

> *They said to the blind man again, "What do you say about Him because He opened your eyes?" He said, "He is a prophet." (John 9:17)*

But they did not believe. They needed additional confirmation of the miracle.

The Interview with the Parents. The Pharisees did not like the answer they got from the blind man, so they tried his parents. The question was direct.

> *And they asked them, saying, "Is this your son, who you say was born blind? How then does he now see?" (John 9:19)*

As direct as the Pharisees' question was, the response of the parents was indirect.

> *His parents answered them and said, "We know that this is our son, and that he was born blind; but by what means he now sees we do not know, or who opened his eyes we do not know. He is of age; ask him. He will speak for himself." (John 9:20-21)*

The reason for their evasion was fear—fear of the power of the religious leaders, fear of excommunication from society. So they do not speak. Soon the Lord will be speaking of the good shepherd and the bad shepherds. What a clear contrast!

The Second Interview with the Pharisees. In the final confrontation with the Pharisees, the blind man takes charge. The Pharisees begin to question him, but he ends up questioning *them.* They inquire about the healing, and he responds,

"I told you already, and you did not listen. Why do you want to hear it again? Do you also want to become His disciples?" (John 9:27)

The man's divinely inspired sarcasm fell on religiously hardened ears. His logical rebuttal is rejected, and they react with hypocritically holy indignation in keeping with their flawed theology.

They answered and said to him, "You were completely born in sins, and are you teaching us?" And they cast him out. (John 9:34)

The Blind Man Meets Jesus. Having given him sight, Jesus now seeks him out. He asks the question of salvation of the now-seeing blind man.

Jesus heard that they had cast him out; and when He had found him, He said to him, "Do you believe in the Son of God?" (John 9:35)

He believed and worshiped Jesus. Blindness yielded to seeing, seeing yielded to faith, and faith resulted in salvation.

And Jesus said, "For judgment I have come into this world, that those who do not see may see, and that those who see may be made blind." Then some of the Pharisees who were with Him heard these words, and said to Him, "Are we blind also?" Jesus said to them, "If you were blind, you would have no sin; but now you say, 'We see.' Therefore your sin remains." (John 9:39-41)

49

The Good Shepherd

John 10:1-21

"Most assuredly, I say to you, he who does not enter the sheepfold by the door, but climbs up some other way, the same is a thief and a robber. But he who enters by the door is the shepherd of the sheep. To him the doorkeeper opens, and the sheep hear his voice; and he calls his own sheep by name and leads them out. And when he brings out his own sheep, he goes before them; and the sheep follow him, for they know his voice. Yet they will by no means follow a stranger, but will flee from him, for they do not know the voice of strangers." Jesus used this illustration, but they did not understand the things which He spoke to them. Then Jesus said to them again, "Most assuredly, I say to you, I am the door of the sheep. All who ever came before Me are thieves and robbers, but the sheep did not hear them. I am the door. If anyone enters by Me, he will be saved, and will go in and out and find pasture. The thief does not come except to steal, and to kill, and to destroy. I have come that they may have life, and that they may have it more abundantly. I am the good shepherd. The good shepherd gives His life for the sheep. But a hireling, he who is not the shepherd, one who does not own the sheep, sees the wolf coming and leaves the sheep and flees; and the wolf catches the sheep and scatters them. The hireling flees because he is a hireling and does not care about the sheep. I am the good shepherd; and I know My sheep, and am known by My own. As the Father knows Me, even so I know the Father; and I lay down My life for the sheep. And other sheep I have which are not of this fold; them also I must bring, and they will hear My voice; and there will be one flock and one shepherd. Therefore My Father loves Me, because I lay down My life that I may take it again. No one takes it from Me, but I lay it down of Myself. I have power to lay it down, and I have power to take it again. This command I have received from My Father." Therefore there was a division again among the Jews because of these sayings. And many of them said, "He has a demon and is mad. Why do you listen to Him?" Others said, "These are not the words of one who has a demon. Can a demon open the eyes of the blind?" (John 10:1-21)

The response growing out of the Feast of Tabernacles was negative, with strong opposition from the Sanhedrin manifested in the excommunication of the healed blind man. Jesus responds.

> *"For judgment I have come into this world, that those who do not see may see, and that those who see may be made blind." Then some of the Pharisees who were with Him heard these words, and said to Him, "Are we blind also?" Jesus said to them, "If you were blind, you would have no sin; but now you say, 'We see.' Therefore your sin remains." (John 9:39-41)*

It is no wonder that Jesus begins His Good Shepherd Discourse following the failure of the shepherds of Israel at the Feast of Tabernacles (a fall festival). Shepherds who cast out the sheep are not good shepherds. The expelled blind man experienced that personally.

It is in contrast to this failure of the religious leaders of Israel that Jesus will describe Himself as the Good Shepherd. Soon He will send the Seventy out to evangelize the province of Judea. They will return just prior to the Feast of Dedication (a winter festival), when Jesus will teach the Good Shepherd Discourse Part 2. While in Jerusalem it is appropriate to teach about shepherds—many "bad" and only one "good."

The teachings of the Lord are laden with theology concerning His work as the Good Shepherd, concerning the response of the sheep to the Good Shepherd, and concerning the detailed plans for the sheep.

The Good Shepherd calls His sheep. This is the divine summons to salvation—all are lost sheep, but He calls His sheep to Himself.

> *All we like sheep have gone astray; we have turned, every one, to his own way; and the LORD has laid on Him the iniquity of us all. (Isaiah 53:6)*

The Good Shepherd knows His sheep by name! The summons to salvation is particular—it is by name—not a corporate, nameless, undefined, collection of humanity. And the name of each sheep is recorded in heaven.

> *"Nevertheless do not rejoice in this, that the spirits are subject to you, but rather rejoice because your names are written in heaven." (Luke 10:20)*

> *All who dwell on the earth will worship him, whose names have not been written in the Book of Life of the Lamb slain from the foundation of the world. (Revelation 13:8)*

> *And anyone not found written in the Book of Life was cast into the lake of fire. (Revelation 20:15)*

The Good Shepherd leads His sheep.

> The LORD is my shepherd; I shall not want. He makes me to lie down
> in green pastures; He leads me beside the still waters. He restores
> my soul; He leads me in the paths of righteousness For His name's
> sake. Yea, though I walk through the valley of the shadow of death,
> I will fear no evil; for You are with me; Your rod and Your staff,
> they comfort me. You prepare a table before me in the presence of
> my enemies; You anoint my head with oil; My cup runs over. Surely
> goodness and mercy shall follow me all the days of my life; and I will
> dwell in the house of the LORD forever. (Psalm 23:1-6)

The Good Shepherd dies for His sheep.

> For if the blood of bulls and goats and the ashes of a heifer, sprinkling
> the unclean, sanctifies for the purifying of the flesh, how much more
> shall the blood of Christ, who through the eternal Spirit offered
> Himself without spot to God, cleanse your conscience from dead
> works to serve the living God? (Hebrews 9:13-14)

> And I looked, and behold, in the midst of the throne and of the four
> living creatures, and in the midst of the elders, stood a Lamb as
> though it had been slain . . . (Revelation 5:6)

The sheep hear His voice, they know His voice, they know Him, and they
follow Him. By divine appointment the wayward sheep hears the voice of
the Shepherd summoning him to salvation. The voice has a familiar, eternal
sound. The call originated in eternity; it catches up in time. It is not the
deceiving tones of false shepherds. It has the ring of truth. Each sheep comes
to know the Good Shepherd experientially, and by knowing Him learns to
trust and follow Him in life.

Jesus announces that He has other sheep not of the fold of Israel. They are
waiting for the future call that reaches beyond the confines of Judaism which
is implemented when the church is started and reaches into all the world. We
who are Gentile believers in Christ are not of the fold of Israel, but there is
one flock of all of God's people. We were His sheep before we knew it.

The response of the Jews was the usual explanation.

> Therefore there was a division again among the Jews because of
> these sayings. And many of them said, "He has a demon and is mad.
> Why do you listen to Him?" (John 10:19-20)

In due time Jesus will conclude His Judean ministry with the second part of
the Good Shepherd Discourse.

50

The Seventy and the Evangelization of Judea

Matthew 11:20-24; Luke 10:1-16

After these things the Lord appointed others also, and sent them two by two before His face into every city and place where He Himself was about to go. Then He said to them, "The harvest truly is great, but the laborers are few; therefore pray the Lord of the harvest to send out laborers into His harvest. Go your way; behold, I send you out as lambs among wolves. Carry neither money bag, knapsack, nor sandals; and greet no one along the road. But whatever house you enter, first say, 'Peace to this house.' And if a son of peace is there, your peace will rest on it; if not, it will return to you. And remain in the same house, eating and drinking such things as they give, for the laborer is worthy of his wages. Do not go from house to house. Whatever city you enter, and they receive you, eat such things as are set before you. And heal the sick there, and say to them, 'The kingdom of God has come near to you.' But whatever city you enter, and they do not receive you, go out into its streets and say, 'The very dust of your city which clings to us we wipe off against you. Nevertheless know this, that the kingdom of God has come near you.' But I say to you that it will be more tolerable in that Day for Sodom than for that city." (Luke 10:1-12)

Then He began to rebuke the cities in which most of His mighty works had been done, because they did not repent: "Woe to you, Chorazin! Woe to you, Bethsaida! For if the mighty works which were done in you had been done in Tyre and Sidon, they would have repented long ago in sackcloth and ashes. But I say to you, it will be more tolerable for Tyre and Sidon in the day of judgment than for you. And you, Capernaum, who are exalted to heaven, will be brought down to Hades; for if the mighty works which were done in you had been done in Sodom, it would have remained until this day. But I say to you that it shall be more tolerable for the land of Sodom in the day of judgment than for you." (Matthew 11:20-24)

"**A**fter these things . . . ." That is, after the Feast of Tabernacles. The events of the first phase of the Judean ministry took place in the capital city Jerusalem with the public confrontation of the Jewish leaders. Now the rest of the province of Judea was to be the object of evangelization in the same way as Galilee to the north had been. In the Galilean ministry, Jesus visited every city and town where He had sent the Twelve, two by two. He had made His mark in Jerusalem just lately, but now it remained to send out the disciples two by two into Judea. Seventy unnamed disciples and the Twelve were sent out, two by two—forty-one teams! Jesus would follow.

His commission is the same to the expanded number as it was to the Twelve in Galilee. The harvest is plentiful due to the larger population of Judea—hence the need for additional laborers. To these laborers who will offer the kingdom to Judea Jesus states the following:

➢ Go your way as lambs among wolves. *You are entering a dangerous and hostile environment.*

➢ Carry no purse, no bag, and no sandals, and don't tarry to greet people along the way. *There is urgency and risk.*

➢ Identify a "son of peace" in a home and bless him with your peace by remaining with him. *Spread the joy of service.*

➢ Take advantage of the generous hospitality you may receive in individual homes as worthy laborers. *Your message has great value.*

➢ Do not wander about from house to house, but make the home in which you are dwelling a regional center of evangelization. *Be organized and efficient.*

➢ When a town receives you, accept their food and heal the sick as a confirming sign that the kingdom of God has come near. *This is an offer of the kingdom.*

➢ When a town does not receive you, make a public declaration of their rejection and coming judgment by shaking the dust of that town off of your sandals. *Some will reject the kingdom offer.*

This outlook on the suburban Judean ministry reflects the negative response of the leadership within Jerusalem. Jesus had already predicted His eventual rejection during His earlier specialized ministry with the Twelve. The enormity of the rejection gives rise to a weighty theological discourse when Jesus upbraids the Galilean cities of His many miracles.

> *"Woe to you, Chorazin! Woe to you, Bethsaida! . . . And you, Capernaum, who are exalted to heaven, will be brought down to Hades." (Matthew 11:21, 23)*

This section contributes to our understanding of God's omniscience in relation to His plan of salvation, and His execution of eternal judgment. God knows all things, past, present, and future; actual and possible; effortlessly and equally well, at once. The enormity of the rejection of Galilee, soon to be duplicated by Judea, is compared to the judgment of Sodom. The omniscience of Jesus sovereignly connects the events of Galilee to the ancient city of Sodom, and Jesus states that repentance would have taken place there if it had witnessed Christ's miracles. He knows all things, real as well has potential, as in this passage. What would happen if . . . ?

Jesus touches on God's sovereign plan of salvation in His comments of rebuke. He states that, given the opportunity of additional light, Tyre and Sidon and Sodom and Gomorrah would have repented. But they were *not* given additional revelation. Even knowing their positive response given the opportunity, they were not given the opportunity.

Two locations, with varying degrees of revelation, both rejecting the revelation, are judged accordingly.

> *"But I say to you, it will be more tolerable for Tyre and Sidon in the day of judgment than for you. . . . But I say to you that it shall be more tolerable for the land of Sodom in the day of judgment than for you."*
> *(Matthew 11:22, 24)*

The final judgment is the Great White Throne judgment at the end of time. It is the judgment of all the unsaved dead, small and great. The book of Revelation adds to our understanding of that judgment:

> *Then I saw a great white throne and Him who sat on it, from whose face the earth and the heaven fled away. And there was found no place for them. And I saw the dead, small and great, standing before God, and books were opened. And another book was opened, which is the Book of Life. And the dead were judged according to their works, by the things which were written in the books. The sea gave up the dead who were in it, and Death and Hades delivered up the dead who were in them. And they were judged, each one according to his works. Then Death and Hades were cast into the lake of fire. This is the second death. And anyone not found written in the Book of Life was cast into the lake of fire. (Revelation 20:11-15)*

There will be variation in judgment based on the nature of the sin and the degree of light rejected. For some it will be "more tolerable" than for others. Jesus tells us more about eternal punishment than any other source in the Scriptures. Here He teaches variation of punishment in the lake of fire.

51

The Good Samaritan, Martha and Mary, and the Lord's Prayer

Luke 10:25-11:13

Then Jesus answered and said: "A certain man went down from Jerusalem to Jericho, and fell among thieves, who stripped him of his clothing, wounded him, and departed, leaving him half dead. Now by chance a certain priest came down that road. And when he saw him, he passed by on the other side. Likewise a Levite, when he arrived at the place, came and looked, and passed by on the other side. But a certain Samaritan, as he journeyed, came where he was. And when he saw him, he had compassion. So he went to him and bandaged his wounds, pouring on oil and wine; and he set him on his own animal, brought him to an inn, and took care of him. On the next day, when he departed, he took out two denarii, gave them to the innkeeper, and said to him, 'Take care of him; and whatever more you spend, when I come again, I will repay you.'" . . . Now it happened as they went that He entered a certain village; and a certain woman named Martha welcomed Him into her house. And she had a sister called Mary, who also sat at Jesus' feet and heard His word. But Martha was distracted with much serving, and she approached Him and said, "Lord, do You not care that my sister has left me to serve alone? Therefore tell her to help me." And Jesus answered and said to her, "Martha, Martha, you are worried and troubled about many things. But one thing is needed, and Mary has chosen that good part, which will not be taken away from her." (Luke 10:30-35, 38-42)

Now it came to pass, as He was praying in a certain place, when He ceased, that one of His disciples said to Him, "Lord, teach us to pray, as John also taught his disciples." So He said to them, "When you pray, say: Our Father in heaven, hallowed be Your name. Your kingdom come. Your will be done on earth as it is in heaven. Give us day by day our daily bread. And forgive us our sins, for we also forgive everyone who is indebted to us. And do not lead us into temptation, but deliver us from the evil one." (Luke 11:1-4)

Between the sending out of the seventy disciples and their return, three great episodes take place in suburban Judea—the story of the Good Samaritan, visiting Mary and Martha, and the second teaching of the Lord's Prayer.

The term *Good Samaritan* has found a place in the English language. It describes a volunteer who comes upon a person in distress and gives aid; it has become a legal term defending such a person; and it is a name affixed to hospitals describing the care given to patients. Yet the term arose out of a story in which the means of inheriting eternal life was the question. Jesus tells the story to convince the questioning lawyer that being neighborly is not the instinctive response of fallen man—but being selfish *is!*

The question is, "What shall I do to inherit eternal life?" We would expect Jesus to put forward the normative response of Scripture—*believe*. Belief is everywhere in the Bible the sole condition for salvation. But here, pre-evangelism takes place before evangelism. A person must recognize that he is lost before he can ever be saved. So Jesus poses a question to the lawyer, a question concerning the law—his field of expertise. The lawyer does know his law and quickly answers:

> *"'You shall love the LORD your God with all your heart, with all your soul, with all your strength, and with all your mind,' and 'your neighbor as yourself.'" (Luke 10:27)*

The Lord says that this is the right answer to the question. "Keep the law!"

> *"You have answered rightly; do this and you will live." (Luke 10:28)*

But the lawyer brings up a legal sticking point—"And who is my neighbor?" The words of Jesus are bringing conviction because the lawyer raises the question in order to justify himself. The lawyer had a narrow interpretation of the law; the Samaritan in the story had a broad interpretation of the term "neighbor." And so Jesus tells the story of the good Samaritan.

Notice, there are two directions in which the lawyer was told to manifest love—to God and to his neighbor. Jesus dealt only with the latter, where the lawyer was failing. His friends were the priests and Levites in the story, not the Samaritan. The Jews had no dealings with Samaritans.

The incident closes without a conclusion. Jesus says, "Go and do likewise." Perhaps the lawyer went away a little closer to recognizing his lost condition, and therefore a little closer to belief.

The second well-known incident recorded in this chapter is Jesus having dinner with Martha and Mary. Martha invited Jesus into her home, and Martha extended her hospitality by serving Jesus, no doubt preparing a meal. She was busy at work for Jesus, manifesting her love for Him by acts of service. Mary was of a different nature, perhaps contemplative and attentive. She sat at the Lord's feet, manifesting her love for Him by her undivided attention. Both were doing the fitting thing for their Savior. But Martha became impatient in the kitchen—not an uncommon scenario! She became irritated with her sister, who seemed to be doing nothing. She voices her complaint to Jesus and then gives a command to Jesus.

> *"Lord, do You not care that my sister has left me to serve alone? Therefore tell her to help me." (Luke 10:40)*

"Do You not care? . . . Tell her to help me." Irritation fosters strange reactions. It was not appropriate to question the Lord's care or to give Him a command. What went wrong in the hospitable home of Mary and Martha and Lazarus, the center of operation for Jesus in the Judean ministry? It was not that one served and the other listened to the Lord's teaching. It was that Martha forgot that she was serving Jesus and then became competitive with her sister. She lost her focus (Jesus) and looked on her sister (Mary) instead. Mary's love for the Lord as she listened to His teaching should have been matched by Martha's love for the Lord as she served.

The third incident in Luke's narrative is an extended lesson on prayer. Here in the Judean ministry the disciples again ask Jesus to teach them to pray. At the beginning of the Galilean ministry, when giving the Sermon on the Mount, Jesus had responded to the same question by teaching them the model prayer, the Lord's Prayer. Here, many months later, His response is the same. Had He not warned at that time about the emptiness of repeated prayers? But He repeats the model because it *is* a model. The four disharmonies of life which become subjects for prayer are summarized in the Lord's Prayer—our relationship to God, our relationship to the necessities of life, our relationship to one another, and our personal holiness.

In expanding His comments, Jesus tells His disciples to be persistent in prayer.

> *"I say to you, though he will not rise and give to him because he is his friend, yet because of his persistence he will rise and give him as many as he needs." (Luke 11:8)*

Jesus tells His disciples to be bold in prayer. God loves to give His people good things, even to the extent of giving the Holy Spirit in a coming day when the Son prays to the Father to send Him.

"So I say to you, ask, and it will be given to you; seek, and you will find; knock, and it will be opened to you. For everyone who asks receives, and he who seeks finds, and to him who knocks it will be opened." (Luke 11:9-10)

How to gain eternal life, how to serve, how to pray—the primary lessons for life are restated in the Judean ministry. A good teacher or preacher must repeat his subject matter until it is learned and practiced in the routine of life. And so Jesus taught in Judea as He had in Galilee.

52

The Beelzebub Theory Is Revisited, and Jesus Visits with a Pharisee

Luke 11:14-54

And He was casting out a demon, and it was mute. So it was, when the demon had gone out, that the mute spoke; and the multitudes marveled. But some of them said, "He casts out demons by Beelzebub, the ruler of the demons." Others, testing Him, sought from Him a sign from heaven. But He, knowing their thoughts, said to them: "Every kingdom divided against itself is brought to desolation, and a house divided against a house falls. If Satan also is divided against himself, how will his kingdom stand? Because you say I cast out demons by Beelzebub. And if I cast out demons by Beelzebub, by whom do your sons cast them out? Therefore they will be your judges. But if I cast out demons with the finger of God, surely the kingdom of God has come upon you." (Luke 11:14-20)

And as He spoke, a certain Pharisee asked Him to dine with him. So He went in and sat down to eat. When the Pharisee saw it, he marveled that He had not first washed before dinner. Then the Lord said to him, "Now you Pharisees make the outside of the cup and dish clean, but your inward part is full of greed and wickedness. Foolish ones! Did not He who made the outside make the inside also? But rather give alms of such things as you have; then indeed all things are clean to you. But woe to you Pharisees! For you tithe mint and rue and all manner of herbs, and pass by justice and the love of God. These you ought to have done, without leaving the others undone. . . . Woe to you lawyers! For you have taken away the key of knowledge. You did not enter in yourselves, and those who were entering in you hindered." And as He said these things to them, the scribes and the Pharisees began to assail Him vehemently, and to cross-examine Him about many things, lying in wait for Him, and seeking to catch Him in something He might say, that they might accuse Him. (Luke 11:37-42, 52-54)

L uke, the physician/historian, is the main contributor to the suburban section of the Judean ministry, just as John is to the urban Jerusalem section of the Judean ministry. Much of Luke's writing recounts similar events to those found in the Galilean ministry; the Master Teacher is teaching the same lessons to a new crowd while He repeats the needed and familiar lessons to His own disciples.

Here, the old accusation of the Pharisees is restated to explain the most recent conflict with the demonic world.

> *And He was casting out a demon, and it was mute. So it was, when the demon had gone out, that the mute spoke; and the multitudes marveled. But some of them said, "He casts out demons by Beelzebub, the ruler of the demons." (Luke 11:14-15)*

This was a strange demonic possession. The demon was mute—what purpose would that serve except to inflict personal harm limited to the man and his world of family and friends? The man could not voice anything because a mute demon had made him mute as well. Satan has many forms of evil, some personal and some public. He would devastate us all with misery but for the control of God!

To explain this wonderful miracle, the opponents of Jesus trot out the official argument. Jesus restates His well-crafted response to that argument—the "house divided" response. How can Satan be fighting with and against demons at the same time? A house so divided will most certainly fall, as in all kingdoms and nations.

Jesus then advances His teaching, connecting the casting out of the demon with the continuing opposition to His ministry and kingdom message. At one time, Israel had been "possessed" by idolatry. Although their "house" had been "swept and put in order," they were refusing to allow Jesus to take up His rightful ownership. In the great tribulation, the nation of Israel will commit the ultimate act of idolatry: worshiping the Antichrist. Thus Jesus warns of the danger that if a demon is cast out and He and His message is rejected, the restless demon will return with seven others and possess the man again, the result being that the latter state of the man will be worse than the first.

And so, with the rejection of Someone greater than Jonah and greater than Solomon, greater judgment will come to the generation that receives a greater sign: Jesus, the Son of God.

> *"Therefore take heed that the light which is in you is not darkness." (Luke 11:35)*

Rejected light brings greater judgment. Judea rejects the repeated shining of the Light, as did Galilee—hence a greater judgment awaits them.

A practical lesson is learned out of this account: a pattern of opposition calls for a restated answer. There are few new approaches in opposition to the light, and therefore a reasoned and developed refutation will serve more often than once. A good answer should be reused. That's what Jesus did!

The next incident Luke records in the suburban Judean ministry grows out of the demon controversy when a Pharisee asks Jesus to dine with him. The motive of the Pharisees is clearly stated in the closing verses of this section.

> *And as He said these things to them, the scribes and the Pharisees began to assail Him vehemently, and to cross-examine Him about many things, lying in wait for Him, and seeking to catch Him in something He might say, that they might accuse Him. (Luke 11:53-54)*

This explains the direct attack Jesus takes on the hypocritical use of hospitality—to invite a person to dinner to trap him. Imagine that! When Jesus fails to practice the ceremonial washing before dinner, the astonishment of the host Pharisee is obvious, and Jesus launches the attack. This "woe attack" is used by Jesus again in Passion Week when He confronts the Sanhedrin in their place of business, the temple.

In an introductory salvo Jesus condemns the outward display of an alms-giving religion, which at the same time is inwardly full of extortion and wickedness:

- ➢ Woe to you for replacing the necessary with the trivial!
- ➢ Woe to you for seeking public prestige!
- ➢ Woe to you for making life intolerable for those you lead without giving aid!
- ➢ Woe to you for being prophet killers like your fathers!
- ➢ Woe to you for rejecting truth and leading others to reject truth as well!

Jesus attacks the Pharisees and their lawyers, bringing reproach to them both.

> *Then one of the lawyers answered and said to Him, "Teacher, by saying these things You reproach us also." (Luke 11:45)*

Jesus constantly challenged the leaders and their people to demonstrate a reality that matches pure motives with righteous works of faith. He continues that challenge to the present day in case *we* become pharisaical in heart and action!

The Judean ministry is finding the same response in the suburbs as it did in Jerusalem, and as it did in Galilee—rejection.

As He said these things to them, the scribes and the Pharisees began to assail Him vehemently, and to cross examine Him about many things, lying in wait for Him, and seeking to catch Him in something He might say, that they might accuse Him. (Luke 11:54)

53

The Sermon on the Mount Restated, and the Olivet Discourse Anticipated

Luke 12:1-59

In the meantime, when an innumerable multitude of people had gathered together, so that they trampled one another, He began to say to His disciples first of all, "Beware of the leaven of the Pharisees, which is hypocrisy." . . . And He said to them, "Take heed and beware of covetousness, for one's life does not consist in the abundance of the things he possesses." . . . Then He said to His disciples, "Therefore I say to you, do not worry about your life, what you will eat; nor about the body, what you will put on. Life is more than food, and the body is more than clothing. Consider the ravens, for they neither sow nor reap, which have neither storehouse nor barn; and God feeds them. Of how much more value are you than the birds? And which of you by worrying can add one cubit to his stature? If you then are not able to do the least, why are you anxious for the rest? Consider the lilies, how they grow: they neither toil nor spin; and yet I say to you, even Solomon in all his glory was not arrayed like one of these. If then God so clothes the grass, which today is in the field and tomorrow is thrown into the oven, how much more will He clothe you, O you of little faith? And do not seek what you should eat or what you should drink, nor have an anxious mind. For all these things the nations of the world seek after, and your Father knows that you need these things. But seek the kingdom of God, and all these things shall be added to you." (Luke 12:1, 15, 22-31)

"Let your waist be girded and your lamps burning; and you yourselves be like men who wait for their master, when he will return from the wedding, that when he comes and knocks they may open to him immediately. Blessed are those servants whom the master, when he comes, will find watching. Assuredly, I say to you that he will gird himself and have them sit down to eat, and will come and serve them. And if he should come in the second watch, or come in the third watch, and find them so, blessed are those servants. But know this, that if the master of the house had known what hour the thief would come, he would have watched and not allowed his house

to be broken into. Therefore you also be ready, for the Son of Man is coming at an hour you do not expect. . . . Do you suppose that I came to give peace on earth? I tell you, not at all, but rather division. For from now on five in one house will be divided: three against two, and two against three. Father will be divided against son and son against father, mother against daughter and daughter against mother, mother-in-law against her daughter-in-law and daughter-in-law against her mother-in-law." (Luke 12:35-40, 51-53)

There were present at that season some who told Him about the Galileans whose blood Pilate had mingled with their sacrifices. (Luke 13:1)

After concluding the confrontational dinner experience in the home of an unnamed Pharisee, Jesus interacts with the disciples and the multitudes as they move through the villages of Judea. The conversations are very animated and unpredictable—with the disciples, with the crowd, with an interrupting individual from the crowd, with the apostle Peter, and with some new arrivals who bring some bad news. It is a day in the life of Jesus in His itinerant Judean ministry—a ministry that will soon be concluded. Let's examine the journey.

Fresh from His encounter with the host Pharisee, Jesus warns His disciples in the midst of the crowds of the fatal flaw of the Pharisees—hypocrisy. Religious hypocrisy pervades their entire being like yeast permeates bread.

In the meantime, when an innumerable multitude of people had gathered together, so that they trampled one another, He began to say to His disciples first of all, "Beware of the leaven of the Pharisees, which is hypocrisy." (Luke 12:1)

How far would this leaven of religious hypocrisy pervade the life and actions of the leadership of Judaism? They will pursue the disciples, they will pry into their private lives, they will bring them before the synagogues and authorities, and they will seek to kill them—all of this as service to God!

But Jesus encourages His disciples with familiar words from the Galilean ministry. It was encouragement for His disciples at that time, and it is now for us, His 21st century disciples!

"And I say to you, My friends, do not be afraid of those who kill the body, and after that have no more that they can do. But I will show you whom you should fear: Fear Him who, after He has killed, has power to cast into hell; yes, I say to you, fear Him! Are not five

sparrows sold for two copper coins? And not one of them is forgotten before God. But the very hairs of your head are all numbered. Do not fear therefore; you are of more value than many sparrows." (Luke 12:4-7)

A man from the crowd interrupts with a plea to settle a family dispute over an earthly inheritance.

"Teacher, tell my brother to divide the inheritance with me." But He said to him, "Man, who made Me a judge or an arbitrator over you?" (Luke 12:13-14)

Jesus deflects the question and reteaches another lesson from the Sermon on the Mount, a lesson of priorities for His disciples then and now.

And He said to them, "Take heed and beware of covetousness, for one's life does not consist in the abundance of the things he possesses. . . . Therefore I say to you, do not worry about your life, what you will eat; nor about the body, what you will put on. . . . Consider the ravens, for they neither sow nor reap, which have neither storehouse nor barn; and God feeds them. Of how much more value are you than the birds? . . . Consider the lilies, how they grow: they neither toil nor spin; and yet I say to you, even Solomon in all his glory was not arrayed like one of these. . . . But seek the kingdom of God, and all these things shall be added to you." (Luke 12:15, 22, 24, 27, 31)

From references to the Sermon on the Mount given during the Galilean ministry, Jesus begins to talk about future events: the return of the Son of Man and the reward of His faithful servants upon His return. This topic becomes more of His focus in the next region of ministry, the Perean ministry. On Tuesday of Passion Week, these initial thoughts will be fully set forth in the Olivet Discourse.

"Let your waist be girded and your lamps burning; and you yourselves be like men who wait for their master, when he will return from the wedding, that when he comes and knocks they may open to him immediately. . . . Therefore you also be ready, for the Son of Man is coming at an hour you do not expect. . . . Blessed is that servant whom his master will find so doing when he comes. Truly, I say to you that he will make him ruler over all that he has." (Luke 12:35-36, 40, 43-44)

At that moment, Jesus was told of a recent tragedy in Jerusalem.

There were present at that season some who told Him about the Galileans whose blood Pilate had mingled with their sacrifices. (Luke 13:1)

Evidently, this was new news. Jesus takes opportunity to address the brevity of life and inevitability of death—consequently, the urgent need for repentance. He reinforces the lesson with the account of another tragedy.

> *"Or those eighteen on whom the tower in Siloam fell and killed them, do you think that they were worse sinners than all other men who dwelt in Jerusalem?" (Luke 13:4)*

Notice, He does not condemn those in the twin stories who were killed as worse sinners than those who were spared. We do well to imitate the gracious words of Jesus.

A closing parable underlines the urgency of responding to the message of grace—because time to respond will not be available forever.

> *He also spoke this parable: "A certain man had a fig tree planted in his vineyard, and he came seeking fruit on it and found none. Then he said to the keeper of his vineyard, 'Look, for three years I have come seeking fruit on this fig tree and find none. Cut it down; why does it use up the ground?' But he answered and said to him, 'Sir, let it alone this year also, until I dig around it and fertilize it. And if it bears fruit, well. But if not, after that you can cut it down.'" (Luke 13:6-9)*

54

Jesus Is Rejected in Judea

Luke 13:10-24; Matthew 11:25-30; John 10:22-39

Now He was teaching in one of the synagogues on the Sabbath. And behold, there was a woman who had a spirit of infirmity eighteen years, and was bent over and could in no way raise herself up. But when Jesus saw her, He called her to Him and said to her, "Woman, you are loosed from your infirmity." And He laid His hands on her, and immediately she was made straight, and glorified God. But the ruler of the synagogue answered with indignation, because Jesus had healed on the Sabbath; and he said to the crowd, "There are six days on which men ought to work; therefore come and be healed on them, and not on the Sabbath day." The Lord then answered him and said, "Hypocrite! Does not each one of you on the Sabbath loose his ox or donkey from the stall, and lead it away to water it?" . . . Then the seventy returned with joy, saying, "Lord, even the demons are subject to us in Your name." . . . In that hour Jesus rejoiced in the Spirit and said, "I thank You, Father, Lord of heaven and earth, that You have hidden these things from the wise and prudent and revealed them to babes. Even so, Father, for so it seemed good in Your sight. All things have been delivered to Me by My Father, and no one knows who the Son is except the Father, and who the Father is except the Son, and the one to whom the Son wills to reveal Him." (Luke 13:10-15, 17, 21-22)

Now it was the Feast of Dedication in Jerusalem, and it was winter. And Jesus walked in the temple, in Solomon's porch. . . . "My sheep hear My voice, and I know them, and they follow Me. And I give them eternal life, and they shall never perish; neither shall anyone snatch them out of My hand. My Father, who has given them to Me, is greater than all; and no one is able to snatch them out of My Father's hand. I and My Father are one." Then the Jews took up stones again to stone Him. . . . Therefore they sought again to seize Him, but He escaped out of their hand. (John 10:22-23, 27-31, 39)

Both the suburban and urban segments of Christ's Judean ministry were coming to an end. In symbolic realism Jesus visits a synagogue of a village of Judea and then makes a final visit to the temple in Jerusalem, thus concluding His Judean ministry. The response is the same in both places—rejection. As in Galilee, so in Judea.

The synagogue encounter would be amusing if it were not so serious. Jesus frees a woman who had been handicapped for eighteen years, and the ruler of the synagogue speaks up in unbridled arrogance.

> *But the ruler of the synagogue answered with indignation, because Jesus had healed on the Sabbath; and he said to the crowd, "There are six days on which men ought to work; therefore come and be healed on them, and not on the Sabbath day." (Luke 13:14)*

It was not his option to invite people for healing and to schedule the Lord's life! He was speaking out of turn, and Jesus responds.

> *"Hypocrite! Does not each one of you on the Sabbath loose his ox or donkey from the stall, and lead it away to water it? So ought not this woman, being a daughter of Abraham, whom Satan has bound—think of it—for eighteen years, be loosed from this bond on the Sabbath?" And when He said these things, all His adversaries were put to shame. (Luke 13:15-17)*

The Seventy return from their evangelization of suburban Judea, having gone into all of the towns and villages of the province with the message of the kingdom. They no doubt met Jesus in Jerusalem in preparation for the coming Feast of Dedication, and they shared their joy of being empowered by the Holy Spirit in their ministry.

> *Then the seventy returned with joy, saying, "Lord, even the demons are subject to us in Your name." (Luke 10:17)*

The contrast of the rejection of the ruler of the synagogue and the exuberance of the Seventy brings pause to Jesus. In a moment of deep spiritual contemplation Jesus finds great joy in the execution of the eternal plan of the triune God.

> *In that hour <u>Jesus</u> rejoiced <u>in the Spirit</u> and said, "I thank You, <u>Father</u>, Lord of heaven and earth, that You have hidden these things from the wise and prudent and revealed them to babes. Even so, Father, for so it seemed good in Your sight. All things have been delivered to Me by My Father, and no one knows who the Son is except the Father, and who the Father is except the Son, and the one to whom the Son wills to reveal Him." (Luke 10:21-22)*

Jesus shares His personal joy with the privileged disciples who were rejoicing in the service of God.

Then He turned to His disciples and said privately, "Blessed are the eyes which see the things you see; for I tell you that many prophets and kings have desired to see what you see, and have not seen it, and to hear what you hear, and have not heard it." (Luke 10:23-24)

We likewise share in the joy of serving God and rejoice in being those to whom God has revealed Himself in His sovereign grace—not to the wise and prudent, but to babes.

Jesus returns to Jerusalem for the Feast of Dedication. Earlier, at the beginning of the Judean ministry, He went up to Jerusalem for the Feast of Tabernacles. It was then that He began the Good Shepherd Discourse. Here at the Feast of Dedication He concludes it.

The Jews provide the introduction to Part 2 of the Good Shepherd Discourse.

Then the Jews surrounded Him and said to Him, "How long do You keep us in doubt? If You are the Christ, tell us plainly." (John 10:24)

The answer of Jesus is direct. "I told you, and you do not believe." Additionally, He points to the multiplied thousands of works and miracles that have testified to His truthfulness. Why did they not believe? Jesus answers that question: They do not belong to His fold . . . His sheep hear His voice and they know Him and follow Him . . . He gives them eternal life, and they are secure forever because the Father gave them to Him . . . He and the Father are one.

The last statement has been the sticking point from the beginning of Jesus' ministry—He forgave sins, making Himself equal to God. Demonstrating that they are not His sheep, they take up stones to stone Him. Jesus interrupts the attempted stoning with an important question:

"Many good works I have shown you from My Father. For which of those works do you stone Me?" (John 10:32)

The response?

The Jews answered Him, saying, "For a good work we do not stone You, but for blasphemy, and because You, being a Man, make Yourself God." (John 10:33)

The Jews try to arrest Him, but in a miraculous way He once again escapes from their hands. Thus ends the Judean ministry; the least populated province, Perea, remains. Rejected in Galilee, rejected in Judea. How will Perea respond? The prospect is not good. It is understandable that an unidentified disciple raises the question, "Lord, are there few who are saved?"

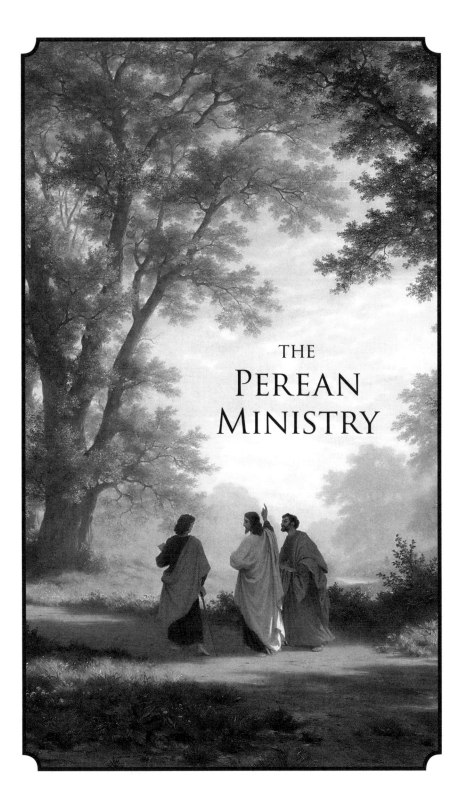

THE
PEREAN
MINISTRY

55

Invitations Given to the Banquet in the Kingdom

John 10:40-42; Luke 13:22-14:35

And He went away again beyond the Jordan to the place where John was baptizing at first, and there He stayed. Then many came to Him and said, "John performed no sign, but all the things that John spoke about this Man were true." (John 10:40-41)

Then one said to Him, "Lord, are there few who are saved?" And He said to them, "Strive to enter through the narrow gate, for many, I say to you, will seek to enter and will not be able. When once the Master of the house has risen up and shut the door, and you begin to stand outside and knock at the door, saying, 'Lord, Lord, open for us,' and He will answer and say to you, 'I do not know you, where you are from,' then you will begin to say, 'We ate and drank in Your presence, and You taught in our streets.' But He will say, 'I tell you I do not know you, where you are from. Depart from Me, all you workers of iniquity.' There will be weeping and gnashing of teeth, when you see Abraham and Isaac and Jacob and all the prophets in the kingdom of God, and yourselves thrust out. They will come from the east and the west, from the north and the south, and sit down in the kingdom of God. And indeed there are last who will be first, and there are first who will be last." (Luke 13:23-30)

Then He also said to him who invited Him, "When you give a dinner or a supper, do not ask your friends, your brothers, your relatives, nor rich neighbors, lest they also invite you back, and you be repaid. But when you give a feast, invite the poor, the maimed, the lame, the blind. And you will be blessed, because they cannot repay you; for you shall be repaid at the resurrection of the just." Now when one of those who sat at the table with Him heard these things, he said to Him, "Blessed is he who shall eat bread in the kingdom of God!" Then He said to him, "A certain man gave a great supper and invited many, and sent his servant at supper time to say to those who were invited, 'Come, for all things are now ready.' But they all with one accord began to make excuses. The first said to him, 'I have bought a piece of ground, and I must go and see it. I ask you to have me excused.' And another said, 'I have bought five yoke of oxen, and I am going to test them. I ask you to have me excused.' Still another said, 'I have married a wife, and therefore I cannot come.' So that servant came and reported these things to his master. Then the master of the house, being angry, said to his servant, 'Go out quickly into the streets and lanes of the city, and bring in here the poor and the maimed and the lame and the blind.' And the servant said, 'Master, it is done as you commanded, and still there is room.' Then the master said to the servant, 'Go out into the highways and hedges, and compel them to come in, that my house may be filled. 'For I say to you that none of those men who were invited shall taste my supper.'" (Luke 14:12-24)

J esus went away again across the Jordan, to the province of Perea. It is here in Perea that the Lord will conclude His evangelization of Israel—first, Galilee, then Judea, and finally Perea. During this closing period of His ministry, Jesus will introduce the concept of the kingdom banquet, which will include Gentile believers. The cross is looming before Him, and Jesus is looking to the other side of it as His rejection grows from province to province.

Now, the Perean ministry. Someone asks the Lord a penetrating question: "Lord, are there few who are saved?" Remember the close of the Galilean ministry.

From that time many of His disciples went back and walked with Him no more. Then Jesus said to the twelve, "Do you also want to go away?" But Simon Peter answered Him, "Lord, to whom shall we go? You have the words of eternal life. Also we have come to believe and know that You are the Christ, the Son of the living God." Jesus answered them, "Did I not choose you, the twelve, and one of you is a devil?" He spoke of Judas Iscariot, the son of Simon, for it was he who would betray Him, being one of the twelve. (John 6:66-71)

Remember the close of the Judean ministry.

Then the Jews took up stones again to stone Him. Jesus answered them, "Many good works I have shown you from My Father. For which of those works do you stone Me?" The Jews answered Him, saying, "For a good work we do not stone You, but for blasphemy, and because You, being a Man, make Yourself God." . . . Therefore they sought again to seize Him, but He escaped out of their hand. (John 10:31-33, 39)

And now, as they move into the least-populated province, Perea, the mood is not optimistic—with good reason! But Jesus introduces an optimistic future—that time when Jews and Gentiles will sit at the banquet table in the kingdom of God.

> *"There will be weeping and gnashing of teeth, when you see Abraham and Isaac and Jacob and all the prophets in the kingdom of God, and yourselves thrust out. They will come from the east and the west, from the north and the south, and sit down [i.e. at the banquet table] in the kingdom of God. And indeed there are last who will be first, and there are first who will be last." (Luke 13:28-30)*

Abraham, and Isaac, and Jacob will be there. And Gentiles from east, west, north, and south will be there. But not those of Galilee or Judea or soon Perea!

> *"Then you will begin to say, 'We ate and drank in Your presence, and You taught in our streets.' But He will say, 'I tell you I do not know you, where you are from, Depart from Me, all you workers of iniquity.'" (Luke 13:26-27)*

The banquet discussion initiated by Jesus is interrupted by a warning by some Pharisees and—once again—confrontation about the Sabbath with one Pharisee.

First, the warning. Some well-meaning Pharisees warned Jesus that Herod Antipas, ruler of Galilee and Perea, was seeking to kill Him. This was the same Herod who had killed John the Baptist at the insistence of Herodias, his illicit wife, and the same Herod who will be in Jerusalem with Pilate conducting the Roman trials of Jesus in Passion Week. With holy sarcasm Jesus responds.

> *"Go, tell that fox, 'Behold, I cast out demons and perform cures today and tomorrow, and the third day I shall be perfected.' Nevertheless I must journey today, tomorrow, and the day following; for it cannot be that a prophet should perish outside of Jerusalem." (Luke 13:32-33)*

Jesus is perfectly safe to conduct His ministry in Perea according to His schedule—today, and tomorrow, and on the third day. He is safe in Perea because prophets die in Jerusalem, not in Perea—it's always that way! This is followed by an ominous declaration.

> *"See! Your house is left to you desolate; and assuredly, I say to you, you shall not see Me until the time comes when you say, 'Blessed is He who comes in the name of the LORD!'" (Luke 13:35)*

Galilee—No! Judea—No! And now, Perea is about to say No! Jesus begins to talk about the withdrawal of the offer of the kingdom until the return of the King following the tribulation. He will say this in a more specific way in Passion Week.

As for Israel, *they* will say in Passion Week, "We will not have this man to rule over us!"

Second, healing on the Sabbath. Perea was like the other provinces when it came to objecting to Sabbath healing. With the healing of the man with dropsy, Jesus repeats the "ox or ass in the ditch" argument. Evidently it was acceptable to help animals on the Sabbath, but not the sons of Abraham. There is weariness to the repetition of the same argument and its logical refutation. "Are there few who are saved?"

Returning to the banquet motif, Jesus teaches proper decorum as to seating and desired guests. Someone at the table exclaims,

> "Blessed is he who shall eat bread in the kingdom of God!" (Luke 14:15)

Jesus responds by teaching about a great banquet to which many were invited to attend. But all those invited sent excuses as to why they would not be coming.

> "'I have bought a piece of ground, and I must go and see it. I ask you to have me excused.' . . . 'I have bought five yoke of oxen, and I am going to test them. I ask you to have me excused.' . . . 'I have married a wife, and therefore I cannot come.'" (Luke 14:18-20)

The banquet *will* be fully attended, however.

> "Then the master said to the servant, 'Go out into the highways and hedges, and compel them to come in, that my house may be filled.'" (Luke 14:23)

The rejection of Israel will make room for many Gentiles at the banquet in the kingdom!

56

The Lost Sheep, the Lost Coin,
and the Lost Son

Luke 15:1-32

Then all the tax collectors and the sinners drew near to Him to hear Him. And the Pharisees and scribes complained, saying, "This Man receives sinners and eats with them." So He spoke this parable to them, saying: "What man of you, having a hundred sheep, if he loses one of them, does not leave the ninety-nine in the wilderness, and go after the one which is lost until he finds it? And when he has found it, he lays it on his shoulders, rejoicing. . . . Or what woman, having ten silver coins, if she loses one coin, does not light a lamp, sweep the house, and search carefully until she finds it? And when she has found it, she calls her friends and neighbors together, saying, 'Rejoice with me, for I have found the piece which I lost!'" . . . Then He said: "A certain man had two sons. And the younger of them said to his father, 'Father, give me the portion of goods that falls to me.' So he divided to them his livelihood. But when he had spent all, there arose a severe famine in that land, and he began to be in want. Then he went and joined himself to a citizen of that country, and he sent him into his fields to feed swine. But when he came to himself, he said, 'How many of my father's hired servants have bread enough and to spare, and I perish with hunger! 'I will arise and go to my father.' And he arose and came to his father. But when he was still a great way off, his father saw him and had compassion, and ran and fell on his neck and kissed him. And the son said to him, 'Father, I have sinned against heaven and in your sight, and am no longer worthy to be called your son.' But the father said to his servants, 'Bring out the best robe and put it on him, and put a ring on his hand and sandals on his feet. 'And bring the fatted calf here and kill it, and let us eat and be merry, 'for this my son was dead and is alive again; he was lost and is found.' And they began to be merry Now his older son was in the field. And as he came and drew near to the house, he heard music and dancing. So he called one of the servants and asked what these things meant. And he said to him, 'Your brother has come, and because he has received him safe and sound, your father has killed the fatted calf.' But he was angry and would not go in. Therefore his father came out and pleaded with him. So he answered and said to his father, 'Lo, these many years I have been serving you; I never transgressed your commandment at any time; and yet you never gave me a young goat, that I might make merry with my friends. 'But as soon as this son of yours came, who has devoured your livelihood with harlots, you killed the fatted calf for him.' And he said to him, 'Son, you are always with me, and all that I have is yours. 'It was right that we should make merry and be glad, for your brother was dead and is alive again, and was lost and is found.'" (Luke 15:1-5, 8-9, 11-32)

The Pharisees were murmuring about Jesus socializing with tax collectors and sinners—those that Jesus came to seek and to save, the lost! So Jesus tells a three-part story about the proper response when the lost are found. The proper response is *joy!* Joy when a lost sheep is found. Joy when a lost coin is found. Joy when a lost son is found.

The setting is important for an understanding of this threefold parable. The self-righteous Pharisees, who cared little for "the people," continually faulted Jesus for welcoming sinners into His presence. These Pharisees fell under the condemnation of the Lord's conclusion of the first movement.

"I say to you that likewise there will be more joy in heaven over one sinner who repents than over ninety-nine righteous persons who need no repentance." (Luke 15:7)

There is no joy in heaven over self-righteousness, over those who delude themselves into thinking that they have no sin and therefore do not need to repent. These are genuinely lost because they will not face the reality of their lost condition. That reality is plainly stated in the Lord's ensuing narrative.

The first story is simple and short. It is about a shepherd with a flock of one hundred, one of which has wandered off. Upon securing the ninety-nine, the shepherd goes into the wilderness to pursue and find the one lost sheep. On finding it he rejoices and then calls his friends and neighbors to rejoice with him. That's the way it is in all of heaven when one sinner repents. Here we have inspired insight into the activities of heaven, where all present rejoice when a person on earth comes to faith. The Pharisees should be rejoicing as well, but they would not.

The second short story is likewise easy to understand. A woman loses one of ten silver coins, worth about a day's wages of a common laborer. The coin is not as valuable as a sheep, but its loss calls for a careful retracing of steps until it is recovered. There is rejoicing, but it is difficult to rejoice alone, so the woman calls her friends for collective rejoicing. The angels in heaven collectively rejoice before God over one repentant sinner. The Pharisees should be rejoicing as well, but they would not!

The third story is an elaborate and beautiful narrative—so much so, that the term "prodigal son" has become part of our secular language. One could pray that the spiritual response of repentance would also become part of the secular experience.

There are three main characters in the story: the father, the younger son, and the elder son. The father is of some means, administering a large estate, with many well cared for servants. The elder son has served for many years in following his father's instructions concerning the management of the farm. But the restless younger son wants to "sow his wild oats." He requests his share of the inheritance. His father divides his living between the sons, and within a few days the younger son takes all of his possessions and departs to a far distant land to escape the oversight of his wise father. The inevitable happens! The rebellious youth squanders his resources with partying friends. His money disappears, and then his friends disappear. To add to his misery, an extensive famine hits the land so that the youthful heir becomes a tender of swine—the Pharisees must have gasped at that! The son reaches rock bottom. He's lost.

But he remembers home: a place of security and provision; a loving father; his older brother; loyal servants who served happily, almost like members of the family. Having come to his senses, a plan comes to mind. Go home. Acknowledge sin. Repent. Volunteer to be a servant.

But he did not really know his father—the father who allowed his son to receive an early inheritance knowing all the risk involved for his son and his own livelihood; the father who longingly looked every day for the return of a repentant son; the father who knew his son so well that he could recognize him from a distance; a father full of love and forgiveness; a father kind and generous in restoration. The young man did not understand the great grace of his father. Only leaving and coming back home would enable him to know that grace. Once lost, being found is wonderful!

The prodigal son is greeted by the father on the road home.

> *"And he arose and came to his father. But when he was still a great*
> *way off, his father saw him and had compassion, and ran and fell on*
> *his neck and kissed him." (Luke 15:20)*

Compassion, a strong embrace, a welcoming kiss. The son begins his previously rehearsed speech.

> *"'Father, I have sinned against heaven and in your sight, and am no longer worthy to be called your son.'" (Luke 15:21)*

Confession finds immediate forgiveness in heaven, yet seldom on earth. Restoration and fellowship ensue and celebration is in order.

> *"But the father said to his servants, 'Bring out the best robe and put it on him, and put a ring on his hand and sandals on his feet. And bring the fatted calf here and kill it, and let us eat and be merry; for this my son was dead and is alive again; he was lost and is found.' And they began to be merry." (Luke 15:22-24)*

He was lost and is found! Joy follows, but not for the elder brother. The proper, elder brother would have no part with the party.

> *"So he answered and said to his father, 'Lo, these many years I have been serving you; I never transgressed your commandment at any time; and yet you never gave me a young goat, that I might make merry with my friends. But as soon as this son of yours came, who has devoured your livelihood with harlots, you killed the fatted calf for him.'" (Luke 15:29-30)*

The elder brother should have rejoiced, but would not. The Pharisees who were so angry with Jesus for eating with repentant sinners should have rejoiced, but would not! They knew nothing of the forgiveness of heaven. They were lost!

57

Money, Marriage, Forgiveness, and Servanthood

Luke 16:1-31; 17:1-10

---

*He also said to His disciples: "There was a certain rich man who had a steward, and an accusation was brought to him that this man was wasting his goods. So he called him and said to him, 'What is this I hear about you? Give an account of your stewardship, for you can no longer be steward.' Then the steward said within himself, 'What shall I do? For my master is taking the stewardship away from me. I cannot dig; I am ashamed to beg. I have resolved what to do, that when I am put out of the stewardship, they may receive me into their houses.' So he called every one of his master's debtors to him, and said to the first, 'How much do you owe my master?' And he said, 'A hundred measures of oil.' So he said to him, 'Take your bill, and sit down quickly and write fifty.' . . . So the master commended the unjust steward because he had dealt shrewdly. For the sons of this world are more shrewd in their generation than the sons of light. And I say to you, make friends for yourselves by unrighteous mammon, that when you fail, they may receive you into an everlasting home."
. . . . Now the Pharisees, who were lovers of money, also heard all these things, and they derided Him. (Luke 16:1-6, 8-9, 14)*

"Whoever divorces his wife and marries another commits adultery; and whoever marries her who is divorced from her husband commits adultery. There was a certain rich man who was clothed in purple and fine linen and fared sumptuously every day. But there was a certain beggar named Lazarus, full of sores, who was laid at his gate, desiring to be fed with the crumbs which fell from the rich man's table. Moreover the dogs came and licked his sores. So it was that the beggar died, and was carried by the angels to Abraham's bosom. The rich man also died and was buried. And being in torments in Hades, he lifted up his eyes and saw Abraham afar off, and Lazarus in his bosom." (Luke 16:18-23)

"Take heed to yourselves. If your brother sins against you, rebuke him; and if he repents, forgive him. And if he sins against you seven

times in a day, and seven times in a day returns to you, saying, 'I repent,' you shall forgive him." (Luke 17:3-4)

"And which of you, having a servant plowing or tending sheep, will say to him when he has come in from the field, 'Come at once and sit down to eat'? But will he not rather say to him, 'Prepare something for my supper, and gird yourself and serve me till I have eaten and drunk, and afterward you will eat and drink'? Does he thank that servant because he did the things that were commanded him? I think not. So likewise you, when you have done all those things which you are commanded, say, 'We are unprofitable servants. We have done what was our duty to do.'" (Luke 17:7-10)

In continuing the evangelization of Perea, Jesus briefly touches on issues of everyday life in teaching His disciples about money, marriage, forgiveness, and servanthood.

There is a somewhat humorous parable developed concerning money—a dishonest steward is caught and fired. What to do?

"Then the steward said within himself, 'What shall I do? For my master is taking the stewardship away from me. I cannot dig; I am ashamed to beg.'" (Luke 16:3)

He immediately goes to the debtors he oversees and reduces their debts drastically—and they pay up! Now the steward has future security with his newly made friends. And his master commends his prudence! Jesus makes application to His disciples, both then and now: use unrighteous money to provide a welcoming committee of friends in heaven. Money should be used for eternal purposes, not only temporal. The materialist Pharisees rejected this teaching.

Next, a brief statement concerning marriage and divorce. There is often a connection between finances and divorce. Here there is a re-statement of the permanence of marriage and a condemnation of adultery, a reminder to His disciples of earlier teaching. The reminder of the standard of the Lord Jesus, who is God, is needed in the present day as well.

Jesus then relates what has become a well-known passage of Scripture—the story of the rich man and a certain Lazarus. It concerns in broad terms to the life of the rich and the poor, both now and in eternity. The story's emphasis is the same as the earlier statement on finances—to live for eternity, not for today. But the details are very significant in the flow of events that will follow. A more detailed discussion of this will be given next time, when we meet another Lazarus.

Forgiveness—another daily necessity! Jesus had already twice taught His disciples to pray, "Forgive us our trespasses as we forgive those who trespass against us." There is an important qualification for forgiveness in this teaching of Jesus—repentance.

> "Take heed to yourselves. If your brother sins against you, rebuke him; and if he repents, forgive him." (Luke 17:3)

Forgiveness requires a forgiver and a forgivee. Forgiveness cannot be executed without repentance. God does not forgive without repentance. The lake of fire will be populated by unrepentant, unforgiven sinners. The forgiving God only forgives those who repent of their sin. This does not justify holding grudges or an attitude of malice and animosity—we should always desire and be ready to forgive—but it requires repentance on the part of the offender. Forgiveness is to be a constantly repeated action by the followers of Jesus. So teaches the gracious Jesus in this brief statement. The disciples cry out for an increase of faith.

Jesus gives an additional lesson in servanthood. This is a frequently repeated subject because it is a difficult lesson to learn for Christ's followers—it's hard to be a servant!

> "And which of you, having a servant plowing or tending sheep, will say to him when he has come in from the field, 'Come at once and sit down to eat'? But will he not rather say to him, 'Prepare something for my supper, and gird yourself and serve me till I have eaten and drunk, and afterward you will eat and drink'? Does he thank that servant because he did the things that were commanded him? I think not." (Luke 17:7-9)

Two observations are made about being a servant: don't expect any privileges, and don't expect to be thanked. Inherently, a servant has no rights. Peter mused on this and addressed it in his first epistle.

> Servants, be submissive to your masters with all fear, not only to the good and gentle, but also to the harsh. For this is commendable, if because of conscience toward God one endures grief, suffering wrongfully. For what credit is it if, when you are beaten for your faults, you take it patiently? But when you do good and suffer, if you take it patiently, this is commendable before God. (1 Peter 2:18-20)

The appropriate attitude of a servant is summarized by Jesus.

> *"So likewise you, when you have done all those things which you are commanded, say, 'We are unprofitable servants. We have done what was our duty to do.'" (Luke 17:10)*

"We are unprofitable servants." And so we are! But it should be noted that God does give His servants enormous privileges and He rewards them generously for services rendered—even when the empowerment comes from Him! God is a gracious Master, and we are His perpetual servants!

58

The Lazarus Connection

John 11:1-46

*Now a certain man was sick, Lazarus of Bethany, the town of Mary
and her sister Martha. . . . He said to them, "Our friend Lazarus
sleeps, but I go that I may wake him up." Then His disciples said,
"Lord, if he sleeps he will get well." However, Jesus spoke of his
death, but they thought that He was speaking about taking rest in
sleep. Then Jesus said to them plainly, "Lazarus is dead. And I
am glad for your sakes that I was not there, that you may believe.
Nevertheless let us go to him." . . . So when Jesus came, He found
that he had already been in the tomb four days. . . . Then Martha
said to Jesus, "Lord, if You had been here, my brother would not
have died. But even now I know that whatever You ask of God, God
will give You." Jesus said to her, "Your brother will rise again." . . .
Then, when Mary came where Jesus was, and saw Him, she fell down
at His feet, saying to Him, "Lord, if You had been here, my brother
would not have died." Therefore, when Jesus saw her weeping, and
the Jews who came with her weeping, He groaned in the spirit and
was troubled. And He said, "Where have you laid him?" They said
to Him, "Lord, come and see." Jesus wept. . . . Then they took away
the stone from the place where the dead man was lying. And Jesus
lifted up His eyes and said, "Father, I thank You that You have heard
Me. And I know that You always hear Me, but because of the people
who are standing by I said this, that they may believe that You sent
Me." Now when He had said these things, He cried with a loud voice,
"Lazarus, come forth!" And he who had died came out bound hand
and foot with graveclothes, and his face was wrapped with a cloth.
Jesus said to them, "Loose him, and let him go." Then many of the
Jews who had come to Mary, and had seen the things Jesus did,
believed in Him. But some of them went away to the Pharisees and
told them the things Jesus did. (John 11:1, 11-15, 17, 21-23, 32-35,
41-46)*

The "Lazarus connection" is twofold, because the name occurs in
juxtaposition to two men named Lazarus—the one in the story of the
rich man and Lazarus and the other being the brother of Mary and Martha.
They are connected in both time sequence and the developing opposition to
Jesus.

First, the story of Lazarus and the rich man. Jesus tells the story of a certain rich man and a certain beggar named Lazarus. In paradise, the rich man sees Lazarus afar off and has a series of requests. From this we receive the teaching of Jesus concerning the eternal state of the lost. Jesus spoke often of eternal punishment.

And what is characteristic of that eternal state? Jesus helps us understand the dreadful situation:

➢ It is a place of eternal torment and anguish.

➢ It is described as an eternal fire, and generating great thirst.

➢ It is a place where the blessings of heaven are visible afar off, being permanently separated from heaven by a great chasm.

➢ It is a place where memory of the past is active, and where spiritual concern for others is active.

➢ It seems to be a place of solitude and reflection.

The eternal state of the lost is a terrible place, to be avoided at all costs. So thinks the rich man, and his final plea is for Abraham to send Lazarus back from the dead to his five brothers so that they might believe. Earlier he asked that Lazarus be sent to him from heaven with a moistened finger to relieve his thirst.

The response of Abraham is dramatic and full of meaning.

"Abraham said to him [the rich man], 'They have Moses and the prophets; let them hear them.' And he said, 'No, father Abraham; but if one goes to them from the dead, they will repent.' But he said to him, 'If they do not hear Moses and the prophets, neither will they be persuaded though one rise from the dead.'" (Luke 16:29-31)

Abraham speaks of two sections of the Old Testament, the law of Moses (the Pentateuch) and the Prophets. Abraham predated Moses and the prophets historically—in fact Moses records Abraham's life and death. But Abraham knows all about Moses and his writings, as well as the writings of the Old Testament prophets. There must be Bible study in heaven—the best of Bible studies.

But Abraham makes an even more amazing statement: "Neither will they be persuaded though one rise from the dead." This is where we turn to the next amazing event in the narrative: the resurrection of a person—of all things, named Lazarus. Another Lazarus! And the Jews will not believe. In fact they will make plans for that Lazarus to die again very soon.

Now, the wonderful story of the resurrection of Lazarus. Almost every funeral takes us to this miracle for comfort and encouragement. Remember,

Jesus is in His Perean ministry, and Bethany is near Jerusalem in Judea. This is where Jesus and the disciples would be based for their Judean ministry. While in Perea, they hear of the serious sickness of Lazarus. The urgent message comes from the sisters, Martha and Mary.

But Jesus remains away two days longer—and Lazarus dies. This delay is out of love for Mary and Martha, and for the glory of God—a very strange connection of motivation and action. Jesus announces to His disciples that Lazarus has died and that they are going to return to Judea to awaken him out of the sleep of death. Four days elapse by the time Jesus responds to the urgent message for help. All parties have the same question:

> *Then Martha said to Jesus, "Lord, if You had been here, my brother would not have died. . . ." Then, when Mary came where Jesus was, and saw Him, she fell down at His feet, saying to Him, "Lord, if You had been here, my brother would not have died." . . . And some of them said, "Could not this Man, who opened the eyes of the blind, also have kept this man from dying?" (John 11:21, 32, 37)*

But it was for the glory of God! It was the setting for Jesus to say:

> *"I am the resurrection and the life. He who believes in Me, though he may die, he shall live. And whoever lives and believes in Me shall never die." (John 11:25-26)*

But it was more! It was for Palm Sunday—for the triumphal entry.

> *Now a great many of the Jews knew that He was there; and they came, not for Jesus' sake only, but that they might also see Lazarus, whom He had raised from the dead. But the chief priests plotted to put Lazarus to death also, because on account of him many of the Jews went away and believed in Jesus. (John 12:9-11)*

The Sanhedrin responds in despair for fear that Rome will intervene and bring destruction on a nation that is out of control. Caiaphas, the high priest, prophesies of the death of Christ.

> *"You know nothing at all, nor do you consider that it is expedient for us that one man should die for the people, and not that the whole nation should perish." Now this he did not say on his own authority; but being high priest that year he prophesied that Jesus would die for the nation, and not for that nation only, but also that He would gather together in one the children of God who were scattered abroad. (John 11:49-52)*

But though one be raised from the dead, they will not believe! The Lazarus connection. God moves in a mysterious way His wonders to perform.

59

One Leper Returns, and the Pharisees Question the Coming of the Kingdom

Luke 17:11-37

Now it happened as He went to Jerusalem that He passed through the midst of Samaria and Galilee. Then as He entered a certain village, there met Him ten men who were lepers, who stood afar off. And they lifted up their voices and said, "Jesus, Master, have mercy on us!" So when He saw them, He said to them, "Go, show yourselves to the priests." And so it was that as they went, they were cleansed. And one of them, when he saw that he was healed, returned, and with a loud voice glorified God, and fell down on his face at His feet, giving Him thanks. And he was a Samaritan. So Jesus answered and said, "Were there not ten cleansed? But where are the nine? Were there not any found who returned to give glory to God except this foreigner?" And He said to him, "Arise, go your way. Your faith has made you well." Now when He was asked by the Pharisees when the kingdom of God would come, He answered them and said, "The kingdom of God does not come with observation; nor will they say, 'See here!' or 'See there!' For indeed, the kingdom of God is in your midst." Then He said to the disciples, "The days will come when you will desire to see one of the days of the Son of Man, and you will not see it. And they will say to you, 'Look here!' or 'Look there!' Do not go after them or follow them. For as the lightning that flashes out of one part under heaven shines to the other part under heaven, so also the Son of Man will be in His day. But first He must suffer many things and be rejected by this generation. And as it was in the days of Noah, so it will be also in the days of the Son of Man. Likewise as it was also in the days of Lot but on the day that Lot went out of Sodom it rained fire and brimstone from heaven and destroyed them all. Even so will it be in the day when the Son of Man is revealed. In that day, he who is on the housetop, and his goods are in the house, let him not come down to take them away. And likewise the one who is in the field, let him not turn back. Remember Lot's wife. Whoever seeks to save his life will lose it, and whoever loses his life will preserve it. I tell you, in that night there will be two men in one bed: the one will be taken and the other will be left. Two women will be grinding together: the one will be taken and the other left. Two men will be in the field: the one will be taken and the other left." And they answered and said to Him, "Where, Lord?" So He said to them, "Wherever the body is, there the eagles will be gathered together." (Luke 17:11-37)

J esus now resumes the conclusion of His Perean ministry, traveling to Perea through a circuitous route via Samaria and Galilee. In Samaria He comes upon ten lepers who cry out for healing. Following the instructions Jesus gives them, they begin the journey to Jerusalem to present themselves to the priest and meet the requirements of the law. In the process of obeying the Lord they are cleansed of the dreaded disease. Only one returns to Jesus to worship and give thanks, and he was a Samaritan.

He was a Samaritan! It was unusual for Samaritans and Jews to mingle together, but leprosy eliminated some barriers of society and established others. When all had leprosy, there was a forced fellowship of exiles. When cured, the Samaritan was alone! But he returns to Jesus and the Lord responds with a logical inquiry:

"Were there not ten cleansed? But where are the nine? Were there not any found who returned to give glory to God except this foreigner?" (Luke 17:17-18)

"Except this foreigner?" The nine Jewish lepers reflected the response of the mass of Judaism; they benefitted from the miracles but gave no praise to God. The Samaritan leper, however, like the woman of Samaria, returned and worshiped God.

It is no wonder that the Pharisees were questioning the coming of the kingdom; even cleansed Jewish lepers did not return to give thanks to One who healed them. Will the kingdom ever come? Jesus responds with information concerning its coming. He the King is in their midst; the kingdom is available upon repentance—but neither the lepers nor Israel will give God the praise.

Then He said to the disciples, "The days will come when you will desire to see one of the days of the Son of Man, and you will not see it." (Luke 17:22)

Please recall the discussion on the title "Son of Man" from an earlier lesson. It is the title that comes from Daniel 7 relating to the receiving of kingdom authority. It is the title the Lord used most when referring to Himself, but it disappears from usage in the epistles except on three occasions when the kingdom is in context. It is a kingdom title. And the offer of the kingdom is falling on stony ground, soon to be rejected altogether. Israel would long for that day. Instead, they will get the invading armies of Rome under Titus.

But the kingdom will come, later. Jesus supplies a bit of the timetable. First, the Son of Man will suffer many things and be rejected. Life will go on as normal, but then judgment will come just like the flood in the time of Noah, and just like the judgment of Sodom in the time of Lot. Jesus is making reference to the great tribulation, which will be the major subject of the Olivet Discourse that He will deliver on Tuesday of Passion Week.

In answer to the disciples' question, "Where, Lord? Where will this carnage take place?" Jesus makes a proverbial statement that is directly repeated in the Olivet Discourse.

> *"Wherever the body is, there the eagles will be gathered together."*
> *(Luke 17:37)*

> *"For wherever the carcass is, there the eagles will be gathered together." (Matthew 24:28)*

The gruesome picture is of devastation during the tribulation, with massive death. The vultures will gather at that time when God's judgment will be poured out on a corrupt world.

The parable that follows is an encouragement to persist in prayer in spite of ungodly judges. Perhaps God will move in mercy on His elect as they continue to cry out for vindication of His holy ones. The Son of Man is seeking to see that faith when He returns for His kingdom. Christ, the Head of the church, desires that the present members of the church be persistent in prayer as well.

> *Then He spoke a parable to them, that men always ought to pray and not lose heart, saying: "There was in a certain city a judge who did not fear God nor regard man. Now there was a widow in that city; and she came to him, saying, 'Get justice for me from my adversary.' And he would not for a while; but afterward he said within himself, 'Though I do not fear God nor regard man, yet because this widow troubles me I will avenge her, lest by her continual coming she weary me.'" Then the Lord said, "Hear what the unjust judge said. And shall God not avenge His own elect who cry out day and night to Him, though He bears long with them? I tell you that He will avenge them speedily. Nevertheless, when the Son of Man comes, will He really find faith on the earth?" (Luke 18:1-8)*

Jesus is restating an earlier teaching concerning His rejection, crucifixion, and return to heaven prior to the establishment of the kingdom. His disciples have difficulty in understanding this concept, and Jesus will continue to teach concerning this as they approach Jerusalem for Passion Week. The cross, that hour, looms closely on the horizon.

60
:

Advice for the Routines of Life: Marriage, Divorce, Celibacy, and Children

Luke 18:9-17; Matthew 19:1-15; Mark 10:1-16

Also He spoke this parable to some who trusted in themselves that they were righteous, and despised others: Two men went up to the temple to pray, one a Pharisee and the other a tax collector. The Pharisee stood and prayed thus with himself, 'God, I thank You that I am not like other men—extortioners, unjust, adulterers, or even as this tax collector. I fast twice a week; I give tithes of all that I possess.' And the tax collector, standing afar off, would not so much as raise his eyes to heaven, but beat his breast, saying, 'God, be merciful to me a sinner!' I tell you, this man went down to his house justified rather than the other; for everyone who exalts himself will be humbled, and he who humbles himself will be exalted." (Luke 18:9-14)

The Pharisees also came to Him, testing Him, and saying to Him, "Is it lawful for a man to divorce his wife for just any reason?" And He answered and said to them, "Have you not read that He who made them at the beginning 'made them male and female,' and said, 'For this reason a man shall leave his father and mother and be joined to his wife, and the two shall become one flesh'? So then, they are no longer two but one flesh. Therefore what God has joined together, let not man separate." They said to Him, "Why then did Moses command to give a certificate of divorce, and to put her away?" He said to them, "Moses, because of the hardness of your hearts, permitted you to divorce your wives, but from the beginning it was not so. And I say to you, whoever divorces his wife, except for sexual immorality, and marries another, commits adultery; and whoever marries her who is divorced commits adultery." His disciples said to Him, "If such is the case of the man with his wife, it is better not to marry." But He said to them, "All cannot accept this saying, but only those to whom it has been given: For there are eunuchs who were born thus from their mother's womb, and there are eunuchs who were made eunuchs by men, and there are eunuchs who have made themselves eunuchs for the kingdom of heaven's sake. He who is able to accept it, let him accept it." Then little children were brought to Him that He might put His hands on them and pray, but the disciples rebuked them. But Jesus said, "Let the little children come to Me, and do not forbid them; for of such is the kingdom of heaven." And He laid His hands on them and departed from there. (Matthew 19:3-15)

A s Jesus re-enters Perea for the conclusion of the evangelization of the third and final province of Israel, He addresses again the routines of life: prayer, marriage and celibacy, children, and finances. Passion Week is only a few weeks away—the confrontations with the religious leaders, the betrayal, Gethsemane, six trials, and the crucifixion. None of this was going to be routine, but it was the focal point of the redemptive plan. Yet Jesus addresses the issues of daily life relationships for those who will hear.

Prayer. Prayer is an acknowledgement of our dependence on God—for understanding God's direction, for daily bread, for human harmony, for deliverance from personal sin. Jesus already taught us that twice in the repeated Lord's Prayer. In the parable of the Pharisee and the tax collector, He teaches us that prayer is not for show and proud public display. Rather, it is the cry of the supplicant who recognizes his need for mercy because of his sinful bent—a universal human plight.

Marriage and divorce. Marriage is the building block of human society. Marriage was created by God in the garden of Eden with specific beneficent guidelines with the wellbeing of the race in mind. It was soon rejected, even by the godly, and multiple marriages, spouses, and subsequent divorces followed with all of the miseries they entailed. To test Jesus, the Pharisees raise the question:

> *"Is it lawful for a man to divorce his wife for just any reason?" (Matthew 19:3)*

Jesus introduces His response by returning to the origins of marriage. Notice the points He makes concerning marriage:

➢ It was created by God in the beginning.
➢ It involves a male and a female.
➢ It involves starting a new entity by leaving father and mother.
➢ It involves a physical consummation.
➢ It is a permanent lifetime relationship.

The Pharisees retort with a pointed argument—"Moses said divorce was alright." And Jesus responds quickly by saying that the action of Moses was a compromise to accommodate the hardness of heart of their ancestors. "But it was not so from the beginning." Jesus then gives His only exception for divorce—unfaithfulness in marriage. Unfaithfulness, like desertion, destroys the very essence of marriage and is a legitimate reason for divorce. So says Jesus.

Celibacy. The disciples of Jesus are shocked by this narrow restriction.

> *His disciples said to Him, "If such is the case of the man with his wife, it is better not to marry." (Matthew 19:10)*

Jesus states, as does Paul in 1 Corinthians 7, that celibacy is a valid option in life if a person can accept that limitation. But not all can! By God's direction, some will choose a celibate life for the sake of the kingdom of God.

Children. Infants and children are brought by their parents to receive a blessing by the Savior's touch. The disciples viewed this as a hindrance to more important issues of communication—and Jesus is indignant with their response.

> *"Let the little children come to Me, and do not forbid them; for of such is the kingdom of God. Assuredly, I say to you, whoever does not receive the kingdom of God as a little child will by no means enter it." And He took them up in His arms, put His hands on them, and blessed them. (Mark 10:14-16)*

Jesus always has time for children, helpless children. All of mankind is helpless!

For many years while driving to Emmaus to teach, I would pass a schoolyard full of children. In the schoolyard was a statue of Jesus with children sitting on His lap. I enjoyed that scene on a daily basis. Jesus loves the little children of the world, and so should His disciples.

TO JERUSALEM,
AND
PASSION WEEK

61

The Young Ruler Stumbles Over Riches

Matthew 19:16-28:16; Mark 10:17-31; Luke 18:18-30

Now behold, one came and said to Him, "Good Teacher, what good thing shall I do that I may have eternal life?" So He said to him, "Why do you call Me good? No one is good but One, that is, God. But if you want to enter into life, keep the commandments." He said to Him, "Which ones?" Jesus said, "'You shall not murder,' 'You shall not commit adultery,' 'You shall not steal,' 'You shall not bear false witness,' 'Honor your father and your mother,' and, 'You shall love your neighbor as yourself.'" The young man said to Him, "All these things I have kept from my youth. What do I still lack?" Jesus said to him, "If you want to be perfect, go, sell what you have and give to the poor, and you will have treasure in heaven; and come, follow Me." But when the young man heard that saying, he went away sorrowful, for he had great possessions. Then Jesus said to His disciples, "Assuredly, I say to you that it is hard for a rich man to enter the kingdom of heaven. And again I say to you, it is easier for a camel to go through the eye of a needle than for a rich man to enter the kingdom of God." When His disciples heard it, they were greatly astonished, saying, "Who then can be saved?" But Jesus looked at them and said to them, "With men this is impossible, but with God all things are possible." Then Peter answered and said to Him, "See, we have left all and followed You. Therefore what shall we have?" So Jesus said to them, "Assuredly I say to you, that in the regeneration, when the Son of Man sits on the throne of His glory, you who have followed Me will also sit on twelve thrones, judging the twelve tribes of Israel." (Matthew 19:16-28)

"For the kingdom of heaven is like a landowner who went out early in the morning to hire laborers for his vineyard. Now when he had agreed with the laborers for a denarius a day, he sent them into his vineyard. . . . And when those came who were hired about the eleventh hour, they each received a denarius. But when the first came, they supposed that they would receive more; and they likewise received

each a denarius. And when they had received it, they complained against the landowner, saying, 'These last men have worked only one hour, and you made them equal to us who have borne the burden and the heat of the day.'" (Matthew 20:1-2, 9-12)

A s Jesus nears Jerusalem the question of materialism becomes a point of teaching. Jesus gives appropriate instruction to His disciples about the outlook a follower of Christ should have relating to material possessions. This subject is introduced as a rich young man (termed "a ruler" in Luke's account) approaches Jesus with life's most important question, "What must I do to inherit eternal life?" The response of Jesus is surprising. He does not go to an instantaneous rebuke and correction, "By faith, not of works, lest any man should boast." Rather, He refers to the keeping of the law to gain the desired eternal life. "If you want to enter into life, keep the commandments." A strange answer! Is the purpose of the answer to point out the deficiency of the character of the rich young ruler, or is it a valid answer? I would suggest both!

The progress of the conversation seems to confirm this conclusion. Jesus identifies a number of the commandments in response to the question, "Which ones?" The listing varies in the three accounts of the gospels, indicating that Jesus gave a sampling of the Ten Commandments. The commandments are taken from both tablets—duty to God and the rights of the individual—and even one of the two summary statements of the law is given, "You shall love your neighbor as yourself." A variety of choices. No bother, the rich young ruler has kept them all. He was either arrogant or strongly deluded.

Gently, Jesus responds again. The rich young ruler only lacks one step to perfection.

> *Jesus said to him, "If you want to be perfect, go, sell what you have and give to the poor, and you will have treasure in heaven; and come, follow Me." (Matthew 19:21)*

The conclusion to the conversation is disappointing. The young man chooses riches over eternal life—a foolish choice.

> *But when the young man heard that saying, he went away sorrowful, for he had great possessions. (Matthew 19:22)*

Clearly, he did not love his neighbor as himself; neither did he love God with all his heart. He did not attain to life-giving perfection. He did have deficiency of character. Was it possible to gain eternal life through keeping the law? After all, Jesus said, "If you want to enter into life, keep the commandments."

One of the attributes of deity is justice; God is not partial. That impartiality is addressed by Paul in Romans 2.

> . . . who "will render to each one according to his deeds": eternal life to those who by patient continuance in doing good seek for glory, honor, and immortality; but to those who are self-seeking and do not obey the truth, but obey unrighteousness—indignation and wrath, tribulation and anguish, on every soul of man who does evil, of the Jew first and also of the Greek; but glory, honor, and peace to everyone who works what is good, to the Jew first and also to the Greek. For there is no partiality with God. (Romans 2:6-11)

It is true. There is salvation through keeping the law. The law is holy, and just, and good; and the flesh is weak, especially for a rich man.

> Then Jesus said to His disciples, "Assuredly, I say to you that it is hard for a rich man to enter the kingdom of heaven." (Matthew 19:23)

Peter's response to the sad event is humorous, and maybe Jesus' initial reaction was to laugh, as the apostles were not rich.

> Then Peter answered and said to Him, "See, we have left all and followed You. Therefore what shall we have?" (Matthew 19:27)

Jesus responded, however, with a wonderful promise for His faithful apostles.

> So Jesus said to them, "Assuredly I say to you, that in the regeneration, when the Son of Man sits on the throne of His glory, you who have followed Me will also sit on twelve thrones, judging the twelve tribes of Israel. And everyone who has left houses or brothers or sisters or father or mother or wife or children or lands, for My name's sake, shall receive a hundredfold, and inherit eternal life." (Matthew 19:28-29)

The apostles will receive a generous reward for their service because God is characterized by generosity. The parable that grows out of the rich young ruler event stresses God's generosity.

> "For the kingdom of heaven is like a householder who went out early in the morning to hire laborers for his vineyard. After agreeing with the laborers for a denarius a day, he sent them into his vineyard. And going out about the third hour he saw others standing idle in the market place; and to them he said, 'You go into the vineyard too, and whatever is right I will give you.' So they went. Going out again about the sixth hour and the ninth hour, he did the same. And about the eleventh hour he went out and found others standing; and he said to them, 'Why do you stand here idle all day?' They said to

him, 'Because no one has hired us.' He said to them, 'You go into the vineyard too.' And when evening came, the owner of the vineyard said to his steward, 'Call the laborers and pay them their wages, beginning with the last, up to the first.' And when those hired about the eleventh hour came, each of them received a denarius. Now when the first came, they thought they would receive more; but each of them also received a denarius. And on receiving it they grumbled at the householder, saying, 'These last worked only one hour, and you have made them equal to us who have borne the burden of the day and the scorching heat.' But he replied to one of them, 'Friend, I am doing you no wrong; did you not agree with me for a denarius? Take what belongs to you, and go; I choose to give to this last as I give to you. Am I not allowed to do what I choose with what belongs to me? Or do you begrudge my generosity?' So the last will be first, and the first last." (Matthew 20:1-16)

Any service for our God will be rewarded generously.

62

Jesus Teaches about
His Death and Servanthood

Matthew 20:17-28; Mark 10:32-45; Luke 18:31-34

*Now Jesus, going up to Jerusalem, took the twelve disciples aside on
the road and said to them, "Behold, we are going up to Jerusalem;
and the Son of Man will be betrayed to the chief priests and to the
scribes; and they will condemn Him to death, and deliver Him to the
Gentiles to mock and to scourge and to crucify. And the third day
He will rise again." Then the mother of Zebedee's sons came to Him
with her sons, kneeling down and asking something from Him. And
He said to her, "What do you wish?" She said to Him, "Grant that
these two sons of mine may sit, one at Your right hand and the other
on the left, in Your kingdom." But Jesus answered and said, "You
do not know what you ask. Are you able to drink the cup that I am
about to drink, and be baptized with the baptism that I am baptized
with?" They said to Him, "We are able." So He said to them, "You
will indeed drink My cup, and be baptized with the baptism that I am
baptized with, but to sit at My right hand and on My left is not Mine
to give, but it is for those for whom it is prepared by My Father."
And when the ten heard it, they were greatly displeased with the
two brothers. But Jesus called them to Himself and said, "You know
that the rulers of the Gentiles lord it over them, and those who are
great exercise authority over them. Yet it shall not be so among you;
but whoever desires to become great among you, let him be your
servant. And whoever desires to be first among you, let him be your
slave—just as the Son of Man did not come to be served, but to serve,
and to give His life a ransom for many." (Matthew 20:17-28)*

Jesus and the disciples were just a few days from entering Jerusalem for the
Passover, for Triumphal Entry Sunday, Palm Sunday. Jesus knew this full
well. The disciples did not understand at all. *They* were going to Jerusalem
to reign in the kingdom; *He* was going to die on a cross on Golgotha. They
will receive additional instruction as to the future, but it will take them well
into the events recorded in the book of Acts before it all comes clear to them.

As Jesus was on His way to Jerusalem, He paused with His disciples to give special instruction concerning His death. Mark points out that He was doing this *again*. He had done this a number of times already, but they did not understand. So how could they miss the teaching? Jesus is even specific as to the nature of His death—it would be by crucifixion. He had stated this same thing after Peter's confession.

> *From that time Jesus began to show to His disciples that he must go to Jerusalem, and suffer many things from the elders and chief priests and scribes, and be killed, and be raised the third day. (Matthew 16:21)*

How could they miss such clear teaching? He identified those who would conduct the trial, the outcome of death by crucifixion by the Roman powers, and His subsequent resurrection after three days. He had spoken of His resurrection after the cleansing of the temple at the beginning of His public ministry. How could they miss all of this specific teaching? Two overlooked verses help us understand.

> *"Let these words sink down into your ears; for the Son of Man is about to be betrayed into the hands of men." But they did not understand this saying, and it was hidden from them so that they did not perceive it; and they were afraid to ask Him about this saying. (Luke 9:44-45)*

> *"For He will be delivered to the Gentiles and be mocked and insulted and spit upon. They will scourge Him and kill Him, and on the third day He will rise again." But they understood none of these things; this saying was hidden from them, and they did not know the things that were spoken. (Luke 18:32-34)*

Dr. Luke, the careful historian, records these interpretive statements that explain the lack of understanding on the part of the apostles. The first statement occurs early after Peter's confession; the second, just before entering Jerusalem for Passion Week. There was a divine fog that descended on the understanding of the apostles that would be dispelled when the Holy Spirit brought to their memory the clear teachings of Jesus.

While Jesus talks about His death, the apostles talk about reigning in the kingdom—an amazing contrast! It was an orchestrated approach for a favored position in the soon-to-come kingdom.

First, Mother Zebedee comes with the request for a favor for her sons, and then the sons come—the Sons of Thunder, the beloved apostle and his to-be-martyred brother. The request is for a place of honor when they reign with Jesus. Having just heard of that promise, they want first place in the kingdom.

When word of the attempt for favorable treatment reaches the rest of the apostles, they are indignant. Jesus calls the men to Himself and counsels them. In short, Jesus rebukes them for acting like political leaders of the world, who are known for their pride, power, and ego. This is not the way of the follower of Christ; this is not the way of Christ.

Out of this embarrassing grab for power by the apostles comes a clear description of the mind of Christ.

> ". . . just as the Son of Man did not come to be served, but to serve, and to give His life a ransom for many." (Matthew 20:28)

The apostle Paul expands on this attitude of mind.

> Let this mind be in you which was also in Christ Jesus, who, being in the form of God, did not consider it robbery to be equal with God, but made Himself of no reputation, taking the form of a bondservant, and coming in the likeness of men. And being found in appearance as a man, He humbled Himself and became obedient to the point of death, even the death of the cross. (Philippians 2:5-8)

Soon they would be witnessing the Son of Man giving His life a ransom for many. Good Friday is near.

63

On the Jericho Road: Blind Bartimaeus and Little Zacchaeus

Matthew 20:29-34; Mark 10:46-52; Luke 18:35-43; Luke 19:1-10

Now they came to Jericho. As He went out of Jericho with His disciples and a great multitude, blind Bartimaeus, the son of Timaeus, sat by the road begging. And when he heard that it was Jesus of Nazareth, he began to cry out and say, "Jesus, Son of David, have mercy on me!" Then many warned him to be quiet; but he cried out all the more, "Son of David, have mercy on me!" So Jesus stood still and commanded him to be called. Then they called the blind man, saying to him, "Be of good cheer. Rise, He is calling you." And throwing aside his garment, he rose and came to Jesus. So Jesus answered and said to him, "What do you want Me to do for you?" The blind man said to Him, "Rabboni, that I may receive my sight." Then Jesus said to him, "Go your way; your faith has made you well." And immediately he received his sight and followed Jesus on the road. (Mark 10:46-52)

Then Jesus entered and passed through Jericho. Now behold, there was a man named Zacchaeus who was a chief tax collector, and he was rich. And he sought to see who Jesus was, but could not because of the crowd, for he was of short stature. So he ran ahead and climbed up into a sycamore tree to see Him, for He was going to pass that way. And when Jesus came to the place, He looked up and saw him, and said to him, "Zacchaeus, make haste and come down, for today I must stay at your house." So he made haste and came down, and received Him joyfully. But when they saw it, they all complained, saying, "He has gone to be a guest with a man who is a sinner." Then Zacchaeus stood and said to the Lord, "Look, Lord, I give half of my goods to the poor; and if I have taken anything from anyone by false accusation, I restore fourfold." And Jesus said to him, "Today salvation has come to this house, because he also is a son of Abraham; for the Son of Man has come to seek and to save that which was lost." (Luke 19:1-10)

Jericho marks the junction of the north-south road with the road to Jerusalem. Jesus was going to Jerusalem—He was going to Jerusalem for "the hour," for Passion Week. On this major route of travel Jesus meets two men (actually, three, as there were two blind men, but both Mark and Luke focus on one, who is named Bartimaeus in Luke's gospel). He is a blind beggar. He is symbolic of the rejecting nation, which was still blind. As Jesus said to the Pharisees earlier, "It would have been better to be born blind, for then you would see." Here on the Jericho road, another "blind" man will see both physically and spiritually.

What is the commotion? Why so many people? Bartimaeus hears the movement of the multitude, and then he hears the wonderful news.

> So they told him that Jesus of Nazareth was passing by. (Luke 18:37)

He cries out and continues to cry out, though rebuked by the crowd. Jesus is passing by, and it will be for the last time, for He is on His way to Jerusalem to die. Bartimaeus does not know that, but he is desperate and he cries out.

The blind man knew a lot about the Savior. He knew He was from Nazareth. He knew He was the Son of David, the King. He knew He could perform miracles. He knew He was the source of mercy. He was crying out to the right Person, and just in time. And Jesus stopped and said, "Call him." The cooperation of the crowd is touching.

> So Jesus stood still and commanded him to be called. Then they called the blind man, saying to him, "Be of good cheer. Rise, He is calling you." (Mark 10:49)

The rest of the story is direct and clear. Bartimaeus throws off his mantle, springs to his feet, and moves toward Jesus!

> So Jesus answered and said to him, "What do you want Me to do for you?" The blind man said to Him, "Rabboni, that I may receive my sight." (Mark 10:51)

The ensuing interaction is full of faith. Jesus performs the miracle and gives instruction to Seeing Bartimaeus, "Go your way, your faith has made you well." On receiving his sight, however, Bartimaeus does not go *his* way; rather, he goes *His* way—he follows Jesus on His way to Jerusalem. After all, he knew He was the Son of David and that He was on His way to Jerusalem where they would welcome the King—at least for a short while!

Bartimaeus would call out "Son of David" one more time—this time seeing Him!

From a blind man to a tax collector—both by the roadside of society. From Bartimaeus to Zacchaeus, outcast and lost. But Mercy came once on the Jericho road, and now He will come again. Tax collectors used to set up their offices on commercial routes, and Zacchaeus was a chief tax collector, so likely a very rich man. He presided over the main route to Jerusalem, the capital of the country.

The story is as well known as the children's chorus about Zacchaeus:

> Zacchaeus was a wee little man,
> A wee little man was he.
> He climbed up into the sycamore tree
> For he wanted his Lord to see.
> And as the Savior passed that way
> He looked up in the tree, and said:
> "Zacchaeus, you come down,
> For I'm going to your house today!
> For I'm going to your house today!"

Jesus was joyfully received by Zacchaeus. His genuine faith was demonstrated in his actions as he made restoration—fourfold—to those he had wronged. Salvation had come to his house, and though previously he was a hated tax collector, now he was a true son of Abraham, the man of faith.

As always, there were murmurers. There were the lost who didn't know they were lost, the blind who didn't know they were blind. And they remained lost and blind even though "the Son of Man came to seek and to save that which was lost." On the Jericho road there was room for just two—Bartimaeus and Zacchaeus—a blind man and a tax collector.

64

Approaching Jerusalem: A Parable about Delay, and an Anointing for Burial

**Luke 19:11-28; John 11:55-57; Matthew 26:6-13;
Mark 14:3-9; John 12:1-11**

Now as they heard these things, He spoke another parable, because He was near Jerusalem and because they thought the kingdom of God would appear immediately. . . . Therefore He said: "A certain nobleman went into a far country to receive for himself a kingdom and to return. So he called ten of his servants, delivered to them ten minas, and said to them, 'Do business till I come.' But his citizens hated him, and sent a delegation after him, saying, 'We will not have this man to reign over us.' And so it was that when he returned, having received the kingdom, he then commanded these servants, to whom he had given the money, to be called to him, that he might know how much every man had gained by trading. Then came the first, saying, 'Master, your mina has earned ten minas.' And he said to him, 'Well done, good servant; because you were faithful in a very little, have authority over ten cities.' . . . And he said to him, 'Out of your own mouth I will judge you, you wicked servant. You knew that I was an austere man, collecting what I did not deposit and reaping what I did not sow. 'Why then did you not put my money in the bank, that at my coming I might have collected it with interest?' And he said to those who stood by, 'Take the mina from him, and give it to him who has ten minas.' (But they said to him, 'Master, he has ten minas.') 'For I say to you, that to everyone who has will be given; and from him who does not have, even what he has will be taken away from him. But bring here those enemies of mine, who did not want me to reign over them, and slay them before me.'" When He had said this, He went on ahead, going up to Jerusalem. (Luke 19:11-17, 22-28)

And being in Bethany at the house of Simon the leper, as He sat at the table, a woman came having an alabaster flask of very costly oil of spikenard. Then she broke the flask and poured it on His head. But there were some who were indignant among themselves, and said, "Why was this fragrant oil wasted? For it might have been sold for more than three hundred denarii and given to the poor." And they criticized her sharply. But Jesus said, "Let her alone. Why do you trouble her? She has done a good work for Me. For you have the poor with you always, and whenever you wish you may do them good; but Me you do not have always. She has done what she could. She has come beforehand to anoint My body for burial. Assuredly, I say to you, wherever this gospel is preached in the whole world, what this woman has done will also be told as a memorial to her." (Mark 14:3-9)

And the Passover of the Jews was near, and many went from the country up to Jerusalem before the Passover, to purify themselves. Then they sought Jesus, and spoke among themselves as they stood in the temple, "What do you think—that He will not come to the feast?" Now both the chief priests and the Pharisees had given a command, that if anyone knew where He was, he should report it, that they might seize Him. . . . Now a great many of the Jews knew that He was there; and they came, not for Jesus' sake only, but that they might also see Lazarus, whom He had raised from the dead. But the chief priests plotted to put Lazarus to death also, because on account of him many of the Jews went away and believed in Jesus. (John 11:55-57; 12:9-11)

The opening statement sets the scene—Jesus was approaching Jerusalem, and the disciples anticipated that the kingdom of God was to appear immediately.

The parable that Jesus tells indicates that there will be a departure and then a return before the kingdom is established. He will depart and then return! The parable addresses the concept, "appear immediately." This may have been based on a local happening when a nobleman went to Rome to receive a political position. His citizens followed him with a petition to reject the nobleman, but their petition was refused. The protesting citizens fell into disfavor. Thus Jesus is saying that the kingdom they have offered in Galilee, in Judea, and of late in Perea, will be rejected by the Jews. The words of Jesus in relating the parable are ominous:

"But his citizens hated him, and sent a delegation after him, saying, 'We will not have this man to reign over us.'" (Luke 19:14)

Soon the multitudes would be voicing the same sentiment, but first they will say,

"Hosanna to the Son of David! 'Blessed is He who comes in the name of the LORD!' Hosanna in the highest!" (Matthew 21:9)

What a change from Palm Sunday to Good Friday! We will see the cause for the abrupt change directly.

In addition to the teaching of His departure, Jesus also teaches about reward and judgment upon His return; about proportional reward for the faithful and judgment for the enemies. This is a vague reference to the "judgment of the goats and the sheep" that will form part of the teaching of the Olivet Discourse on Tuesday of Passion Week. Only after the death and resurrection of Christ will the disciples understand this teaching of a departure and return of the Savior.

Prior to entering Jerusalem, Jesus stays at His Judean home in Bethany. It was where Mary and Martha and Lazarus lived (and died, and lived again!). Simon the leper hosted the occasion. The anointing by Mary follows.

There they made Him a supper; and Martha served, but Lazarus was one of those who sat at the table with Him. Then Mary took a pound of very costly oil of spikenard, anointed the feet of Jesus, and wiped His feet with her hair. And the house was filled with the fragrance of the oil. (John 12:2-3)

Judas opposed the extravagant act, as did the rest of the disciples. Occasionally, extravagance is the appropriate response—after all, how often will the Savior die? Jesus rebukes the disciples and commends Mary. She did what she could. She anointed Him for His burial. What a comforting commendation for Mary, and for all who would serve the Savior: "She did what she could."

Behind the scenes, the Jewish leaders were plotting.

Now both the chief priests and the Pharisees had given a command, that if anyone knew where He was, he should report it, that they might seize Him. (John 11:57)

Now a great many of the Jews knew that He was there; and they came, not for Jesus' sake only, but that they might also see Lazarus, whom He had raised from the dead. But the chief priests plotted to put Lazarus to death also, because on account of him many of the Jews went away and believed in Jesus. (John 12:9-11)

Cheering and then jeering crowds, a plotting Sanhedrin, the arrival of the King, the powers of the Roman empire—all gathering for the week of weeks, for the day of redemption, for "the hour." "For this hour have I come into the world!"

> *"For truly against Your holy Servant Jesus, whom You anointed, both Herod and Pontius Pilate, with the Gentiles and the people of Israel, were gathered together to do whatever Your hand and Your purpose determined before to be done." (Acts 4:27-28)*

65

Triumphal Entry Sunday:
The King Comes to Jerusalem

Matthew 21:1-11; Mark 11:1-11; Luke 19:29-44; John 12:12-19

The next day a great multitude that had come to the feast, when they heard that Jesus was coming to Jerusalem, took branches of palm trees and went out to meet Him, and cried out: "Hosanna! 'Blessed is He who comes in the name of the Lord!' The King of Israel!" (John 12:12-13)

Now when they drew near Jerusalem, and came to Bethphage, at the Mount of Olives, then Jesus sent two disciples, saying to them, "Go into the village opposite you, and immediately you will find a donkey tied, and a colt with her. Loose them and bring them to Me. And if anyone says anything to you, you shall say, 'The Lord has need of them,' and immediately he will send them." All this was done that it might be fulfilled which was spoken by the prophet, saying: "Tell the daughter of Zion, 'Behold, your King is coming to you, lowly, and sitting on a donkey, a colt, the foal of a donkey.'" So the disciples went and did as Jesus commanded them. They brought the donkey and the colt, laid their clothes on them, and set Him on them. And a very great multitude spread their clothes on the road; others cut down branches from the trees and spread them on the road. Then the multitudes who went before and those who followed cried out, saying: "Hosanna to the Son of David! 'Blessed is He who comes in the name of the Lord!' Hosanna in the highest!" (Matthew 21:1-9)

Therefore the people, who were with Him when He called Lazarus out of his tomb and raised him from the dead, bore witness. For this reason the people also met Him, because they heard that He had done this sign. (John 12:17-18)

Then, as He was now drawing near the descent of the Mount of Olives, the whole multitude of the disciples began to rejoice and praise God with a loud voice for all the mighty works they had seen, saying: "'Blessed is the King who comes in the name of the Lord!' Peace in heaven and glory in the highest!" And some of the Pharisees called to Him from the crowd, "Teacher, rebuke Your disciples." But He answered and said to them, "I tell you that if these should keep silent, the stones would immediately cry out." (Luke 19:37-40)

And Jesus went into Jerusalem and into the temple. So when He had looked around at all things, as the hour was already late, He went out to Bethany with the twelve. (Mark 11:11)

Passion Week has arrived. All the provinces of Israel have heard the message, "Repent, the kingdom of heaven is at hand." And now the King is entering Israel's capital city, Jerusalem. It is Passover time, and the Lamb of God is on the scene. Many prophetic statements from the Old Testament are converging on this appointed Palm Sunday. The angel Gabriel who had appeared to Zacharias announcing the birth of John the forerunner, and to Mary announcing the miraculous birth of Jesus, had appeared to Daniel over five hundred years earlier. Gabriel had given to Daniel a series of detailed prophetic revelations from God. One of them related to the triumphal entry.

"Seventy weeks are determined for your people and for your holy city, to finish the transgression, to make an end of sins, to make reconciliation for iniquity, to bring in everlasting righteousness, to seal up vision and prophecy, and to anoint the Most Holy. Know therefore and understand, that from the going forth of the command to restore and build Jerusalem until Messiah the Prince, there shall be seven weeks and sixty-two weeks; the street shall be built again, and the wall, even in troublesome times. And after the sixty-two weeks Messiah shall be cut off, but not for Himself; and the people of the prince who is to come shall destroy the city and the sanctuary. The end of it shall be with a flood, and till the end of the war desolations are determined." (Daniel 9:24-26)

After sixty-nine weeks of years, or 483 years, the Messiah would be cut off. The decree of Artaxerxes in the days of Nehemiah activated the prophetic clock. Another emperor, Caesar Augustus of Rome, also cooperated unknowingly by decreeing that all the world should be taxed, thus moving Mary and Joseph from Nazareth to Bethlehem in fulfillment of Micah's prophecy.

And it came to pass in the month of Nisan, in the twentieth year of King Artaxerxes, when wine was before him, that I took the wine and gave it to the king. Now I had never been sad in his presence before. . . . Then the king said to me (the queen also sitting beside him), "How long will your journey be? And when will you return?" So it pleased the king to send me; and I set him a time. Furthermore I said to the king, "If it pleases the king, let letters be given to me for the governors of the region beyond the River, that they must permit me to pass through till I come to Judah, and a letter to Asaph the keeper of the king's forest, that he must give me timber to make beams for the gates of the citadel which pertains to the temple, for the city wall, and for the house that I will occupy." And the king granted them to me according to the good hand of my God upon me. (Nehemiah 2:1, 6-8)

Doing careful analysis of the specific dates of Nehemiah and the prophecy of Daniel relating to the 483 years, it turns out that 173,880 days are fulfilled at the date of the triumphal entry. The timing is according to God's specific plan.

The prophecy of Zechariah is also fulfilled on this important Sunday.

"Rejoice greatly, O daughter of Zion! Shout, O daughter of Jerusalem! Behold, your King is coming to you; He is just and having salvation, lowly and riding on a donkey, a colt, the foal of a donkey. I will cut off the chariot from Ephraim and the horse from Jerusalem; the battle bow shall be cut off. He shall speak peace to the nations; His dominion shall be 'from sea to sea, and from the River to the ends of the earth.'" (Zechariah 9:9-10)

This prophecy describes the peaceful entrance of the King into His kingdom on a lowly donkey, not a warhorse! The details of the narrative show that Jesus had made arrangements for the humble transportation. It was an animal which had never borne a burden, which immediately became subject to the Master without objection. Messiah Jesus arrives to the acclaim of the crowds, to a path decorated with their garments and paved with palm branches. They were welcoming their King!

Notice that the Jews were anticipating the establishment of David's kingdom through the coming of their King, Jesus! The Pharisees who had sought to destroy Him from the beginning were perplexed.

And some of the Pharisees called to Him from the crowd, "Teacher, rebuke Your disciples." But He answered and said to them, "I tell you that if these should keep silent, the stones would immediately cry out." (Luke 19:39-40)

The Pharisees therefore said among themselves, "You see that you are accomplishing nothing. Look, the world has gone after Him!" (John 12:19)

Why were the crowds so favorable? John's gospel gives the reason.

> *Therefore the people, who were with Him when He called Lazarus out of his tomb and raised him from the dead, bore witness. For this reason the people also met Him, because they heard that He had done this sign. (John 12:17-18)*

But remember the statement of Abraham to the rich man in Hades:

> *"But he said to him, 'If they do not hear Moses and the prophets, neither will they be persuaded though one rise from the dead.'" (Luke 16:31)*

Jesus enters the city, looks around at everything, and leaves with His disciples to retire to His Judean home at Bethany. What did He see late Sunday? He saw the temple, and He will return there on Monday to His Father's House— to *His* House.

66

No Fruit on the Fig Tree
or in the Temple

Matthew 21:12-19; Mark 11:12-26; Luke 19:45-48

Now in the morning, as He returned to the city, He was hungry. And seeing a fig tree by the road, He came to it and found nothing on it but leaves, and said to it, "Let no fruit grow on you ever again." Immediately the fig tree withered away. (Matthew 21:18-19)

So they came to Jerusalem. Then Jesus went into the temple and began to drive out those who bought and sold in the temple, and overturned the tables of the money changers and the seats of those who sold doves. And He would not allow anyone to carry wares through the temple. Then He taught, saying to them, "Is it not written, 'My house shall be called a house of prayer for all nations'? But you have made it a 'den of thieves.'" And the scribes and chief priests heard it and sought how they might destroy Him; for they feared Him, because all the people were astonished at His teaching. When evening had come, He went out of the city. Now in the morning, as they passed by, they saw the fig tree dried up from the roots. And Peter, remembering, said to Him, "Rabbi, look! The fig tree which You cursed has withered away." So Jesus answered and said to them, "Have faith in God. For assuredly, I say to you, whoever says to this mountain, 'Be removed and be cast into the sea,' and does not doubt in his heart, but believes that those things he says will be done, he will have whatever he says. Therefore I say to you, whatever things you ask when you pray, believe that you receive them, and you will have them. And whenever you stand praying, if you have anything against anyone, forgive him, that your Father in heaven may also forgive you your trespasses. But if you do not forgive, neither will your Father in heaven forgive your trespasses." (Mark 11:15-26)

The second cleansing of the temple is bracketed by the cursing of the fig tree and the lesson from that action. The first cleansing took place at the very beginning of the Lord's public ministry, following His baptism and temptation in the desert by Satan. Now, just three days before Good Friday, He cleanses the temple again. But first, the fig tree incident.

At the close of Palm Sunday, Jesus, having entered Jerusalem, observes what is going on in the temple and leaves. As He returns to Jerusalem on Monday morning, He passes a fig tree. He is hungry and He approaches the tree for figs, but he finds no fruit. He has approached Judaism for three years, but obtained no fruit there either. Jesus curses the tree. He will enter the temple soon and find no evidence of fruit there either. And within a generation, only the wall of the temple will remain.

After three years of ministry and teaching, the spiritual level of Judaism remains the same. The temple is still a place of business. The same people are at the money-changers' tables, sacrifices are being sold—and Jesus once again drives them out of the temple area. Once again He overturns the tables. Once again He drives out the animals. Once again He condemns selling religion.

> And He said to them, "It is written, 'My house shall be called a house of prayer,' but you have made it a 'den of thieves.'" (Matthew 21:13)

Nothing had changed in Judaism.

After the second cleansing of the temple, Jesus remains in the city for a short while and continues His gracious ministry of healing.

> Then the blind and the lame came to Him in the temple, and He healed them. (Matthew 21:14)

The response of the chief priests and scribes is predictable—they always misrepresented His miracles, ascribing them to Beelzebub. They were indignant that He continued His miracles of compassion.

> But when the chief priests and scribes saw the wonderful things that He did, and the children crying out in the temple and saying, "Hosanna to the Son of David!" they were indignant and said to Him, "Do You hear what these are saying?" (Matthew 21:15)

> But the chief priests, the scribes, and the leaders of the people sought to destroy Him, and were unable to do anything; for all the people were very attentive to hear Him. (Luke 19:47-48)

They sought a way to destroy Him—but how could that be accomplished, especially after the royal welcome He had received just the day before? How could His removal be accomplished with the populace hanging on His every word? How could it be accomplished with everyone saying,

"Hosanna to the Son of David! 'Blessed is He who comes in the name of the LORD!' Hosanna in the highest!" (Matthew 21:9)

How could they stop His growing popularity? Soon the answer will come—on Wednesday. That, later.

Jesus and the disciples return to Bethany and lodge there overnight on Monday, just as they had on Sunday night. With a night of rest, the Lord and His disciples return to Jerusalem on Tuesday for a day of confrontation and teaching. As they pass the fig tree, His disciples notice it has withered overnight. The obvious is assumed—no fruit on the fig tree, no fruit in Israel. Hence, judgment. Jesus then uses the withered tree for teaching a lesson on prayer.

> *And when the disciples saw it, they marveled, saying, "How did the fig tree wither away so soon?" So Jesus answered and said to them, "Assuredly, I say to you, if you have faith and do not doubt, you will not only do what was done to the fig tree, but also if you say to this mountain, 'Be removed and be cast into the sea,' it will be done. And whatever things you ask in prayer, believing, you will receive." (Matthew 21:20-22)*

Believing prayer can produce miraculous results—it can even change topography. One should be certain of his request when requesting God to rearrange His creation! But that power is available for the disciples—and in the coming days of despair, that power will be needed.

67

A Dispute Over Authority, and a Parable of Two Sons

Matthew 21:23-32; Mark 11:27-33; Luke 20:1-8

Then they came again to Jerusalem. And as He was walking in the temple, the chief priests, the scribes, and the elders came to Him. And they said to Him, "By what authority are You doing these things? And who gave You this authority to do these things?" But Jesus answered and said to them, "I also will ask you one question; then answer Me, and I will tell you by what authority I do these things: The baptism of John—was it from heaven or from men? Answer Me." And they reasoned among themselves, saying, "If we say, 'From heaven,' He will say, 'Why then did you not believe him?' But if we say, 'From men'—they feared the people, for all counted John to have been a prophet indeed. so they answered and said to Jesus, "We do not know." And Jesus answered and said to them, "Neither will I tell you by what authority I do these things." (Mark 11:27-33)

"But what do you think? A man had two sons, and he came to the first and said, 'Son, go, work today in my vineyard.' He answered and said, 'I will not,' but afterward he regretted it and went. Then he came to the second and said likewise. And he answered and said, 'I go, sir,' but he did not go. Which of the two did the will of his father?" They said to Him, "The first." Jesus said to them, "Assuredly, I say to you that tax collectors and harlots enter the kingdom of God before you. For John came to you in the way of righteousness, and you did not believe him; but tax collectors and harlots believed him; and when you saw it, you did not afterward relent and believe him." (Matthew 21:28-32)

Tuesday is the day of confrontation in Passion Week. The chief priests, the scribes, the Pharisees, the Herodians, and the Sadducees all come with entrapping questions—and Jesus silences them all. He then ministers to His disciples in presenting the Olivet Discourse, which deals with the prophetic future of the kingdom.

Now, the first confrontation.

> *Then they came again to Jerusalem. And as He was walking in the temple, the chief priests, the scribes, and the elders came to Him. And they said to Him, "By what authority are You doing these things? And who gave You this authority to do these things?" (Mark 11:27-28)*

The question was about authority. The issue always been about authority. Lucifer, Adam and Eve, government and citizens, employers and employees, husbands and wives, children and parents. Remember the incident in Capernaum of the centurion who had a sick servant?

> *The centurion answered and said, "Lord, I am not worthy that You should come under my roof. But only speak a word, and my servant will be healed. For I also am a man under authority, having soldiers under me. And I say to this one, 'Go,' and he goes; and to another, 'Come,' and he comes; and to my servant, 'Do this,' and he does it." When Jesus heard it, He marveled, and said to those who followed, "Assuredly, I say to you, I have not found such great faith, not even in Israel!" (Matthew 8:8-10)*

"I have not found such great faith, not even in Israel!" The Jews questioned Christ's authority, but the feeble intellect of Israel's leadership was no match for the King. *He* sets the trap this time.

> *But Jesus answered and said to them, "I also will ask you one question; then answer Me, and I will tell you by what authority I do these things: "The baptism of John—was it from heaven or from men? Answer Me." (Mark 11:29-30)*

A simple question with a simple answer. "The baptism of John—from heaven or man?" It was John who introduced water baptism and prophesied about Spirit baptism. Both of these have impacted believers, in the time of Jesus and continuing into the church era. Did baptism come from heaven or man? Clearly, from heaven. The response should have been immediate.

But the chief priests, scribes, and elders hold a caucus to figure out a politically correct answer.

> *And they reasoned among themselves, saying, "If we say, 'From heaven,' He will say, 'Why then did you not believe him?' But if we say, 'From men'—they feared the people, for all counted John to have been a prophet indeed. So they answered and said to Jesus, "We do not know." (Mark 11:31-33)*

They did not only not speak the truth, they lied! Jesus springs the trap—"Neither will I tell you by what authority I do these things." He had told them often before and they did not respond to truth. He will not tell them again. Soon He will say to Pilate,

> *"You could have no power at all against Me unless it had been given you from above." (John 19:11)*

From the beginning they would not accept His authority. "He forgives sins making Himself equal to God." Now their response is determined by the consequences rather than truth. So much for religious integrity!

The first confrontation on Tuesday was clearly a victory for Jesus and a frustration for the leaders of Judaism. Jesus then takes the offensive in the debate and teaches by means of entrapping parables. The first is a simple one about two sons.

> *"But what do you think? A man had two sons, and he came to the first and said, 'Son, go, work today in my vineyard.' He answered and said, 'I will not,' but afterward he regretted it and went. Then he came to the second and said likewise. And he answered and said, 'I go, sir,' but he did not go." (Matthew 21:28-30)*

The question raised by Jesus brings an easy and immediate response. The trap is now sprung.

> *"Which of the two did the will of his father?" They said to Him, "The first." Jesus said to them, "Assuredly, I say to you that tax collectors and harlots enter the kingdom of God before you. For John came to you in the way of righteousness, and you did not believe him; but tax collectors and harlots believed him; and when you saw it, you did not afterward relent and believe him." (Matthew 21:31-32)*

As it turns out, the tax collectors and sinners were equivalent to the first son, and the chief priests scribes, and elders were equivalent to the second son. The second confrontation was also a clear victory for Jesus. But it added to the growing frustration of the leaders of Judaism, underlining their total inability to gain control.

It seems as though Jesus was continuing to gain the upper hand, and the coming events on Tuesday will reinforce that perception. But Wednesday is coming.

68

The King Withdraws His Offer of the Kingdom

Matthew 21:33-46; Mark 12:1-12; Luke 20:9-19

*"Hear another parable: There was a certain landowner who planted
a vineyard and set a hedge around it, dug a winepress in it and built
a tower. And he leased it to vinedressers and went into a far country.
Now when vintage-time drew near, he sent his servants to the
vinedressers, that they might receive its fruit. And the vinedressers
took his servants, beat one, killed one, and stoned another. Again
he sent other servants, more than the first, and they did likewise
to them. Then last of all he sent his son to them, saying, 'They will
respect my son.' But when the vinedressers saw the son, they said
among themselves, 'This is the heir. Come, let us kill him and seize
his inheritance.' So they took him and cast him out of the vineyard
and killed him. Therefore, when the owner of the vineyard comes,
what will he do to those vinedressers?" They said to Him, "He will
destroy those wicked men miserably, and lease his vineyard to other
vinedressers who will render to him the fruits in their seasons." Jesus
said to them, "Have you never read in the Scriptures: 'The stone
which the builders rejected has become the chief cornerstone. This
was the LORD's doing, and it is marvelous in our eyes'? Therefore I
say to you, the kingdom of God will be taken from you and given to
a nation bearing the fruits of it. And whoever falls on this stone will
be broken; but on whomever it falls, it will grind him to powder."
Now when the chief priests and Pharisees heard His parables, they
perceived that He was speaking of them. But when they sought to lay
hands on Him, they feared the multitudes, because they took Him for
a prophet. (Matthew 21:33-46)*

The second confrontational parable on Tuesday is quickly stated. The
storyline is direct. A landowner rents out his vineyards to tenants, and
when harvest time is completed, he sends his representatives to collect the
profits. They are received with escalating violence, concluding with murder.
In a strange expression of logic, the landowner sends his son, thinking they
will honor him. Instead, they kill him.

Now Jesus asks the trap question.

> *"Therefore, when the owner of the vineyard comes, what will he do to those vinedressers?" (Matthew 21:40)*

The chief priests, the scribes, and the elders respond immediately and correctly.

> *They said to Him, "He will destroy those wicked men miserably, and lease his vineyard to other vinedressers who will render to him the fruits in their seasons." (Matthew 21:41)*

The parable and its message are understood. Now Jesus makes the theological application revealing the redemptive plan of God. With a sarcastic question, Jesus opens the message of judgment, "Have you never read in the Scriptures . . . ?" Chief priests and scribes and elders—never read their Bible? They would be insulted!

> *I will praise You, for You have answered me, and have become my salvation. The stone which the builders rejected has become the chief cornerstone. This was the LORD's doing; it is marvelous in our eyes. This is the day the LORD has made; we will rejoice and be glad in it. (Psalm 118:21-24)*

Never read *this?* Psalms 113-118 were called "the Egyptian Hallel" and were sung in conjunction with the feasts of Israel—Psalm 118 particularly with the Passover. The leaders of Israel would be singing this psalm shortly as Passover approached. Never read this?

But what did this psalm teach? It taught about a rejected Stone, and it talked about the builders who rejected the Stone. In God's great plan of redemption history revealed in the book of Daniel, the Stone concept is expanded.

> *"And in the days of these kings the God of heaven will set up a kingdom which shall never be destroyed; and the kingdom shall not be left to other people; it shall break in pieces and consume all these kingdoms, and it shall stand forever. Inasmuch as you saw that the stone was cut out of the mountain without hands, and that it broke in pieces the iron, the bronze, the clay, the silver, and the gold—the great God has made known to the king what will come to pass after this. The dream is certain, and its interpretation is sure." (Daniel 2:44-45)*

The book of Daniel presents the parade of kingdoms and empires according to God's sovereign plan. First, Babylon; then Medo-Persia, Greece, Rome, and finally the millennial kingdom of Christ—that kingdom being offered by Christ up until this very moment of history. But it was about to be rejected by the builders. And who were the builders that rejected the Stone? Let the text answer.

> *Now when the chief priests and Pharisees heard His parables, they perceived that He was speaking of them. But when they sought to lay hands on Him, they feared the multitudes, because they took Him for a prophet. (Matthew 21:45-46)*

The Pharisees and chief priests perceived He was speaking of them, and He was! The King makes a devastating statement:

> *"Therefore I say to you, the kingdom of God will be taken from you and given to a nation bearing the fruits of it." (Matthew 21:43)*

And so it was! The offer was withdrawn until a later date—much later!

The theology growing out of this event is expanded in Peter's first epistle.

> *Coming to Him as to a living stone, rejected indeed by men, but chosen by God and precious, you also, as living stones, are being built up a spiritual house, a holy priesthood, to offer up spiritual sacrifices acceptable to God through Jesus Christ. Therefore it is also contained in the Scripture, "Behold, I lay in Zion a chief cornerstone, elect, precious, and he who believes on Him will by no means be put to shame." Therefore, to you who believe, He is precious; but to those who are disobedient, "The stone which the builders rejected has become the chief cornerstone," and "A stone of stumbling and a rock of offense." They stumble, being disobedient to the word, to which they also were appointed. But you are a chosen generation, a royal priesthood, a holy nation, His own special people, that you may proclaim the praises of Him who called you out of darkness into His marvelous light; who once were not a people but are now the people of God, who had not obtained mercy but now have obtained mercy. (1 Peter 2:4-10)*

Peter advances the progress of God's plan of redemption. He identifies the same builders as Jesus did—the leaders of Israel—and adds the truth that they were sovereignly appointed to this disobedience. Also, that a new nation and a new priesthood were formed with the beginning of the church through Peter's preaching on the day of Pentecost.

The confrontation of Tuesday continues and increases—and Jesus continues to win the day. And the day has only begun. Bring on the Herodians, bring on the Sadducees, bring on the lawyers. Gather together for a collective scathing denunciation of Judaism. Tuesday is the high-water mark for Jesus and the disciples. But Wednesday is coming.

69

The Invitation to the Kingdom
Rejected by the Jewish Leaders

Matthew 22:1-46; Mark 12:13-37; Luke 20:20-44

And Jesus answered and spoke to them again by parables and said: "The kingdom of heaven is like a certain king who arranged a marriage for his son, and sent out his servants to call those who were invited to the wedding; and they were not willing to come. . . . Then he said to his servants, 'The wedding is ready, but those who were invited were not worthy. 'Therefore go into the highways, and as many as you find, invite to the wedding.'" (Matthew 22:1-3, 8-9)

When they had come, they said to Him, "Teacher, we know that You are true, and care about no one; for You do not regard the person of men, but teach the way of God in truth. Is it lawful to pay taxes to Caesar, or not? Shall we pay, or shall we not pay?" But He, knowing their hypocrisy, said to them, "Why do you test Me? Bring Me a denarius that I may see it." . . . And Jesus answered and said to them, "Render to Caesar the things that are Caesar's, and to God the things that are God's." And they marveled at Him. (Mark 12:14-15, 17)

Then some Sadducees, who say there is no resurrection, came to Him; and they asked Him, saying: "Teacher, Moses wrote to us that if a man's brother dies, and leaves his wife behind, and leaves no children, his brother should take his wife and raise up offspring for his brother. Now there were seven brothers. The first took a wife; and dying, he left no offspring. And the second took her, and he died; nor did he leave any offspring. And the third likewise. So the seven had her and left no offspring. Last of all the woman died also. Therefore, in the resurrection, when they rise, whose wife will she be? For all seven had her as wife." Jesus answered and said to them, "Are you not therefore mistaken, because you do not know the Scriptures nor the power of God? For when they rise from the dead, they neither marry nor are given in marriage, but are like angels in heaven. But concerning the dead, that they rise, have you not read in the book of Moses, in the burning bush passage, how God spoke to him, saying,

'I am the God of Abraham, the God of Isaac, and the God of Jacob'?
He is not the God of the dead, but the God of the living. You are
therefore greatly mistaken." (Mark 12:18-27)

But when the Pharisees heard that He had silenced the Sadducees,
they gathered together. Then one of them, a lawyer, asked Him a
question, testing Him, and saying, "Teacher, which is the great
commandment in the law?" Jesus said to him, "'You shall love the
LORD your God with all your heart, with all your soul, and with
all your mind.' This is the first and great commandment. And the
second is like it: 'You shall love your neighbor as yourself.' On these
two commandments hang all the Law and the Prophets." (Matthew
22:34-40)

These words—"Therefore I say to you, the kingdom of God will be taken from you and given to a nation bearing the fruits of it"—concluded the last encounter with the Pharisees, and led Jesus to the parable of the marriage of the king's son. The story is clear and direct. The guests invited by the king refuse to come, and so he invites other guests. This wedding and banquet motif was introduced in the Perean ministry, the last province to be evangelized. Jesus was anticipating the final rejection of Israel and was looking beyond to the inclusion of the Gentiles—to that promised church which He would build. But He has more to say to those invited—the Pharisees, the Herodians, the Sadducees, the scribes, and lawyers—to Israel.

The Pharisees and Herodians (strange collaborators!) try to entrap Him in a political and religious conflict.

"Is it lawful to pay taxes to Caesar, or not? Shall we pay, or shall we
not pay?" But He, knowing their hypocrisy, said to them, "Why do
you test Me? Bring Me a denarius that I may see it." (Mark 12:14-15)

Is Christ loyal to Israel, or to Rome, or to that illusive kingdom He was offering to Israel? Surely there was no way to escape this clever trap without the Lord being embarrassed. He could choose Rome and lose His appeal to Israel. He could choose Israel and suffer the wrath of Rome. Nor could He deny His own kingdom and His message of repentance and deliverance. But they underestimated the wisdom of the Messiah they were rejecting. A simple everyday coin answered the question. It had Caesar's picture on it— therefore, give Caesar what was his. Mankind has God's image impressed on it; therefore, render to God what is God's. The result of this irrefutable argument?

And they marveled at His answer and kept silent. (Luke 20:26)

The Pharisees and Herodians had refused the invitation to the marriage feast, but what about the Sadducees? They had a trick question as well, one that grew out of their liberal theological stance. They did not believe in life after death, in resurrection. But they quoted the law of Moses regarding marriage in an attempt to show the irrational nature of the law in relation to marriage and resurrection.

> *"Teacher, Moses wrote to us that if a man's brother dies, and leaves his wife behind, and leaves no children, his brother should take his wife and raise up offspring for his brother. Now there were seven brothers. The first took a wife; and dying, he left no offspring. Therefore, in the resurrection, when they rise, whose wife will she be? For all seven had her as wife." (Mark 12:19-20, 23)*

The answer of Jesus is twofold.

> *"Are you not therefore mistaken, <u>because</u> you do not know the Scriptures nor the power of God?" (Mark 12:24)*

Two mistakes—not knowing the teaching of Scripture, and not knowing the power of God—two huge mistakes. Concerning the power of God, He will initiate an entirely new relationship in the eternal state. Those who have a resurrected body will not have the physical marriage arrangement of the present earthly experience—rather, an angelic one. Concerning the power of God, death has no lasting victory because God is the God of the living, as proven by the recurring statement concerning the patriarchs.

> *"But concerning the dead, that they rise, have you not read in the book of Moses, in the burning bush passage, how God spoke to him, saying, 'I am the God of Abraham, the God of Isaac, and the God of Jacob'?" (Mark 12:26)*

Notice the verb tense. "I am the God of . . . ." Not, "I *was* the God of . . . ." The resurrection will confirm and finalize the living relationship between the living God and those who have died as believers. There is life after death: eternal life for the believers and the second death for the unbeliever—for unbelievers like the Sadducees, whether or not they believe in the resurrection. So the Sadducees likewise reject the invitation to the banquet.

A final attempt at entrapment is organized. A lawyer from the Pharisees, no doubt the top lawyer, was appointed to test the Messiah—a futile attempt! The question is the essence of the Mosaic law. "Teacher, which is the great commandment in the law?" The response of the Lord is brilliant, as would be expected.

Jesus said to him, "'You shall love the LORD your God with all your heart, with all your soul, and with all your mind.' This is the first and great commandment. And the second is like it: 'You shall love your neighbor as yourself.' On these two commandments hang all the Law and the Prophets." (Matthew 22:37-40)

A summary statement of all of the law in under thirty words—yet there were 613 commandments in Old Testament Judaism. All of the Ten Commandments of the moral law, and all of the ceremonial law, and all of the civil law, summarized in under thirty words. The first tablet of the Ten Commandments covers man's responsibility to God; the second tablet, his responsibility to his fellow man. This was a brilliant and insightful answer, and the lawyer acknowledged it in a praiseworthy way.

So the scribe said to Him, "Well said, Teacher. You have spoken the truth, for there is one God, and there is no other but He. And to love Him with all the heart, with all the understanding, with all the soul, and with all the strength, and to love one's neighbor as oneself, is more than all the whole burnt offerings and sacrifices." (Mark 12:32-33)

The response of Jesus to this honest evaluation is touching. "You are not far from the kingdom of God." The best of the Jewish lawyers was close to conversion, close to the King. There were no more questions from the opposition—at least, for the moment.

But the Lord has a question for them; that seems fair. "What do you think of the Christ? Whose Son is He?" The immediate theological response is correct—"The Son of David"—and the logical trap is sprung.

"How then does David in the Spirit call Him 'Lord,' saying: 'The LORD said to my Lord, Sit at My right hand, till I make Your enemies Your footstool'? If David then calls Him 'Lord,' how is He his Son?" And no one was able to answer Him a word, nor from that day on did anyone dare question Him anymore. (Matthew 22:41-46)

How could David call one of his descendants his "Lord"? The obvious answer is an acknowledgement of the incarnation—God had come in the flesh. This they would not accept. They were silent! The invitation is turned down. And to this rejection of the invitation, Jesus would say,

"The wedding is ready, but those who were <u>invited</u> were not worthy. Therefore go into the highways, and as many as you find, invite to the wedding." (Matthew 22:8-9)

The invitation has gone out to each of us. RSVP

70

About the Pharisees

Matthew 23:1-44; Mark 12:38-44; Luke 20:45-21:4

Then Jesus spoke to the multitudes and to His disciples, saying: "The scribes and the Pharisees sit in Moses' seat. Therefore whatever they tell you to observe, that observe and do, but do not do according to their works; for they say, and do not do. . . . But woe to you, scribes and Pharisees, hypocrites! For you shut up the kingdom of heaven against men; for you neither go in yourselves, nor do you allow those who are entering to go in. . . . Woe to you, scribes and Pharisees, hypocrites! For you travel land and sea to win one proselyte, and when he is won, you make him twice as much a son of hell as yourselves. Woe to you, blind guides, who say, 'Whoever swears by the temple, it is nothing; but whoever swears by the gold of the temple, he is obliged to perform it.' . . . Woe to you, scribes and Pharisees, hypocrites! For you pay tithe of mint and anise and cummin, and have neglected the weightier matters of the law: justice and mercy and faith. These you ought to have done, without leaving the others undone. . . . Woe to you, scribes and Pharisees, hypocrites! For you cleanse the outside of the cup and dish, but inside they are full of extortion and self-indulgence. . . . Woe to you, scribes and Pharisees, hypocrites! For you are like whitewashed tombs which indeed appear beautiful outwardly, but inside are full of dead men's bones and all uncleanness. . . . Woe to you, scribes and Pharisees, hypocrites! Because you build the tombs of the prophets and adorn the monuments of the righteous, therefore you are witnesses against yourselves that you are sons of those who murdered the prophets. . . . See! Your house is left to you desolate; for I say to you, you shall see Me no more till you say, 'Blessed is He who comes in the name of the LORD!'" (Matthew 23:1-3, 13, 15-16, 23, 25, 27, 29, 31, 38-39)

With the end of His earthly ministry at hand, Jesus addresses the Pharisees in direct and scathing terms. First, He warns His disciples about the pharisaical mindset.

> *"The scribes and the Pharisees sit in Moses' seat. Therefore whatever they tell you to observe, that observe and do, but do not do according to their works; for they say, and do not do." (Matthew 23:2-3)*

An important principle grows out of this warning. Truth is truth and should be followed no matter the lifestyle of the teacher. All spiritual teachers except Jesus teach above the level of their own spiritual reality. There was an enormous gap between what the Pharisees taught and how they conducted their own lives, but when the teaching reflected the truth of God, the teaching was to be followed. Truth is always truth!

Jesus attacked the Pharisees' gaping reality gap with vigor. "Woe to you, scribes and Pharisees, hypocrites!" Seven times over Jesus introduces His rebuke with this caustic evaluation of their empty religious formalism.

> *"But woe to you, scribes and Pharisees, hypocrites! For you shut up the kingdom of heaven against men; for you neither go in yourselves, nor do you allow those who are entering to go in." (Matthew 23:13)*

It is one thing to reject the message of the truth personally, but a far more serious thing to block others from coming to the truth. By rejecting the offer of the kingdom, by inventing the Beelzebub theory as an explanation of the miraculous, by seeking to kill the Messiah, they had hindered the people of Israel from responding to their Messiah.

> *"Woe to you, scribes and Pharisees, hypocrites! For you travel land and sea to win one proselyte, and when he is won, you make him twice as much a son of hell as yourselves." (Matthew 23:15)*

By proselytizing from the surrounding nations, they made the converts more guilty than they were before, leaving behind a false religion to be replaced by a perverted form of Judaism. They were twice cursed.

> *"Woe to you, blind guides, who say, 'Whoever swears by the temple, it is nothing; but whoever swears by the gold of the temple, he is obliged to perform it.' Fools and blind!" (Matthew 23:16-17)*

Establishing personal rules of ethics to justify ungodly behavior in the name of religion made a mockery of the altar, the holy temple, and the God of heaven before whom all oaths are uttered.

> *"Woe to you, scribes and Pharisees, hypocrites! For you pay tithe of mint and anise and cummin, and have neglected the weightier matters of the law: justice and mercy and faith. These you ought to have done, without leaving the others undone. Blind guides, who strain out a gnat and swallow a camel!" (Matthew 23:23-24)*

There is a difference between tithing the spice cabinet and being a person of spiritual integrity, a person characterized by justice and mercy and faith. Reality of life rather than a ritual of rule keeping of the insignificant is true godliness. In fact, more attention was given to the minor points of the law than to the essence of the law. It is important to note that Jesus attaches different levels of importance to God's commandments individually, but urges obedience to all as the goal. A verbal cartoon of gagging on a gnat and swallowing a camel shows a slightly humorous side of Jesus.

> *"Woe to you, scribes and Pharisees, hypocrites! For you cleanse the outside of the cup and dish, but inside they are full of extortion and self-indulgence." (Matthew 23:25)*

Concern for ceremonial washings, forms of worship, liturgical garments rather than personal spiritual integrity—these characteristics of the Pharisees compelled the condemnation of Jesus.

> *"Woe to you, scribes and Pharisees, hypocrites! For you are like whitewashed tombs which indeed appear beautiful outwardly, but inside are full of dead men's bones and all uncleanness." (Matthew 23:27)*

Cemeteries are places of ordered beauty and solemnity honoring the blessed dead. In the hidden places of the dead, however, are the decayed remains of lifeless bodies—the corruption of death. Within the very being of the Pharisees were the remains of personal corruption.

> *"Woe to you, scribes and Pharisees, hypocrites! Because you build the tombs of the prophets and adorn the monuments of the righteous, and say, 'If we had lived in the days of our fathers, we would not have been partakers with them in the blood of the prophets.'" (Matthew 23:29-30)*

Cemeteries are also places where the greats are honored by their descendants. The tombs of the prophets testified to the continuous rejection of the nation of the message of God and the messengers of God. And the living descendants were moving in the same direction, as they were about to reject the greatest of all of the prophets, the Word!

In a closing burst of righteous anger Jesus condemns the hypocrites.

> *"Fill up, then, the measure of your fathers' guilt. Serpents, brood of vipers! How can you escape the condemnation of hell? Therefore, indeed, I send you prophets, wise men, and scribes: some of them you will kill and crucify, and some of them you will scourge in your synagogues and persecute from city to city, that on you may come all the righteous blood shed on the earth, from the blood of righteous Abel to the blood of Zechariah, son of Berechiah, whom you murdered between the temple and the altar. Assuredly, I say to you, all these things will come upon this generation." (Matthew 23:32-36)*

But then a lament from the loving Savior and soon-to-be-rejected Messiah.

> *"O Jerusalem, Jerusalem, the one who kills the prophets and stones those who are sent to her! How often I wanted to gather your children together, as a hen gathers her chicks under her wings, but you were not willing! See! Your house is left to you desolate; for I say to you, you shall see Me no more till you say, 'Blessed is He who comes in the name of the LORD!'" (Matthew 23:37-39)*

"Your house is left to you desolate"! It is Tuesday, and rejection is but a few days away—Good Friday is coming.

71

A Generous Widow, Inquiring Greeks, Secret Disciples, and a Final Statement

Matthew 12:41-44; Luke 21:1-4; John 12:20-50

And He looked up and saw the rich putting their gifts into the treasury, and He saw also a certain poor widow putting in two mites. So He said, "Truly I say to you that this poor widow has put in more than all; for all these out of their abundance have put in offerings for God, but she out of her poverty put in all the livelihood that she had." (Luke 21:1-4)

Now there were certain Greeks among those who came up to worship at the feast. Then they came to Philip, who was from Bethsaida of Galilee, and asked him, saying, "Sir, we wish to see Jesus." Philip came and told Andrew, and in turn Andrew and Philip told Jesus. But Jesus answered them, saying, "The hour has come that the Son of Man should be glorified. . . . Now My soul is troubled, and what shall I say? 'Father, save Me from this hour'? But for this purpose I came to this hour. Father, glorify Your name." Then a voice came from heaven, saying, "I have both glorified it and will glorify it again." . . . "And I, if I am lifted up from the earth, will draw all peoples to Myself." . . . Nevertheless even among the rulers many believed in Him, but because of the Pharisees they did not confess Him, lest they should be put out of the synagogue. . . . Then Jesus cried out and said, "He who believes in Me, believes not in Me but in Him who sent Me. And he who sees Me sees Him who sent Me. I have come as a light into the world, that whoever believes in Me should not abide in darkness." (John 12:20-23, 27-28, 32, 42, 44-46)

As the public ministry of the Lord draws to a conclusion, the rejection of His message is pathetically apparent: A poor widow gives out of a genuine heart in contrast to the hypocritical giving of the wealthy; the Greeks express a desire to come to Jesus while the Jews reject their Messiah; rulers who believe lack courage to confess their Messiah openly; and Jesus makes His last public statement.

"The widow's mite" has become proverbial—a proverb of reality versus hypocrisy, but also a negative measurement of the response of Judaism to the penetrating ministry of Jesus. The empty form of religion was still in place as it was at the beginning when He confronted the business going on in the temple. Again, He watches the multitude in the temple going through their empty, meaningless, religious form.

> *Now Jesus sat opposite the treasury and saw how the people put money into the treasury. And many who were rich put in much. (Mark 12:41)*

The form of the masses is contrasted to the widow's reality. Also, an important principle of giving is established here and later restated in the epistles.

> *For if there is first a willing mind, it is accepted according to what one has, and not according to what he does not have. . . . So let each one give as he purposes in his heart, not grudgingly or of necessity; for God loves a cheerful giver. (2 Corinthians 8:12; 9:7)*

There is an element of encouragement as the Greeks come to Jesus. This causes the Lord to think of the nearness of the cross and the other side of Calvary. Whereas the Jews have rejected their Messiah, the Greeks seek Him out. They come via the familiar team of Philip and Andrew, welcoming names to some Greeks who would see Jesus. The coming of the Greeks was a signal—a signal of the divine appointment of Calvary.

> *But Jesus answered them, saying, "The hour has come that the Son of Man should be glorified." (John 12:23)*

The hour has come—it is that appointed hour!

At twelve years of age in the temple, not yet:

> *And He said to them, "Why did you seek Me? Did you not know that I must be about My Father's business?" (Luke 2:49)*

With His mother at Cana and the water-to-wine miracle, not yet:

> *Jesus said to her, "Woman, what does your concern have to do with Me? My hour has not yet come." (John 2:4)*

In Nazareth of Galilee after the synagogue service, not yet:

> *So all those in the synagogue, when they heard these things, were filled with wrath, and rose up and thrust Him out of the city; and they led Him to the brow of the hill on which their city was built, that they might throw Him down over the cliff. Then passing through the midst of them, He went His way. (Luke 4:28-30)*

In the temple in the Judean ministry, not yet:

> Therefore they sought to take Him; but no one laid a hand on Him, because His hour had not yet come. (John 7:30)

But with the coming of the Greeks, the hour had come. And the response of Jesus is a mix of emotion and determination.

> "Now My soul is troubled, and what shall I say? 'Father, save Me from this hour'? But for this purpose I came to this hour." (John 12:27)

The assuring voice of the Father echoes from heaven.

> "Father, glorify Your name." Then a voice came from heaven, saying, "I have both glorified it and will glorify it again." (John 12:28)

And Jesus responds with a profound statement. When He is crucified, He will draw all men to Himself—all categories of men—Jews and Gentiles! No longer will the message be limited to the lost sheep of Israel.

Although public confessions of Christ were scarce, there were some believers among the authorities. We will meet two of them shortly at the foot of the cross: Joseph of Arimathea and Nicodemus. But for fear of the Pharisees they would not speak. They represent the many who love the praise of men and who continue to be virtually secret disciples. But thanks to the grace of God, still believers, then and now!

One final statement to the general public remains, then Gethsemane, the trials, and the cross.

> Then Jesus cried out and said, "He who believes in Me, believes not in Me but in Him who sent Me. And he who sees Me sees Him who sent Me. I have come as a light into the world, that whoever believes in Me should not abide in darkness. And if anyone hears My words and does not believe, I do not judge him; for I did not come to judge the world but to save the world. He who rejects Me, and does not receive My words, has that which judges him—the word that I have spoken will judge him in the last day. For I have not spoken on My own authority; but the Father who sent Me gave Me a command, what I should say and what I should speak. And I know that His command is everlasting life. Therefore, whatever I speak, just as the Father has told Me, so I speak." (John 12:44-50)

So ends the public ministry of Jesus, the Christ.

72

The Olivet Discourse: The Tribulation, and Christ's Second Advent

Matthew 24:1-14; Mark 13:1-13; Luke 21:5-19

Then Jesus went out and departed from the temple, and His disciples came up to show Him the buildings of the temple. And Jesus said to them, "Do you not see all these things? Assuredly, I say to you, not one stone shall be left here upon another, that shall not be thrown down." Now as He sat on the Mount of Olives, the disciples came to Him privately, saying, "Tell us, when will these things be? And what will be the sign of Your coming, and of the end of the age?" And Jesus answered and said to them: "Take heed that no one deceives you. For many will come in My name, saying, 'I am the Christ,' and will deceive many. And you will hear of wars and rumors of wars. See that you are not troubled; for all these things must come to pass, but the end is not yet. For nation will rise against nation, and kingdom against kingdom. And there will be famines, pestilences, and earthquakes in various places. All these are the beginning of sorrows. Then they will deliver you up to tribulation and kill you, and you will be hated by all nations for My name's sake. And then many will be offended, will betray one another, and will hate one another. Then many false prophets will rise up and deceive many. And because lawlessness will abound, the love of many will grow cold. But he who endures to the end shall be saved. And this gospel of the kingdom will be preached in all the world as a witness to all the nations, and then the end will come." (Matthew 24:1-14)

Thanks to the miraculous resurrection of Lazarus, all was going well—at least, that's what the apostles were thinking. A welcoming triumphal entry on Sunday. An authoritative cleansing and claiming of the temple on Monday. Refuting every trick question and plot of the Pharisees, the Herodians, the lawyers, and the Sadducees on Tuesday. Yes, all was going well. The apostles could sense the nearness of the kingdom. Their excitement is evident in their appraisal of the beauty of the temple—the soon-to-be seat of government for the King, the Son of David. This temple would surely be where each apostle would rule one of the twelve tribes of Israel. Jesus had promised them that role with the coming of the King and the kingdom.

But Jesus responds,

> *"Do you not see all these things? Assuredly, I say to you, not one stone shall be left here upon another, that shall not be thrown down."* *(Matthew 24:2)*

This astonishing announcement must have produced a stunned silence as the Lord and the disciples descended the Kidron Valley and ascended to the Mount of Olives. They sat down with the view of the temple to the west and the disciples asked,

> *"Tell us, when will these things be? And what will be the sign of Your coming, and of the end of the age?"* *(Matthew 24:3)*

Jesus responds to these three questions in reverse order—first He addresses the signs of the end of the age, then the sign of the coming of the Son of Man. He does not answer the first question directly but responds with exhortations as to how to live until that time.

First, the signs of the close of the age. There is the immediate instruction to the disciples.

> *"But before all these things, they will lay their hands on you and persecute you, delivering you up to the synagogues and prisons. You will be brought before kings and rulers for My name's sake. But it will turn out for you as an occasion for testimony. Therefore settle it in your hearts not to meditate beforehand on what you will answer."* *(Luke 21:12-14)*

This persecution would begin after the church was formed and continue throughout the church age—it comes "before" all these things.

Also, "before all these things," Jerusalem would be destroyed by Roman forces under Titus, in AD 70.

> *"But when you see Jerusalem surrounded by armies, then know that its desolation is near. And they will fall by the edge of the sword, and be led away captive into all nations. And Jerusalem will be trampled by Gentiles until the times of the Gentiles are fulfilled."* *(Luke 21:20, 24)*

The things that characterize the beginning of the tribulation, marking the close of the age, follow: wars and rumors of war, famines, earthquakes, pestilences, terrors from the heavens, betrayal of the faith, and false prophets.

But there will be many who will endure through the tribulation and be saved as a result of the preaching of the gospel of the kingdom. They will subsequently enter into that millennial kingdom offered so long before by Christ Jesus.

"But he who endures to the end shall be saved. And this gospel of the kingdom will be preached in all the world as a witness to all the nations, and then the end will come." (Matthew 24:13-14)

What will be the signs of the close of the age? In summary:

➢ The disciples will be persecuted.

➢ Jerusalem will be destroyed.

➢ The times of the Gentiles will be fulfilled.

➢ The tribulation will occur.

With the conclusion of the tribulation the close of "this age" will take place, and the new and glorious age of the millennium will begin.

The second question, "What will be the sign of Your coming?" is answered next: As the final phases of the judgments of the tribulation are being poured out on the earth, the second advent of the Messiah is at hand.

"For as the lightning comes from the east and flashes to the west, so also will the coming of the Son of Man be. For wherever the carcass is, there the eagles will be gathered together. Immediately after the tribulation of those days the sun will be darkened, and the moon will not give its light; the stars will fall from heaven, and the powers of the heavens will be shaken. Then the sign of the Son of Man will appear in heaven, and then all the tribes of the earth will mourn, and they will see the Son of Man coming on the clouds of heaven with power and great glory." (Matthew 24:27-29)

Terrifying atmospheric conditions provide a dark backdrop for the blaze of glory of the return of Christ! First, the sign of the coming of the Son of Man, and then the Son of Man returning as promised. The sign is the return of the *shekinah* glory to Israel (which departed the temple prior to the Babylonian captivity).

So the cherubim lifted up their wings, and the glory of the God of Israel was high above them. And the glory of the LORD went up from the midst of the city and stood on the mountain, which is on the east side of the city. (Ezekiel 11:22-23)

And the glory of the LORD came into the temple by way of the gate which faces toward the east. The Spirit lifted me up and brought me into the inner court; and behold, the glory of the LORD *filled the temple. (Ezekiel 43:4-5)*

Then the Son of Man will appear in power and great glory on the clouds of heaven coming with his holy angels—this in fulfillment of Daniel's prophecy.

"I was watching in the night visions, And behold, One like the Son of Man, coming with the clouds of heaven! He came to the Ancient of Days, and they brought Him near before Him. Then to Him was given dominion and glory and a kingdom, that all peoples, nations, and languages should serve Him. His dominion is an everlasting dominion, which shall not pass away, and His kingdom the one which shall not be destroyed." (Daniel 7:13-14)

In contrast to the rapture, which will be secret and instantaneous, the return of the Lord to earth at the end of the tribulation will be deliberate and visible to the entire planet. Having waited at God's right hand until His enemies are made His footstool, He returns in power and great glory to claim His promised kingdom.

"Ask of Me, and I will give You The nations for Your inheritance, and the ends of the earth for Your possession." (Psalm 2:8)

And He asks!

73

The Olivet Discourse: The "When" of Christ's Return

Matthew 24:32-25:36; Mark 13:1-37; Luke 21:5-36

"Now learn this parable from the fig tree: When its branch has already become tender and puts forth leaves, you know that summer is near. So you also, when you see all these things, know that it is near—at the doors! Assuredly, I say to you, this generation will by no means pass away till all these things take place. Heaven and earth will pass away, but My words will by no means pass away. But of that day and hour no one knows, not even the angels of heaven, but My Father only. But as the days of Noah were, so also will the coming of the Son of Man be. For as in the days before the flood, they were eating and drinking, marrying and giving in marriage, until the day that Noah entered the ark, and did not know until the flood came and took them all away, so also will the coming of the Son of Man be. . . . Watch therefore, for you do not know what hour your Lord is coming. But know this, that if the master of the house had known what hour the thief would come, he would have watched and not allowed his house to be broken into. . . . Who then is a faithful and wise servant, whom his master made ruler over his household, to give them food in due season?" (Matthew 24:32-39, 42-43, 45)

"Then the kingdom of heaven shall be likened to ten virgins who took their lamps and went out to meet the bridegroom. Watch therefore, for you know neither the day nor the hour in which the Son of Man is coming. For the kingdom of heaven is like a man traveling to a far country, who called his own servants and delivered his goods to them. When the Son of Man comes in His glory, and all the holy angels with Him, then He will sit on the throne of His glory. All the nations will be gathered before Him, and He will separate them one from another, as a shepherd divides his sheep from the goats. And He will set the sheep on His right hand, but the goats on the left." (Matthew 25:1, 13-14, 31-33)

Finally, the Lord addresses the disciples' first question—"When will this be?" He does not answer the time aspect, however, but instead addresses the attitudes and actions of all who await His return. He does this by telling seven parables:

- ➤ The parable of the fig tree
- ➤ The parable of the days of Noah
- ➤ The parable of the thief in the night
- ➤ The parable of the faithful and wicked servants
- ➤ The parable of the ten virgins
- ➤ The parable of the talents
- ➤ The parable of the sheep and the goats

In general, two themes become apparent—watch, and be faithful!

The parable of *the fig tree* teaches that the generation of people who enter the tribulation will soon see the return of the Lord to establish His kingdom. But as to the day and hour,

> *". . . no one knows, not even the angels in heaven, nor the Son, but only the Father." (Mark 13:32)*

Jesus restates this concept just before His ascension:

> *And He said to them, "It is not for you to know times or seasons which the Father has put in His own authority." (Acts 1:7)*

The parable of *the days of Noah* teaches that life will go forward in normal practices and habits, both good and bad. The exhortation is to not be ensnared by the concerns of the age, but to watch for the deliverance that the Son of Man will bring when He comes.

The parable of *the faithful and wicked servants* emphasizes the need for continued faithfulness in relating to others while the Master is away. Upon the Master's return there will be the reward of additional responsibilities based on past performance.

The parable of *the ten virgins* teaches preparedness rather than slumber and sleep. The unwise virgins will not participate in the marriage feast because they were not watching.

The parable of *the talents* relates to the entrustment of the use of money in the absence of the Master. Upon His return, generous rewards will be given to the servants who were faithful.

The parable of *the sheep and goats* contains a significant contribution to the events at the end of the tribulation and the beginning of the millennium. The Gentiles and the Jews surviving the tribulation will be gathered and divided according to the evidence of their faith. Their true faith will have been demonstrated in providing for the faithful of the tribulation, and these sheep are welcomed into the newly established kingdom. On the other hand, the unbelievers will be banished to "eternal fire prepared for the devil and his angels."

It is interesting to note that Jesus clearly states the judgment that is to come for those who reject His kingdom message.

> ". . . *and will cut him in two and appoint him his portion with the hypocrites. There shall be weeping and gnashing of teeth. . . . And cast the unprofitable servant into the outer darkness. There will be weeping and gnashing of teeth. . . . And these will go away into everlasting punishment, but the righteous into eternal life."* (Matthew 24:51; 25:30, 46)

Thus Jesus concludes His great prophetic discourse as He responds to the three questions of the apostles.

An exhausting Tuesday has finally come to an end. The crowds are still for Jesus; the leaders of Judaism have been silenced by the debates and denounced by the Lord's attack on their hypocrisy. The Greeks have come seeking Jesus—an anticipation of the coming church era. The destruction of Jerusalem, the coming of the tribulation, and the coming of the King and His kingdom have been predicted.

How will these details be integrated into the plan of redemption? The remainder of Passion Week will answer that question—first, Wednesday, the dark day of the betrayal plot of Judas with the Sanhedrin!

74

The Betrayal Room with Judas, and the Upper Room with Jesus

Matthew 26:3-5, 14-19; Mark 14:1-2,10-16; Luke 22:1-13, 24-20

Now the Feast of Unleavened Bread drew near, which is called Passover. And the chief priests and the scribes sought how they might kill Him, for they feared the people. Then Satan entered Judas, surnamed Iscariot, who was numbered among the twelve. So he went his way and conferred with the chief priests and captains, how he might betray Him to them. And they were glad, and agreed to give him money. So he promised and sought opportunity to betray Him to them in the absence of the multitude. Then came the Day of Unleavened Bread, when the Passover must be killed. And He sent Peter and John, saying, "Go and prepare the Passover for us, that we may eat." So they said to Him, "Where do You want us to prepare?" And He said to them, "Behold, when you have entered the city, a man will meet you carrying a pitcher of water; follow him into the house which he enters. Then you shall say to the master of the house, 'The Teacher says to you, Where is the guest room where I may eat the Passover with My disciples?' Then he will show you a large, furnished upper room; there make ready." So they went and found it just as He had said to them, and they prepared the Passover. (Luke 22:1-13)

Wednesday is a quiet day for Jesus and His disciples, except for Judas. It is the day of the betrayal plot! Jesus has known from the beginning who would betray Him. He spoke of this at the close of the Galilean ministry.

"But there are some of you who do not believe." For Jesus knew from the beginning who they were who did not believe, and who would betray Him. And He said, "Therefore I have said to you that no one can come to Me unless it has been granted to him by My Father. . . . Did I not choose you, the twelve, and one of you is a devil?" He spoke of Judas Iscariot, the son of Simon, for it was he who would betray Him, being one of the twelve. (John 6:64-65, 70-71)

And now the betrayer will execute the plan. Judas was the treasurer of the little band of disciples—no doubt, the trusted one, as they make the best treasurers. Yet he loved money. Earlier, when Mary anointed Jesus, he complained about the money not being given to the poor. This was because he had his hand in the bag. He was a thief driven by the love of money. Perhaps on a human level this was why he had identified with Jesus: Judas saw Jesus as the provider, the miracle worker, a good candidate to be a revolutionary king—in short, a road for him to gain wealth and power and control. Perhaps Judas was trying to force Jesus into an overt act of power to seize government from the Sanhedrin. Perhaps it was simply theological insanity common to Judas and the power behind Judas, Satan. Satanic revolt started in heaven, and now would be executed on earth. On Thursday night, Satan would enter into Judas, and the plot would be put into action. But on the divine side, an earlier eternal covenant had a controlling timeline that was being executed by the sovereign God.

> *"The kings of the earth took their stand, and the rulers were gathered together against the LORD and against His Christ. For truly against Your holy Servant Jesus, whom You anointed, both Herod and Pontius Pilate, with the Gentiles and the people of Israel, were gathered together to do whatever Your hand and Your purpose determined before to be done." (Acts 4:26-28)*

So Judas goes to the Jewish officials with plot in hand to betray the Messiah. It was a happy opportunity for the Jews.

> *And when they heard it, they were glad, and promised to give him money. So he sought how he might conveniently betray Him. (Mark 14:11)*

On Friday the three Jewish trials will find Jesus guilty, condemn Him, and deliver Him to Pilate for execution. At this point, Judas goes through some level of repentance for the plot he had suggested. The Jewish officials have no interest in his repentance or receiving back the blood money that Judas returns. He throws the thirty silver coins on the temple floor, rushes out, and hangs himself! A perfect set up for the Sanhedrin—the trusted treasurer agrees with them about the fraud Messiah, and in his shame and remorse he commits suicide. A perfect set up! But these subsequent events will come to pass directly.

To return to the schedule, plans must be made to celebrate Passover. Jesus has already made arrangements for the Upper Room and He commissions Peter and John to prepare for the Passover meal. Specific directions are given to find the location by following a man carrying a vessel of water (a strange practice for a man in the society of that day). And so the room was prepared by Peter, the apostolic spokesman, and John, the beloved apostle. The preparation would include securing the unblemished lamb, the bitter herbs, the unleavened bread, the wine, and dipping sauce, as well as necessary dishes and utensils. It would also include the basin, water, and towels for the customary washing of feet. Peter and John were instructed to take care of these details, and by Thursday afternoon everything was ready for the Passover feast.

Well, almost everything was ready. The disciples themselves were not ready to celebrate this feast—they were disputing with one another.

> *Now there was also a dispute among them, as to which of them should be considered the greatest. And He said to them, "The kings of the Gentiles exercise lordship over them, and those who exercise authority over them are called 'benefactors.' But not so among you; on the contrary, he who is greatest among you, let him be as the younger, and he who governs as he who serves. For who is greater, he who sits at the table, or he who serves? Is it not he who sits at the table? Yet I am among you as the One who serves. But you are those who have continued with Me in My trials. And I bestow upon you a kingdom, just as My Father bestowed one upon Me, that you may eat and drink at My table in My kingdom, and sit on thrones judging the twelve tribes of Israel." (Luke 22:24-30)*

The disciples were not ready for the Passover. They were once again arguing about their personal greatness, not the greatness of God in delivering the nation from Egyptian slavery or the greatness of God in sending His Son as His Passover Lamb to deliver the world from sin. They were not beholding the Lamb of God who would bear away the sin of the world on the following day. In the presence of Greatness and the greatest act of power and grace, they were arguing about personal greatness. They were not ready for Passover, and they certainly were not ready to wash feet. The basin and water and towel of humility were disregarded by the arrogant disciples. But Jesus would humble Himself in the Upper Room, and even more so on the cross.

75
.
.
.

Jesus Teaches His Disciples about Servanthood

John 13:1-38

Now before the feast of the Passover, when Jesus knew that His hour had come that He should depart from this world to the Father, having loved His own who were in the world, He loved them to the end. And supper being ended, the devil having already put it into the heart of Judas Iscariot, Simon's son, to betray Him, Jesus, knowing that the Father had given all things into His hands, and that He had come from God and was going to God, rose from supper and laid aside His garments, took a towel and girded Himself. After that, He poured water into a basin and began to wash the disciples' feet, and to wipe them with the towel with which He was girded. Then He came to Simon Peter. And Peter said to Him, "Lord, are You washing my feet?" Jesus answered and said to him, "What I am doing you do not understand now, but you will know after this." Peter said to Him, "You shall never wash my feet!" Jesus answered him, "If I do not wash you, you have no part with Me." Simon Peter said to Him, "Lord, not my feet only, but also my hands and my head!" Jesus said to him, "He who is bathed needs only to wash his feet, but is completely clean; and you are clean, but not all of you." For He knew who would betray Him; therefore He said, "You are not all clean." So when He had washed their feet, taken His garments, and sat down again, He said to them, "Do you know what I have done to you? You call me Teacher and Lord, and you say well, for so I am. If I then, your Lord and Teacher, have washed your feet, you also ought to wash one another's feet. For I have given you an example, that you should do as I have done to you. Most assuredly, I say to you, a servant is not greater than his master; nor is he who is sent greater than he who sent him. If you know these things, blessed are you if you do them." (John 13:1-17)

Now as they were eating, He said, "Assuredly, I say to you, one of you will betray Me." And they were exceedingly sorrowful, and each of them began to say to Him, "Lord, is it I?" He answered and said,

"He who dipped his hand with Me in the dish will betray Me. The Son of Man indeed goes just as it is written of Him, but woe to that man by whom the Son of Man is betrayed! It would have been good for that man if he had not been born." Then Judas, who was betraying Him, answered and said, "Rabbi, is it I?" He said to him, "You have said it." (Matthew 26:21-25)

It is the day before crucifixion and Jesus was still teaching His disciples—this time, about humility and servanthood. Remember, they were arguing about which of them was the greatest. Late into the Passover supper, Jesus could wait no longer for His disciples to take the servant's place that they were avoiding. In a picture of His laying aside His glory of deity and becoming a man, Jesus lays aside His seamless robe and girds Himself with the servant's towel. He begins to wash their feet, and then He comes to Peter. Those He served before Peter were speechless, but Peter was never speechless. Peter was familiar with the towel, and the basin, and the water; he had placed them in the room being used for the Passover. He had not yet learned servanthood, but he was learning. He recognizes that the Master should not be washing feet, and he objects to the Lord's action on his behalf. It was a noble reaction, but late.

The Lord insists on continuing the visual teaching in strongest terms.

Peter said to Him, "You shall never wash my feet!" Jesus answered him, "If I do not wash you, you have no part with Me." (John 13:8)

Peter responds in an equally strong tone, again with good but misguided motivation.

"Lord, not my feet only, but also my hands and my head!" (John 13:9)

The teaching of Jesus that Peter's response solicits is complex on three levels. First, to be ceremonially clean for Passover, only the feet needed to be washed. The bath was already completed; only the feet were unclean because of the walk on the dusty streets. Second, on a spiritual level, Peter and the rest of the disciples (except for one) had already received the "bath" of salvation. They were all clean. Third, Judas was not spiritually clean.

Having concluded the object lesson, the Savior will now make the pointed application to the disciples. He begins with an arresting question:

"Do you know what I have done to you?" (John 13:12)

The Lord speaks in clear terms, summoning all would-be disciples to servanthood.

"You call me Teacher and Lord, and you say well, for so I am. If I then, your Lord and Teacher, have washed your feet, you also ought to wash one another's feet. For I have given you an example, that you should do as I have done to you. Most assuredly, I say to you, a servant is not greater than his master; nor is he who is sent greater than he who sent him." (John 13:13-16)

Knowing we are called to servanthood is one thing; *being* a servant is another. And the Lord addresses this dichotomy.

"If you know these things, blessed are you if you do them." (John 13:17)

To be a servant is to be blessed and happy! In this first part of the Upper Room Discourse, Jesus answers the psychological question for the disciples, "Who am I?" The answer: a servant.

Jesus reveals that a betrayer was at the table. Now he addresses this troubling issue in detail. Notice the cadence of the solemn statements:

"But behold, the hand of My betrayer is with Me on the table. And truly the Son of Man goes as it has been determined, but woe to that man by whom He is betrayed!" (Luke 22:21-22)

"It is one of the twelve, who dips with Me in the dish. The Son of Man indeed goes just as it is written of Him, but woe to that man by whom the Son of Man is betrayed! It would have been good for that man if he had never been born." (Mark 14:20-21)

"It is he to whom I shall give a piece of bread when I have dipped it." And having dipped the bread, He gave it to Judas Iscariot, the son of Simon. Now after the piece of bread, Satan entered him. Then Jesus said to him, "What you do, do quickly." . . . Having received the piece of bread, he then went out immediately. And it was night. (John 13:26-27, 30)

The group of disciples now purified with the departure of Judas receives a commandment from Jesus which Christians have obeyed throughout history—the ordinance of the Lord's Supper. "Do this in remembrance of Me."

And He took bread, gave thanks and broke it, and gave it to them, saying, "This is My body which is given for you; do this in remembrance of Me." Likewise He also took the cup after supper, saying, "This cup is the new covenant in My blood, which is shed for you." (Luke 22:19-20)

Jesus institutes a simple symbol with depth of imagery full of theological content.

- ➤ There is one loaf as there is one universal body: the church.
- ➤ There is the body given and the blood shed: His sacrificial death.
- ➤ There is salvation by eating His flesh and drinking His blood at conversion—by believing.
- ➤ There is the sustaining ministry of Christ—a repeated feast.
- ➤ There is a future celebration when the New Covenant is enacted.

From teaching the important lesson of servanthood through washing the disciples' feet, the Lord will extend His teaching to the next great question of life—the emotional question. This will be the next lesson of the Upper Room Discourse.

76

Jesus Teaches His Disciples about Serenity

Matthew 26:31-35; Mark 14:27-31; Luke 22:31-38; John 13:33-14:30

"Little children, I shall be with you a little while longer. You will seek Me; and as I said to the Jews, 'Where I am going, you cannot come,' so now I say to you. A new commandment I give to you, that you love one another; as I have loved you, that you also love one another. By this all will know that you are My disciples, if you have love for one another." Simon Peter said to Him, "Lord, where are You going?" Jesus answered him, "Where I am going you cannot follow Me now, but you shall follow Me afterward." Peter said to Him, "Lord, why can I not follow You now? I will lay down my life for Your sake." Jesus answered him, "Will you lay down your life for My sake? Most assuredly, I say to you, the rooster shall not crow till you have denied Me three times. Let not your heart be troubled; you believe in God, believe also in Me. In My Father's house are many mansions; if it were not so, I would have told you. I go to prepare a place for you. And if I go and prepare a place for you, I will come again and receive you to Myself; that where I am, there you may be also. And where I go you know, and the way you know." Thomas said to Him, "Lord, we do not know where You are going, and how can we know the way?" Jesus said to him, "I am the way, the truth, and the life. No one comes to the Father except through Me. . . . And whatever you ask in My name, that I will do, that the Father may be glorified in the Son. If you ask anything in My name, I will do it. . . . But the Helper, the Holy Spirit, whom the Father will send in My name, He will teach you all things, and bring to your remembrance all things that I said to you. Peace I leave with you, My peace I give to you; not as the world gives do I give to you. Let not your heart be troubled, neither let it be afraid." (John 13:33-14:6, 13-14, 26-27)

Peter is a troubled disciple. He has just heard the Lord say He is going away and His disciples cannot follow Him.

"Little children, I shall be with you a little while longer. You will seek Me; and as I said to the Jews, 'Where I am going, you cannot come.'" (John 13:33)

Jesus goes on to predict that Peter will deny Him. Three items are in place relating to his denial. First, the Lord refers to a prophecy in Zechariah concerning His disciples.

"Awake, O sword, against My Shepherd, against the Man who is My Companion," says the LORD of hosts. "Strike the Shepherd, and the sheep will be scattered; then I will turn My hand against the little ones." (Zechariah 13:7)

Peter and all the disciples will be scattered in fear—it was prophesied.

Second, Satan had demanded to "sift" Peter (and the other apostles), and God had granted that desire.

And the Lord said, "Simon, Simon! Indeed, Satan has asked . . . that he may sift you [plural] as wheat . . ." (Luke 22:31)

And finally, the Lord Himself predicts that before sunrise Peter will deny Him three times. Most certainly the denial is forthcoming. Peter is a troubled disciple, as are all of the disciples.

Against this background of anxiety, Jesus calls His disciples to an attitude of peace and serenity. And He gives reasons for this blessed serenity and peace.

First, the future is secure.

"Let not your heart be troubled; you believe in God, believe also in Me. In My Father's house are many mansions; if it were not so, I would have told you. I go to prepare a place for you. And if I go and prepare a place for you, I will come again and receive you to Myself; that where I am, there you may be also." (John 14:1-3)

The future is secure for the believer. When he is absent from the body, he is at home with the Lord.

"The dead in Christ shall rise first, then we who are alive shall be caught up together with them in the clouds to meet the Lord in the air. And thus we shall always be with the Lord" (1 Thessalonians 4:16-17).

We shall be a kingdom of priests and we shall rule with Him on the earth for ever and ever! The future is secure; therefore, "Let not your heart be troubled."

Second, we have been granted to know the truth.

Jesus said to him, "I am the way, the truth, and the life. No one comes to the Father except through Me." (John 14:6)

This statement by Jesus is both gracious and narrow. The grace of God is seen in revealing Himself and His truth to fallen man.

Truth is an illusive matter. Because God is truth, His revelation is true, and a worldview based on this truth is the only true worldview, the only true religion. Jesus is full of grace and truth. Later in this same Upper Room Discourse Jesus will pray to His Father, "Sanctify them through Your word, Your word is truth." Truth is narrow, and the narrow truth states that access to God, heaven, and eternal life can only be gained through the Lord Jesus Christ. He who knows the truth is free. Therefore, "Let not your heart be troubled."

Third, Jesus invites the disciples to pray in His name.

"And whatever you ask in My name, that I will do, that the Father may be glorified in the Son. . . . I say to you, whatever you ask the Father in My name He will give you. Until now you have asked nothing in My name. Ask, and you will receive, that your joy may be full." (John 14:13; 16:23-24)

A new, direct access is available to the Father in prayer—in the name of Jesus. The norm in the coming church era is that everyone has access to the Father, through the Spirit, in the name of the Son.

For through Him we both [Jews and Gentiles] have access by one Spirit to the Father. (Ephesians 2:18)

Asking in the name of Jesus does not, however, imply we have a blank check. It means praying as Jesus would pray in a given situation. Knowing Jesus through the Word of Truth will enable us to pray as He would—not according to our desires or limited understanding, but according to the principles of prayer in the life of the Savior. We have direct access to God in prayer. Therefore, "Let not your heart be troubled."

Fourth, Jesus promises to send the Holy Spirit upon His departure to heaven.

"And I will pray the Father, and He will give you another Helper, that He may abide with you forever— the Spirit of truth, whom the world cannot receive, because it neither sees Him nor knows Him; but you know Him, for He dwells with you and will be in you. . . . But the Helper, the Holy Spirit, whom the Father will send in My name, He will teach you all things, and bring to your remembrance all things that I said to you." (John 14:16-17, 26)

The Holy Spirit, who has been *with* them, will be *in* them forever. The Holy Spirit will bring to remembrance and teach all things of the Father and the Son. The Holy Spirit will become the active member of the Trinity on earth as directed by the Father and the Son. The church will be formed on Pentecost by the baptism of the Holy Spirit and concluded at the rapture when "He who hinders" is taken with the church, thus ending the church age. The Holy Spirit will indwell us forever. Therefore, "Let not your heart be troubled."

"Peace I leave with you, My peace I give to you; not as the world gives do I give to you. Let not your heart be troubled, neither let it be afraid." (John 14:27)

How am I to be? At peace!

77

Jesus Teaches His Disciples about Bearing Fruit

John 15:1-16:3

"I am the true vine, and My Father is the vinedresser. Every branch in Me that does not bear fruit He takes away; and every branch that bears fruit He prunes, that it may bear more fruit. You are already clean because of the word which I have spoken to you. Abide in Me, and I in you. As the branch cannot bear fruit of itself, unless it abides in the vine, neither can you, unless you abide in Me. I am the vine, you are the branches. He who abides in Me, and I in him, bears much fruit; for without Me you can do nothing. If anyone does not abide in Me, he is cast out as a branch and is withered; and they gather them and throw them into the fire, and they are burned. If you abide in Me, and My words abide in you, you will ask what you desire, and it shall be done for you. By this My Father is glorified, that you bear much fruit; so you will be My disciples. As the Father loved Me, I also have loved you; abide in My love. If you keep My commandments, you will abide in My love, just as I have kept My Father's commandments and abide in His love. These things I have spoken to you, that My joy may remain in you, and that your joy may be full. This is My commandment, that you love one another as I have loved you. Greater love has no one than this, than to lay down one's life for his friends. You are My friends if you do whatever I command you. No longer do I call you servants, for a servant does not know what his master is doing; but I have called you friends, for all things that I heard from My Father I have made known to you. You did not choose Me, but I chose you and appointed you that you should go and bear fruit, and that your fruit should remain, that whatever you ask the Father in My name He may give you. These things I command you, that you love one another. If the world hates you, you know that it hated Me before it hated you. If you were of the world, the world would love its own. Yet because you are not of the world, but I chose you out of the world, therefore the world hates you." (John 15:18-19)

The third lesson of the Upper Room Discourse is about bearing fruit. The serene servant is to bear fruit—fruit of character, and then fruit of converts. The analogy is of a fruit-bearing vine and its branches. There is an interesting parallel with a brief parable in Ezekiel:

> *Then the word of the LORD came to me, saying, "Son of man, how is the wood of the vine better than any other wood, the vine branch which is among the trees of the forest? Is wood taken from it to make any object? Or can men make a peg from it to hang any vessel on? Instead, it is thrown into the fire for fuel; the fire devours both ends of it, and its middle is burned. Is it useful for any work?" (Ezekiel 15:1-4)*

A vine has a single use—to bear fruit. Fruit-bearing is the subject: fruit, more fruit, much fruit, and abiding fruit.

The fruit under discussion is the fruit of character as seen in the concluding commandment—the fruit of love. It is the fruit of the Spirit as seen in Galatians 5:25-26—love, joy, peace, longsuffering, kindness, goodness, faithfulness, gentleness, and self control. All of these are the desirable traits of a Spirit-directed life. The question is, how is it possible to attain these characteristics?

Jesus gives the answer in the next often repeated word—abide.

> *"Abide in Me, and I in you. As the branch cannot bear fruit of itself, unless it abides in the vine, neither can you, unless you abide in Me. I am the vine, you are the branches. He who abides in Me, and I in him, bears much fruit; for without Me you can do nothing. . . . If you abide in Me, and My words abide in you, you will ask what you desire, and it shall be done for you. . . . As the Father loved Me, I also have loved you; abide in My love. If you keep My commandments, you will abide in My love, just as I have kept My Father's commandments and abide in His love." (John 15:4-5, 7, 9-10)*

Abide in Christ, in His Word, in His love. Abiding is a mystical concept, difficult to define, differently expressed by every individual. Abiding in Christ is the life of personal communion with Christ. This communion has several basic components: worship, prayer, thanksgiving, confession of sin, and the personal reading and study of the Bible. These are the routine elements of communion life, of abiding in Christ.

But abiding is moved from the intangible to the measurable by the Lord's next oft repeated word—commandment.

"If you keep My commandments, you will abide in My love, just as I have kept My Father's commandments and abide in His love. . . . This is My commandment, that you love one another as I have loved you. . . . You are My friends if you do whatever I command you. . . . These things I command you, that you love one another." (John 15:10, 12, 14, 17)

He who abides in Christ keeps His commandments. This is not mystical; it is measurable and specific. It is not only an external keeping of rules because the greatest motivation of all—love—is one of the commandments, the highest commandment. Yes, abiding in Christ is obeying Him with the highest of all motivations—the love of Christ constraining us. While the world will hate us, we are to love one another.

The apostle John echoes these words in his first epistle.

Whoever believes that Jesus is the Christ is born of God, and everyone who loves Him who begot also loves him who is begotten of Him. By this we know that we love the children of God, when we love God and keep His commandments. For this is the love of God, that we keep His commandments. And His commandments are not burdensome. (1 John 5:1-3)

Fruit-bearing is made possible through abiding in Christ. Abiding in Christ is demonstrated by knowing and keeping His commandments. And the greatest of all of the commandments is the motivating commandment of love.

The servant at peace is to bear fruit of character, but he is also to bear fruit of converts. This will be the next section of the Upper Room Discourse.

78

The Coming of the Holy Spirit, and the Departure of Jesus

John 15:26-16:33

"But when the Helper comes, whom I shall send to you from the Father, the Spirit of truth who proceeds from the Father, He will testify of Me. And you also will bear witness, because you have been with Me from the beginning. . . . Nevertheless I tell you the truth. It is to your advantage that I go away; for if I do not go away, the Helper will not come to you; but if I depart, I will send Him to you. And when He has come, He will convict the world of sin, and of righteousness, and of judgment: of sin, because they do not believe in Me; of righteousness, because I go to My Father and you see Me no more; of judgment, because the ruler of this world is judged. I still have many things to say to you, but you cannot bear them now. However, when He, the Spirit of truth, has come, He will guide you into all truth; for He will not speak on His own authority, but whatever He hears He will speak; and He will tell you things to come. He will glorify Me, for He will take of what is Mine and declare it to you. All things that the Father has are Mine. Therefore I said that He will take of Mine and declare it to you. A little while, and you will not see Me; and again a little while, and you will see Me, because I go to the Father." Then some of His disciples said among themselves, "What is this that He says to us, 'A little while, and you will not see Me; and again a little while, and you will see Me'; and, 'because I go to the Father'?" They said therefore, "What is this that He says, 'A little while'? We do not know what He is saying." Now Jesus knew that they desired to ask Him, and He said to them, "Are you inquiring among yourselves about what I said, 'A little while, and you will not see Me; and again a little while, and you will see Me'? . . . I came forth from the Father and have come into the world. Again, I leave the world and go to the Father." His disciples said to Him, "See, now You are speaking plainly, and using no figure of speech!" (John 15:26-27; 16:7-19, 28-29)

F ruit-bearing also involves the fruit of conversion—the conversion of individuals out of the world. For this, the world hates the followers of Christ. And Jesus again states that He is going away, returning to His Father. A hostile world and the absence of the Savior—how will evangelism take place? Jesus has a wonderful answer.

> *"But when the Helper comes, whom I shall send to you from the Father, the Spirit of truth who proceeds from the Father, He will testify of Me. . . . Nevertheless I tell you the truth. It is to your advantage that I go away; for if I do not go away, the Helper will not come to you; but if I depart, I will send Him to you." (John 15:26; 16:7)*

The solution to the crisis of evangelism is the coming of the Holy Spirit— the indwelling-every-believer Holy Spirit, the omnipresent Holy Spirit, the hindering-sin-in-the-world Holy Spirit, the convicting-the-world Holy Spirit!

The theology of the promise of the Holy Spirit in this context is significant. The functioning order of the Trinity is implicitly stated in Jesus' promise. The Father and the Son send the Holy Spirit on this divine mission. In the next movement of the Upper Room Discourse Jesus states that the Father has sent Him.

> *"As You sent Me into the world, I also have sent them into the world. . . . That they all may be one, as You, Father, are in Me, and I in You; that they also may be one in Us, that the world may believe that You sent Me." (John 17:18, 21)*

The Father sends the Son and the Spirit, and the Son sends the Spirit. Hence, the first, second, and third members of the Trinity—the harmonious functioning order of the submission of Equals within the Godhead. Mystery upon mystery!

Jesus tells His disciples that, when the Holy Spirit comes, He will have an extensive ministry in the world.

> *"And when He has come, He will convict the world of sin, and of righteousness, and of judgment: of sin, because they do not believe in Me; of righteousness, because I go to My Father and you see Me no more; of judgment, because the ruler of this world is judged." (John 16:8-11)*

The critical sin is the sin of rejecting the Savior—it is the unforgivable sin! The Holy Spirit incessantly asks the question, "Do you believe in Jesus?"

Second, the Holy Spirit will convict of the standard of perfect righteousness. In the absence of Jesus Himself, the only perfectly righteous human being to ever live, it is the Holy Spirit who continually convicts the world, "You fall short of the righteousness of God."

Third, the Holy Spirit will convict of the doom of impending judgment. Satan has been judged—the execution of his judgment is certain; his destiny is the lake of fire. And so the Holy Spirit urgently convicts the world, "Eternal judgment awaits you, the demons, and Satan."

In addition, the Holy Spirit will have a ministry toward man and toward God.

> *"However, when He, the Spirit of truth, has come, He will guide you into all truth; for He will not speak on His own authority, but whatever He hears He will speak; and He will tell you things to come. He will glorify Me, for He will take of what is Mine and declare it to you." (John 16:13-14)*

The Holy Spirit will guide believers into all truth and He will glorify Christ. This is why Jesus could say,

> *"Nevertheless I tell you the truth. It is to your advantage that I go away; for if I do not go away, the Helper will not come to you; but if I depart, I will send Him to you." (John 16:7)*

Having promised the coming of the Holy Spirit with all of the advantages of that great exchange, Jesus now introduces a riddle-like statement.

> *"A little while, and you will not see Me; and again a little while, and you will see Me, because I go to the Father." Then some of His disciples said among themselves, "What is this that He says to us, 'A little while, and you will not see Me; and again a little while, and you will see Me'; and, 'because I go to the Father'? . . . We do not know what He is saying." (John 16:16-18)*

"Now you see Me. Now you don't. Then you will." The disciples don't get it. So Jesus speaks plainly to them.

> *"I came forth from the Father and have come into the world. Again, I leave the world and go to the Father." His disciples said to Him, "See; now You are speaking plainly, and using no figure of speech!" (John 16:28-29)*

The coming ministry of the Holy Spirit would enable the disciples of Jesus, then and now, to bear the fruit of converts through His ministry of convicting the world. He would also teach the believers, then and now, and bring glorify Christ.

79

For the Glory of God

John 17:1-26

Jesus spoke these words, lifted up His eyes to heaven, and said: "Father, the hour has come. Glorify Your Son, that Your Son also may glorify You, as You have given Him authority over all flesh, that He should give eternal life to as many as You have given Him. And this is eternal life, that they may know You, the only true God, and Jesus Christ whom You have sent. I have glorified You on the earth. I have finished the work which You have given Me to do. And now, O Father, glorify Me together with Yourself, with the glory which I had with You before the world was. I have manifested Your name to the men whom You have given Me out of the world. They were Yours, You gave them to Me, and they have kept Your word. Now they have known that all things which You have given Me are from You. For I have given to them the words which You have given Me; and they have received them, and have known surely that I came forth from You; and they have believed that You sent Me. I pray for them. I do not pray for the world but for those whom You have given Me, for they are Yours. And all Mine are Yours, and Yours are Mine, and I am glorified in them. Now I am no longer in the world, but these are in the world, and I come to You. Holy Father, keep through Your name those whom You have given Me, that they may be one as We are. . . . I do not pray that You should take them out of the world, but that You should keep them from the evil one. They are not of the world, just as I am not of the world. . . . I do not pray for these alone, but also for those who will believe in Me through their word; that they all may be one, as You, Father, are in Me, and I in You; that they also may be one in Us, that the world may believe that You sent Me. And the glory which You gave Me I have given them, that they may be one just as We are one." (John 17:1-11, 15-16, 20-22)

The Upper Room Discourse closes with the prayer of Christ Jesus to His Father. It is a prayer for the glory of God through unity and love among God's people. The chief end of man is to glorify God and enjoy Him forever. Why do I exist? To glorify God! And it is this subject that marks the content of Jesus' prayer.

There are three parts to the prayer: Jesus prays for Himself, for His disciples, and then for those who will believe through the testimony—both spoken and written—of the disciples. First, the prayer of Jesus for Himself.

> *Jesus spoke these words, lifted up His eyes to heaven, and said: "Father, the hour has come. Glorify Your Son, that Your Son also may glorify You. . . . I have glorified You on the earth. I have finished the work which You have given Me to do. And now, O Father, glorify Me together with Yourself, with the glory which I had with You before the world was." (John 17:1, 4-5)*

The hour of His appointment from eternity past has arrived—the hour of His death. And He prays that He may be glorified by the Father so that He could glorify the Father. Glory is not an attribute of God. Rather, it is the manifestation of the attributes of God, the manifestation of the nature of God, of God Himself. And the hour of the death of Christ will manifest the attributes of God in this one great event as no other event in all of time. Consider His holiness, His justice, His love, His omniscience, His omnipotence, His infinitude and eternality, His immutability, His freedom of will, His sovereignty—all working harmoniously within the Trinity. Pause and consider!

Jesus speaks as from the other side of the cross, "I have finished the work which You have given Me to do." Soon those very words "It is finished!" would be spoken from the cross. And His prayer is for the restoration of the glory that was His before He laid it aside at His incarnation. When He comes to establish His kingdom, He will manifest a continuous transfiguration-like glory.

The second part of the prayer of Jesus is for His apostles.

> *"I have manifested Your name to the men whom You have given Me out of the world. They were Yours, You gave them to Me, and they have kept Your word. I pray for them. I do not pray for the world but for those whom You have given Me, for they are Yours. And all Mine are Yours, and Yours are Mine, and I am glorified in them. Now I am no longer in the world, but these are in the world, and I come to You. Holy Father, keep through Your name those whom You have given Me, that they may be one as We are. . . . I do not pray that You should take them out of the world, but that You should keep them from the evil one. They are not of the world, just as I am not of the world. Sanctify them by Your truth. Your word is truth." (John 17:6, 9-11, 15-17)*

The Lord gives lessons for prayer in His prayer. He makes a distinction in His prayer by praying for His own and not for the world. His "own" were given to Him by the Father. In praying for His own, He prays that He be *glorified* in them. The apostles will glorify God by maintaining their apostolic unity, reflecting the unity of the Trinity. This was accomplished in the life and death of every apostle. Jesus also prays for the sanctification of the apostles, the progressive sanctification of a maturing life. He gives the key to growth in holiness—the Word of God.

> *"Sanctify them by Your truth. Your word is truth." (John 17:17)*

This request in prayer was also fulfilled as witnessed by the Word of God itself.

> *... having been built on the foundation of the apostles and prophets, Jesus Christ Himself being the chief cornerstone. (Ephesians 2:20)*

Jesus also prays for biblical separation, not isolation. "In the world but not of the world" is the standard of operation. The apostles present this truth in their writings—the Christian is a pilgrim and stranger on a journey, the Christian is a citizen of heaven, the Christian is an ambassador for Christ. Their lives confirmed their teaching.

The third section of the prayer is for future believers.

> *"I do not pray for these alone, but also for those who will believe in Me through their word." (John 17:20)*

These unnamed—and even unborn—people are the focus of Jesus' prayer. The prayer for the church is the same as the prayer for the apostles—unity and love—that they would glorify God.

> *"And the glory which You gave Me I have given them, that they may be one just as We are one: And I have declared to them Your name, and will declare it, that the love with which You loved Me may be in them, and I in them." (John 17:22, 26)*

The chief end of man is to glorify God, and this is seen in the unity and love of the church.

In the Upper Room Discourse Jesus teaches us that we are to be serene servants, bearing fruit of character and converts, for the glory of God.

> *And when they had sung a hymn, they went out. (Matthew 26:30)*

80

Gethsemane: The Prayer

Matthew 26:36-44; Mark 14:32-42; Luke 22:39-46

*Then Jesus came with them to a place called Gethsemane, and said
to the disciples, "Sit here while I go and pray over there." And He
took with Him Peter and the two sons of Zebedee, and He began to be
sorrowful and deeply distressed. Then He said to them, "My soul is
exceedingly sorrowful, even to death. Stay here and watch with Me."
He went a little farther and fell on His face, and prayed, saying, "O
My Father, if it is possible, let this cup pass from Me; nevertheless,
not as I will, but as You will." Then He came to the disciples and
found them asleep, and said to Peter, "What? Could you not watch
with Me one hour? Watch and pray, lest you enter into temptation.
The spirit indeed is willing, but the flesh is weak." Again, a second
time, He went away and prayed, saying, "O My Father, if this cup
cannot pass away from Me unless I drink it, Your will be done." And
He came and found them asleep again, for their eyes were heavy. So
He left them, went away again, and prayed the third time, saying the
same words. Then He came to His disciples and said to them, "Are
you still sleeping and resting? Behold, the hour is at hand, and the
Son of Man is being betrayed into the hands of sinners. Rise, let us be
going. See, My betrayer is at hand." (Matthew 26:36-46)*

Acknowledging that "the hour had come" in his prayer to His Father,
Jesus enters into that familiar place—Gethsemane. The "hour" of
eternity had come finally. It was the focus of the life of Christ.

At age twelve in the temple:

*And He said to them, "Why did you seek Me? Did you not know that
I must be about My Father's business?" (Luke 2:49)*

In Cana at the first miracle:

*And when they ran out of wine, the mother of Jesus said to Him,
"They have no wine." Jesus said to her, "Woman, what does your
concern have to do with Me? My hour has not yet come." (John 2:3-4)*

In Galilee in His home synagogue:

So all those in the synagogue, when they heard these things, were filled with wrath, and rose up and thrust Him out of the city; and they led Him to the brow of the hill on which their city was built, that they might throw Him down over the cliff. Then passing through the midst of them, He went His way. (Luke 4:28-30)

In the temple in the Judean ministry:

Therefore they sought to take Him; but no one laid a hand on Him, because His hour had not yet come. . . . These words Jesus spoke in the treasury, as He taught in the temple; and no one laid hands on Him, for His hour had not yet come. (John 7:30; 8:20)

On Tuesday of Passion Week:

"The hour has come that the Son of Man should be glorified. . . . Now My soul is troubled, and what shall I say? 'Father, save Me from this hour'? But for this purpose I came to this hour." (John 12:23, 27)

Yes, now the hour *had* come—that dreadful hour. He takes His three closest disciples—Peter, James, and John—to join in prayer as the hour approaches. He instructs them to pray to avoid temptation and then goes a bit deeper into the garden to pray alone.

His emotions are tense. Hear the words describing the struggle—He is sorrowful, troubled, perplexed, distressed, alarmed—even to death. He needs the help of an angel to strengthen Him.

So He prays, "Father, save Me from this hour!" Three times He prays this request. Where is the determination of His entire earthly ministry? What caused this pleading with the Father to avoid the hour of eternal destiny? What was in the cup that He was appointed to drink?

. . . who Himself bore our sins in His own body on the tree, that we, having died to sins, might live for righteousness. (1 Peter 2:24)

And He Himself is the propitiation for our sins, and not for ours only but also for the whole world. (1 John 2:2)

God was in Christ reconciling the world to Himself, not imputing their trespasses to them. . . . For He made Him who knew no sin to be sin for us, that we might become the righteousness of God in Him. (2 Corinthians 5:19, 21)

What was in the cup? Sin, all the sin of all the world, every individual sin, the guilt, the shame, the unholiness of it all—the eternal punishment for every person in the space of three hours. It was a deep cup!

So He prays. He prays three times—the same prayer, but with a progression. Having been focused on the hour from the beginning, He now prays to be delivered from that hour. Amazing humanity!

> *He went a little farther and fell on His face, and prayed, saying, "O My Father, if it is possible, let this cup pass from Me; nevertheless, not as I will, but as You will." . . . Again, a second time, He went away and prayed, saying, "O My Father, if this cup cannot pass away from Me unless I drink it, Your will be done." . . . So He left them, went away again, and prayed the third time, saying the same words. (Matthew 26:39, 42, 44)*

Jesus is asking that the cup would pass from Him. Notice, "Not as I will, but as You will." This is a statement of contrast, not comparison. It is My will *but* Your will, not My will *and* Your will. The author of Hebrews exegetes this event in his epistle.

> *. . . who, in the days of His flesh, when He had offered up prayers and supplications, with vehement cries and tears to Him who was able to save Him from death, and was heard because of His godly fear, though He was a Son, yet He learned obedience by the things which He suffered. (Hebrews 5:7-8)*

Jesus learned obedience through the things which He suffered in the Gethsemane struggle. Notice the progress in the prayers—the progress of obedience—"not My will, but Yours be done!" We know the wording of the first and second prayer, not the third. Notice:

> *"O My Father, if it is possible, let this cup pass Me . . ."*

> *"O My Father, if this cup cannot pass from Me . . ."*

There is progress in these two similar statements—from, "If it is possible . . ." to "If it is not possible . . ." The answer from heaven from the Father is, "It is not possible." The final statement is seen a little later when obedience acts.

> *So Jesus said to Peter, "Put your sword into the sheath. Shall I not drink the cup which My Father has given Me?" (John 18:11)*

Fully God, yet perfectly Man, Jesus learned obedience to do the will of God in the same way His followers learn trust and obedience. That is why the passage quoted from Hebrews 5 is prefaced by the following:

> *For we do not have a High Priest who cannot sympathize with our weaknesses, but was in all points tempted as we are, yet without sin. (Hebrews 4:15)*

We, like Jesus, learn obedience to do the will of God.

81

The Betrayal by Judas, and the Arrest of Jesus

Matthew 26:47-56; Mark 14:43-52; Luke 22:47-54; John 18:2-12

And Judas, who betrayed Him, also knew the place; for Jesus often met there with His disciples. Then Judas, having received a detachment of troops, and officers from the chief priests and Pharisees, came there with lanterns, torches, and weapons. Jesus therefore, knowing all things that would come upon Him, went forward and said to them, "Whom are you seeking?" They answered Him, "Jesus of Nazareth." Jesus said to them, "I am He." And Judas, who betrayed Him, also stood with them. Now when He said to them, "I am He," they drew back and fell to the ground. Then He asked them again, "Whom are you seeking?" And they said, "Jesus of Nazareth." Jesus answered, "I have told you that I am He. Therefore, if you seek Me, let these go their way," that the saying might be fulfilled which He spoke, "Of those whom You gave Me I have lost none." Then Simon Peter, having a sword, drew it and struck the high priest's servant, and cut off his right ear. The servant's name was Malchus. So Jesus said to Peter, "Put your sword into the sheath. Shall I not drink the cup which My Father has given Me?" Then the detachment of troops and the captain and the officers of the Jews arrested Jesus and bound Him. (John 18:2-12)

The plot between Judas and the chief priests made on Wednesday is about to be carried out. Having just returned to the company of His disciples, Jesus must have heard the betrayal crowd coming. In controlled tones He arouses the sleeping disciples.

Then He came to His disciples and said to them, "Are you still sleeping and resting? Behold, the hour is at hand, and the Son of Man is being betrayed into the hands of sinners. Rise, let us be going. See, My betrayer is at hand." (Matthew 26:45-46)

The hour is at hand!

It is late Thursday night, probably after midnight. The darkness of the garden of Gethsemane is dispelled by the torches of the coming gang: Roman soldiers, Jewish temple police, and a great crowd with swords and clubs, all sent by the chief priests and elders of the people. And leading the crowd is one of the Twelve, the treasurer, Judas! The plot thickens. Jesus steps out of the shadows of the garden. Notice His composure, having been in communion with His Father in intense prayer—having learned obedience.

> *Jesus therefore, knowing all things that would come upon Him, went forward and said to them, "Whom are you seeking?" (John 18:4)*

"Whom are you seeking?" Judas was with the crowd, the leader of the group. The crowd responded to the Lord's question: "Jesus of Nazareth." A simple, short statement comes from the lips of Jesus: "I am He!" And they all step back and fall to the ground. Perhaps a mini-burst of transfiguration glory? They all bow in the presence of the God-Man, but in an act of grace He repeats the question and Judas steps forward to betray Him. He betrays Him with a kiss. Hear the hurt of Jesus in His question:

> *"Friend, why have you come? Judas, are you betraying the Son of Man with a kiss?" (Matthew 26:50; Luke 22:48)*

And they seize Jesus!

Now the fishermen become warriors. "Lord, shall we strike with the sword?" Where did the swords come from? It was their interpretation of the Lord's instruction earlier that day:

> *And He said to them, "When I sent you without money bag, knapsack, and sandals, did you lack anything?" So they said, "Nothing." Then He said to them, "But now, he who has a money bag, let him take it, and likewise a knapsack; and he who has no sword, let him sell his garment and buy one. "For I say to you that this which is written must still be accomplished in Me: 'And He was numbered with the transgressors.' For the things concerning Me have an end." So they said, "Lord, look, here are two swords." And He said to them, "It is enough." (Luke 22:35-38)*

He was telling them that they would no longer be viewed as representing a king who was offering a kingdom; instead, they would be identified with an outlaw, a transgressor. The scepter would be replaced by a sword, the symbol of an outlaw. They had produced two swords and Jesus had said, "That's enough." They had missed the symbolism and taken His words literally.

Peter now takes the literal sword and swings into action. A fisherman with a sword is a dangerous person, as the high priest's servant Malchus soon finds out: with one swipe of his sword, Peter cuts off the man's right ear. And with one word of rebuke Jesus quells the violence and then restores the ear to Malchus.

But Jesus said to him, "Put your sword in its place, for all who take the sword will perish by the sword. Or do you think that I cannot now pray to My Father, and He will provide Me with more than twelve legions of angels?" . . . And He touched his ear and healed him. (Matthew 26:52-54; Luke 22:51)

It is at this point that Jesus displays the serenity of obedience to the Father's will.

"Shall I not drink the cup which My Father has given Me?" (John 18:11)

Jesus then begins an inquiry of His accusers.

Then Jesus said to the chief priests, captains of the temple, and the elders who had come to Him, "Have you come out, as against a robber, with swords and clubs? When I was with you daily in the temple, you did not try to seize Me. But this is your hour, and the power of darkness." (Luke 22:52-53)

This was a good question. Why hadn't they arrested Him in the temple? Answer: The people would not have allowed it. The chief priests said that earlier.

And the chief priests and the scribes sought how they might take Him by trickery and put Him to death. But they said, "Not during the feast, lest there be an uproar of the people." (Mark 14:1-2)

Trickery! Betrayal by Judas, the treasurer of the disciples, in the darkness of night, then three quick trials before the Jewish authorities by early Friday morning—that is trickery! Illegal trickery! And the supporting multitudes of the triumphal entry would now join in the opposition to Jesus, thinking they had been defrauded.

A footnote is added by Mark in his gospel.

Then they all forsook Him and fled. Now a certain young man followed Him, having a linen cloth thrown around his naked body. And the young men laid hold of him, and he left the linen cloth and fled from them naked. (Mark 14:50-52)

They all fled—all the disciples fled. Some did not go very far: young Mark returned home, naked; John was allowed into the courtyard of the high priest as an observer; Peter followed at a distance and was caught out; and Judas lurked in the shadows to see if his plot would work out as imagined.

82

Three Jewish Trials for Jesus, and Three Trials for Peter

**Matthew 26:57-75; Mark 14:53-72;
Luke 22:54-71; John 18:13-27**

*And they led Him away to Annas first, for he was the father-in-law
of Caiaphas who was high priest that year. Now it was Caiaphas
who advised the Jews that it was expedient that one man should die
for the people. And Simon Peter followed Jesus, and so did another
disciple. Now that disciple was known to the high priest, and went
with Jesus into the courtyard of the high priest. But Peter stood at
the door outside. Then the other disciple, who was known to the high
priest, went out and spoke to her who kept the door, and brought
Peter in. Then the servant girl who kept the door said to Peter, "You
are not also one of this Man's disciples, are you?" He said, "I am
not." Now the servants and officers who had made a fire of coals
stood there, for it was cold, and they warmed themselves. And Peter
stood with them and warmed himself. The high priest then asked
Jesus about His disciples and His doctrine. Jesus answered him,
"I spoke openly to the world. I always taught in synagogues and in
the temple, where the Jews always meet, and in secret I have said
nothing. Why do you ask Me? Ask those who have heard Me what I
said to them. Indeed they know what I said." And when He had said
these things, one of the officers who stood by struck Jesus with the
palm of his hand, saying, "Do You answer the high priest like that?"
Jesus answered him, "If I have spoken evil, bear witness of the evil;
but if well, why do you strike Me?" Then Annas sent Him bound to
Caiaphas the high priest. (John 18:13-24)*

*And the high priest stood up in the midst and asked Jesus, saying,
"Do You answer nothing? What is it these men testify against You?"
But He kept silent and answered nothing. Again the high priest asked
Him, saying to Him, "Are You the Christ, the Son of the Blessed?"
Jesus said, "I am. And you will see the Son of Man sitting at the right
hand of the Power, and coming with the clouds of heaven." Then the
high priest tore his clothes and said, "What further need do we have
of witnesses? You have heard the blasphemy! What do you think?"*

And they all condemned Him to be deserving of death. . . . Then he [Peter] began to curse and swear, "I do not know this Man of whom you speak!" A second time the rooster crowed. Then Peter called to mind the word that Jesus had said to him, "Before the rooster crows twice, you will deny Me three times." And when he thought about it, he wept. (Mark 14:60-64, 71-72)

As soon as it was day, the elders of the people, both chief priests and scribes, came together and led Him into their council, saying, "If You are the Christ, tell us." But He said to them, "If I tell you, you will by no means believe. And if I also ask you, you will by no means answer Me or let Me go. Hereafter the Son of Man will sit on the right hand of the power of God." Then they all said, "Are You then the Son of God?" So He said to them, "You rightly say that I am." And they said, "What further testimony do we need? For we have heard it ourselves from His own mouth." (Luke 22:66-71)

Two storylines intertwine in the early, dark hours of Good Friday—the three Jewish trials of Jesus and the personal trials of Peter as he observes at a distance.

The First Jewish Trial of Jesus. The temple police deliver their bound prisoner to the house of the high priest where his father-in-law Annas presided. He is going to preside over the first, preliminary pre-sunrise trial—an illegal one. The chief priests, elders, and scribes have assembled.

Peter's First Personal Trial. Peter, in the other storyline, is watching. Thanks to the connections of the apostle John, he is invited to a closer setting, where he is identified.

And Simon Peter followed Jesus, and so did another disciple. Now that disciple was known to the high priest, and went with Jesus into the courtyard of the high priest. But Peter stood at the door outside. Then the other disciple, who was known to the high priest, went out and spoke to her who kept the door, and brought Peter in. Then the servant girl who kept the door said to Peter, "You are not also one of this Man's disciples, are you?" He said, "I am not." Now the servants and officers who had made a fire of coals stood there, for it was cold, and they warmed themselves. And Peter stood with them and warmed himself. (John 18:15-18)

Peter fails his first personal trial—he denies that he is a disciple of Jesus in the face of the inquiry of a servant girl—"I am not." And he takes a seat by the fire to warm himself.

The preliminary trial of Jesus before Annas was brief, and involved questions from the high priest about the teachings of Jesus and His disciples. The Lord's response is direct and precise.

> *Jesus answered him, "I spoke openly to the world. I always taught in synagogues and in the temple, where the Jews always meet, and in secret I have said nothing. Why do you ask Me? Ask those who have heard Me what I said to them. Indeed they know what I said." (John 18:20-21)*

In response to this honest answer an officer of the high priest slaps Jesus in the face. "Is that how you answer the high priest?" Jesus responds,

> *"If I have spoken evil, bear witness of the evil; but if well, why do you strike Me?" (John 18:23)*

Thus ends the first Jewish trial.

The Second Jewish Trial of Jesus. The Sanhedrin, the whole council, had gathered by now. Perhaps two were absent (we'll meet them later). The sun had not yet risen—it was another illegal trial. False witnesses were gathered and made accusations—all false.

> *"We heard Him say, 'I will destroy this temple made with hands, and within three days I will build another made without hands.'" (Mark 14:58)*

Jesus does not respond to the false charge. Caiaphas then puts Jesus under oath.

> *"I put You under oath by the living God: Tell us if You are the Christ, the Son of God!" Jesus said to him, "It is as you said. Nevertheless, I say to you, hereafter you will see the Son of Man sitting at the right hand of the Power, and coming on the clouds of heaven." (Matthew 26:63-64)*

The Sanhedrin's verdict: guilty, deserving of the death sentence.

> *Then the high priest tore his clothes, saying, "He has spoken blasphemy! What further need do we have of witnesses? Look, now you have heard His blasphemy! What do you think?" They answered and said, "He is deserving of death." (Matthew 26:65-66)*

Peter's Second and Third Personal Trials. Another servant girl identifies Peter sitting by the light of the fire. And he again denies his association with Jesus. An hour later he is identified for the third time by his Galilean accent and by a relative of Malchus. Ouch! And Peter fails.

Then he began to curse and swear, "I do not know this Man of whom you speak!" The rooster crowed. Then Peter called to mind the word that Jesus had said to him, "Before the rooster crows twice, you will deny Me three times." And when he thought about it, he wept. (Mark 14:71-72)

The Third Jewish Trial. Finally morning comes! "As soon as it was day . . ." A quick restatement of the previous trial is made, this time legally. And the Jewish trials end.

"If You are the Christ, tell us." But He said to them, "If I tell you, you will by no means believe. And if I also ask you, you will by no means answer Me or let Me go. Hereafter the Son of Man will sit on the right hand of the power of God." Then they all said, "Are You then the Son of God?" So He said to them, "You rightly say that I am." And they said, "What further testimony do we need? For we have heard it ourselves from His own mouth." (Luke 22:67-71)

Peter fails three times, but Jesus never fails. The Jewish Sanhedrin had manipulated the legal system to their end. The three Roman trials remain. It is still early in the morning on Friday—enough time to hold three Roman trials by 9 a.m. The "hour" is but a short time away.

83

The Three Roman Trials of Jesus

Matthew 27:1-31; Mark 15:1-20; Luke 23:1-25; John 18:28-19:16

Then Judas, His betrayer, seeing that He had been condemned, was remorseful and brought back the thirty pieces of silver to the chief priests and elders, saying, "I have sinned by betraying innocent blood." And they said, "What is that to us? You see to it!" Then he threw down the pieces of silver in the temple and departed, and went and hanged himself. (Matthew 27:3-5)

Then the whole multitude of them arose and led Him to Pilate. And they began to accuse Him, saying, "We found this fellow perverting the nation, and forbidding to pay taxes to Caesar, saying that He Himself is Christ, a King." Then Pilate asked Him, saying, "Are You the King of the Jews?" He answered him and said, "It is as you say." (Luke 23:1-3)

Jesus answered, "My kingdom is not of this world. If My kingdom were of this world, My servants would fight, so that I should not be delivered to the Jews; but now My kingdom is not from here." Pilate therefore said to Him, "Are You a king then?" Jesus answered, "You say rightly that I am a king. For this cause I was born, and for this cause I have come into the world, that I should bear witness to the truth. Everyone who is of the truth hears My voice." Pilate said to Him, "What is truth?" And when he had said this, he went out again to the Jews, and said to them, "I find no fault in Him at all." (John 18:36-38)

And as soon as he knew that He belonged to Herod's jurisdiction, he sent Him to Herod, who was also in Jerusalem at that time. Now when Herod saw Jesus, he was exceedingly glad; for he had desired for a long time to see Him, because he had heard many things about Him, and he hoped to see some miracle done by Him. Then he questioned Him with many words, but He answered him nothing. And the chief priests and scribes stood and vehemently accused Him. (Luke 23:7-10)

So then Pilate took Jesus and scourged Him. And the soldiers twisted a crown of thorns and put it on His head, and they put on Him a purple robe. Then they said, "Hail, King of the Jews!" And they struck Him with their hands. Pilate then went out again, and said to them, "Behold, I am bringing Him out to you, that you may know that I find no fault in Him." Then Jesus came out, wearing the crown of thorns and the purple robe. And Pilate said to them, "Behold the Man!" Therefore, when the chief priests and officers saw Him, they cried out, saying, "Crucify Him, crucify Him!" Pilate said to them, "You take Him and crucify Him, for I find no fault in Him." . . . and he went again into the Praetorium, and said to Jesus, "Where are You from?" But Jesus gave him no answer. Then Pilate said to Him, "Are You not speaking to me? Do You not know that I have power to crucify You, and power to release You?" Jesus answered, "You could have no power at all against Me unless it had been given you from above. Therefore the one who delivered Me to you has the greater sin." . . . When Pilate therefore heard that saying, he brought Jesus out and sat down in the judgment seat in a place that is called The Pavement, but in Hebrew, Gabbatha. . . . But they cried out, "Away with Him, away with Him! Crucify Him!" Pilate said to them, "Shall I crucify your King?" The chief priests answered, "We have no king but Caesar!" (John 19:1-6, 9-11, 13, 15)

But they were insistent, demanding with loud voices that He be crucified. And the voices of these men and of the chief priests prevailed. So Pilate gave sentence that it should be as they requested. (Luke 23:23-24)

With the condemnation of Jesus by the Sanhedrin, Judas the betrayer commits suicide.

The First Roman Trial. The Sanhedrin delivers Jesus to Pilate, the Roman governor, for trial. To maintain their ceremonial holiness they could not enter the Praetorium.

Then they led Jesus from Caiaphas to the Praetorium, and it was early morning. But they themselves did not go into the Praetorium, lest they should be defiled, but that they might eat the Passover. (John 18:28)

Illegal trials, false witnesses, and ceremonial holiness. Strange juxtaposition! They bring charges, though not the charges from the Jewish trials.

And they began to accuse Him, saying, "We found this fellow perverting the nation, and forbidding to pay taxes to Caesar, saying that He Himself is Christ, a King." (Luke 23:2)

The first and second charges are clearly untrue. The third charge, that He is "Christ, a King" is true, and this is the charge that Pilate pursues.

Then Pilate entered the Praetorium again, called Jesus, and said to Him, "Are You the King of the Jews?" (John 18:33)

Jesus gives a convincing answer and Pilate declares Him innocent.

Jesus answered, "My kingdom is not of this world. If My kingdom were of this world, My servants would fight, so that I should not be delivered to the Jews; but now My kingdom is not from here." Pilate therefore said to Him, "Are You a king then?" Jesus answered, "You say rightly that I am a king. For this cause I was born, and for this cause I have come into the world, that I should bear witness to the truth. Everyone who is of the truth hears My voice." Pilate said to Him, "What is truth?" And when he had said this, he went out again to the Jews, and said to them, "I find no fault in Him at all." (John 18:36-38)

The Second Roman Trial. When Pilate hears that Jesus was a Galilean he opts for involving Herod Antipas, who was in Jerusalem at the time. So the second Roman trial of Jesus takes place before Herod. Even after extensive questioning, Jesus refuses to respond to him. Silent righteousness! So Herod returns Jesus to Pilate for the final trial.

The Third Roman Trial. Pilate tries his best to have Jesus released. He brings Jesus before the priests, the rulers, and the people, and again declares Him innocent.

Then Pilate, when he had called together the chief priests, the rulers, and the people, said to them, "You have brought this Man to me, as one who misleads the people. And indeed, having examined Him in your presence, I have found no fault in this Man concerning those things of which you accuse Him; no, neither did Herod, for I sent you back to him; and indeed nothing deserving of death has been done by Him. I will therefore chastise Him and release Him." (Luke 23:13-16)

He proposes an alternative: releasing Jesus instead of Barabbas. After the Jews decisively reject Jesus, he washes his hands of the whole legal process. He scourges an innocent man hoping that the Jews would be satisfied with a little blood. But they are not.

Then Pilate said to Him, "Are You not speaking to me? Do You not know that I have power to crucify You, and power to release You?" Jesus answered, "You could have no power at all against Me unless it had been given you from above. Therefore the one who delivered Me to you has the greater sin." (John 19:10-11)

Pilate is frightened by the Lord's claim of power so he seeks to release Him. But the Jews have saved their strongest argument till the end.

"If you let this Man go, you are not Caesar's friend. Whoever makes himself a king speaks against Caesar." . . . "Let Him be crucified." (John 19:12; Matthew 27:23)

Pilate gives in.

When Pilate saw that he could not prevail at all, but rather that a tumult was rising, he took water and washed his hands before the multitude, saying, "I am innocent of the blood of this just Person. You see to it." . . . And all the people answered and said, "His blood be on us and on our children." But they were insistent, demanding with loud voices that He be crucified. And the voices of these men and of the chief priests prevailed. So Pilate gave sentence that it should be as they requested. (Matthew 27:24-25; Luke 23:23-24)

The hour has arrived.

"For truly against Your holy Servant Jesus, whom You anointed, both Herod and Pontius Pilate, with the Gentiles and the people of Israel, were gathered together to do whatever Your hand and Your purpose determined before to be done." (Acts 4:27-28)

84

Good Friday: The Crucifixion of Jesus—It Is Finished!

Matthew 27:31-56; Mark 15:20-41;
Luke 23:26-49; John 19:17-30

And when they had mocked Him, they took the robe off Him, put His own clothes on Him, and led Him away to be crucified. Now as they came out, they found a man of Cyrene, Simon by name. Him they compelled to bear His cross. And when they had come to a place called Golgotha, that is to say, Place of a Skull. . . . There they crucified Him, and two others with Him, one on either side, and Jesus in the center. (Matthew 27:31-33; John 19:18)

Then Jesus said, "Father, forgive them, for they do not know what they do." . . . Then one of the criminals who were hanged blasphemed Him, saying, "If You are the Christ, save Yourself and us." . . . Then [the other] said to Jesus, "Lord, remember me when You come into Your kingdom." And Jesus said to him, "Assuredly, I say to you, today you will be with Me in Paradise." (Luke 23:34, 39, 42-43)

When Jesus therefore saw His mother, and the disciple whom He loved standing by, He said to His mother, "Woman, behold your son!" Then He said to the disciple, "Behold your mother!" And from that hour that disciple took her to his own home. (John 19:26-27)

And about the ninth hour Jesus cried out with a loud voice, saying, "Eli, Eli, lama sabachthani?" that is, "My God, My God, why have You forsaken Me?" (Matthew 27:46)

After this, Jesus, knowing that all things were now accomplished, that the Scripture might be fulfilled, said, "I thirst!" . . . So when Jesus had received the sour wine, He said, "It is finished!" And bowing His head, He gave up His spirit. (John 19:28, 30)

And when Jesus had cried out with a loud voice, He said, "Father, 'into Your hands I commit My spirit.'" Having said this, He breathed His last. (Luke 23:46)

T he hour has come, the hour decreed from eternity past in the eternal councils of the Godhead.

> *. . . How much more shall the blood of <u>Christ</u>, who through the eternal <u>Spirit</u> offered Himself without spot to <u>God</u>, cleanse your conscience from dead works to serve the living God? (Hebrews 9:14)*

The entire Trinity is active in providing salvation for fallen man at this solemn hour of time.

The sufferings of Christ are beyond human comprehension.

> *And without controversy great is the mystery of godliness: God was manifested in the flesh. (1 Timothy 3:16)*

"Amazing love, how can it be, that Thou my God shouldst die for me?"

Christ suffered physically. From the arrest onward He suffered brutal harm—in the garden, in the Jewish trials, from the Roman platoon of soldiers, from the scourgings, from the crown of thorns—marred more than any man, according to Isaiah's prophecy. And then He was crucified—that severe form of execution devised by the powerful Roman empire but prophesied by a more powerful Ruler.

> *They pierced My hands and My feet. (Psalm 22:16)*

Without the shedding of blood there is no remission of sin.

> *Therefore, when He came into the world, He said: "Sacrifice and offering You did not desire, but a body You have prepared for Me." (Hebrews 10:5)*

> *Knowing that you were not redeemed with corruptible things, like silver or gold, but with the precious blood of Christ, as of a lamb without blemish and without spot. (1 Peter 1:18-19)*

The humanity of Christ and the shedding of blood were necessary components of our eternal salvation from the penalty of sin, and His "bearing our sins *in His own body* on the tree" was the means of forgiveness. Redemption necessitated the incarnation.

At noon it became dark. Jesus was being made sin for us. He was bearing our sins in His own body on the tree. He was paying for all the sins of all the world of sinners. He was viewed as guilty before God. He was satisfying the wrath and vengeance of a holy God against sin. He endured eternal punishment in three hours—the hour had come!

From the cross Jesus makes seven statements.

> ➤ ***Father, forgive them for they do not know what they do.*** This is a statement of redemption. Forgiveness can only take place when the price has been paid. We have redemption through Christ, the forgiveness of sins. Redemption!

> ➤ ***Today you will be with Me in paradise.*** What an incredible journey for the repentant thief. From a jail cell, to a cross, to paradise—in the same day. What an incredible journey, from being an enemy of God to being a child of God. What a change. God was in Christ reconciling us to Himself (2 Corinthians 5:19). Reconciliation!

> ➤ ***Woman, behold your son. Son, behold your mother.*** Jesus makes provision for His mother with His trusted disciple, not with His yet unbelieving half-brothers. The spiritual family is closer than the natural family, and more to be trusted!

> ➤ ***My God, My God, why have You forsaken Me?*** Jesus takes up the plaintive lament of Psalm 22. But God is holy, and Jesus is bearing the sins of the world. He is suffering the vengeance of God, the accumulated wrath of God upon all the sins of mankind. God's holy wrath against sin is satisfied. Propitiation!

> ➤ ***I thirst.*** The intense suffering would produce intense thirst. His tongue would cleave to the roof of His mouth—as prophesied.

> ➤ ***It is finished.*** The "hour" is over. Propitiation, reconciliation, redemption—the Finished Work of Christ. The glory of the cross. A final burst of victory!

> ➤ ***Father, into Your hands I commit My spirit.*** Having finished His work He addresses His Father in these final words of trust and breathes His last—for three days!

"I have glorified You on the earth. I have finished the work which You have given Me to do." (John 17:4)

85

Joseph of Arimathea and Nicodemus

Matthew 25:57-60; Mark 15:42-46;
Luke 23:50-54; John 19:38-42

After this, Joseph of Arimathea, being a disciple of Jesus, but secretly, for fear of the Jews, asked Pilate that he might take away the body of Jesus; and Pilate gave him permission. So he came and took the body of Jesus. And Nicodemus, who at first came to Jesus by night, also came, bringing a mixture of myrrh and aloes, about a hundred pounds. Then they took the body of Jesus, and bound it in strips of linen with the spices, as the custom of the Jews is to bury. Now in the place where He was crucified there was a garden, and in the garden a new tomb in which no one had yet been laid. So there they laid Jesus, because of the Jews' Preparation Day, for the tomb was nearby. (John 19:38-42)

It must have been a strange meeting of two members of the Sanhedrin at the foot of the cross. They were secret believers, but for fear of the Jews they stayed in the shadows of faith. Now, however, as evening comes, they take courage and step out of the shadows.

Nicodemus probably had come to faith before Joseph, at that significant meeting with Jesus (recorded in John 3) at the beginning of His public ministry just after He cleansed the temple the first time.

That discussion must have come to mind when he stood with Joseph on Calvary.

> *"And as Moses lifted up the serpent in the wilderness, even so must the Son of Man be lifted up, that whoever believes in Him should not perish but have eternal life. For God so loved the world that He gave His only begotten Son, that whoever believes in Him should not perish but have everlasting life." (John 3:14-16)*

Surely he now fully understood the typology of the wilderness experience of Moses and the serpent of brass as he and Joseph removed the lifeless body of Jesus, the Son of Man, who had been lifted up on a cross. Look and live!

During the Judean ministry of Jesus it seems that Nicodemus came into contact with Jesus again. The Sanhedrin had been seeking to arrest Jesus, and the temple police returned without a prisoner.

> *Then the officers came to the chief priests and Pharisees, who said to them, "Why have you not brought Him?" The officers answered, "No man ever spoke like this Man!" Then the Pharisees answered them, "Are you also deceived? Have any of the rulers or the Pharisees believed in Him? But this crowd that does not know the law is accursed." Nicodemus (he who came to Jesus by night, being one of them) said to them, "Does our law judge a man before it hears him and knows what he is doing?" They answered and said to him, "Are you also from Galilee? Search and look, for no prophet has arisen out of Galilee." (John 7:45-52)*

Without doubt Nicodemus tried to respond positively to the question raised, "Have any of the rulers or the Pharisees believed in Him?" But he lacked courage—he was a secret disciple. So he responded with a legal technicality. Even for this he was rebuked by the Sanhedrin.

Now he joins with Joseph, the other secret follower of Jesus, and they become two disciples willing to confess their allegiance to Christ Jesus openly. The apostles, meanwhile, are still scattered.

Who is this Joseph? We know only this single public event in his life, but we know a little about him.

> *Now behold, there was a man named Joseph, a council member, a good and just man. He had not consented to their decision and deed. He was from Arimathea, a city of the Jews, who himself was also waiting for the kingdom of God. (Luke 23:50-51)*

We also know that he was a rich man, that he had a large tomb, hewn out of rock, no doubt for him and his family.

Joseph initiates the contact with Pilate to remove Jesus' body and provide for a proper burial. Permission is granted, and Joseph and Nicodemus meet at the foot of the cross. Joseph had a linen shroud for wrapping the body. Nicodemus had a generous weight of spices, myrrh, and aloes for anointing the body. Did the two men cooperate to provide the necessities for burial? Perhaps. But remember, they were secret disciples. I wonder if Joseph knew he was fulfilling a prophecy of Isaiah? Probably not!

> *They made his grave with the wicked and his tomb with the rich, although he had done no violence, and there was no deceit in his mouth. (Isaiah 53:9)*

The secret disciples do what the public disciples do not. They remove the body with care, wash and anoint it, wrap it with the linen shroud, provide a separate headpiece, and carry the body to the tomb. Then the large disc-like stone is rolled into place securing the body safely in the tomb. The Romans would seal the tomb and provide a guard, soon to be overcome by angelic power!

The next meeting of the Sanhedrin must have been interesting. The Sanhedrin by that time would have bribed the Roman guards with the "stolen body" hoax. The news of the two new disciples, Joseph and Nicodemus, would be common knowledge to them. Their world of intrigue was coming undone. Truth will set you free, but lies entangle!

Nicodemus and Joseph were not anticipating the resurrection of Christ any more than the rest of the disciples. In a few days they would all understand and believe, but not yet. What then was the purpose of "going public" at this late date? If it was all over, why make a public gesture that would exclude them from the synagogue, the Sanhedrin, and Jewish society? Because it was the righteous thing to do, and the resurrection would confirm that. The truth will set you free.

The secret life of Nicodemus and Joseph is an encouragement to any who have been secret disciples. And at one time or another, all disciples of Jesus have been secret ones. Yes, it is possible to be both a secret disciple and a true follower of Jesus Christ.

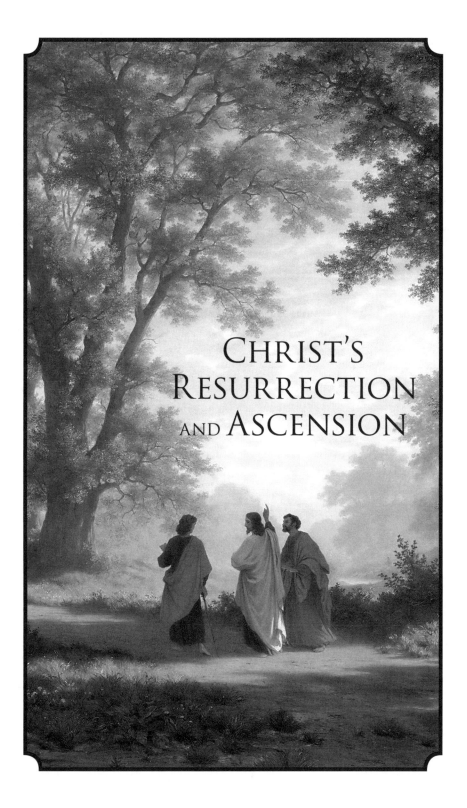

CHRIST'S
RESURRECTION
AND ASCENSION

86

The First Witnesses
of the Empty Tomb

Matthew 28:1-10; Luke 24:1-8; Mark 16:1-9; John 20:1-18

---

*Now on the first day of the week Mary Magdalene went to the tomb
early, while it was still dark, and saw that the stone had been taken
away from the tomb. Then she ran and came to Simon Peter, and to
the other disciple, whom Jesus loved, and said to them, "They have
taken away the Lord out of the tomb, and we do not know where they
have laid Him." Peter therefore went out, and the other disciple,
and were going to the tomb. So they both ran together, and the other
disciple outran Peter and came to the tomb first. And he, stooping
down and looking in, saw the linen cloths lying there; yet he did not
go in. Then Simon Peter came, following him, and went into the tomb;
and he saw the linen cloths lying there, and the handkerchief that
had been around His head, not lying with the linen cloths, but folded
together in a place by itself. Then the other disciple, who came to the
tomb first, went in also; and he saw and believed. For as yet they did
not know the Scripture, that He must rise again from the dead. Then
the disciples went away again to their own homes. But Mary stood
outside by the tomb weeping, and as she wept she stooped down and
looked into the tomb. And she saw two angels in white sitting, one at
the head and the other at the feet, where the body of Jesus had lain.
Then they said to her, "Woman, why are you weeping?" She said to
them, "Because they have taken away my Lord, and I do not know
where they have laid Him." Now when she had said this, she turned
around and saw Jesus standing there, and did not know that it was
Jesus. Jesus said to her, "Woman, why are you weeping? Whom are
you seeking?" She, supposing Him to be the gardener, said to Him,
"Sir, if You have carried Him away, tell me where You have laid
Him, and I will take Him away." Jesus said to her, "Mary!" She
turned and said to Him, "Rabboni!" (which is to say, Teacher). Jesus
said to her, "Do not cling to Me, for I have not yet ascended to My
Father; but go to My brethren and say to them, 'I am ascending to
My Father and your Father, and to My God and your God.'" Mary
Magdalene came and told the disciples that she had seen the Lord,
and that He had spoken these things to her. (John 20:1-18)*

And as they went to tell His disciples, behold, Jesus met them, saying, "Rejoice!" So they came and held Him by the feet and worshiped Him. Then Jesus said to them, "Do not be afraid. Go and tell My brethren to go to Galilee, and there they will see Me." (Matthew 28:9-10)

The body of Jesus had been laid to rest by Joseph and Nicodemus. It was to be a short-lived rest! But the followers of Jesus were not at rest. Some were concerned about a proper burial. Some were returning home in discouragement. Most of the apostles were hiding in fear of the Jews. Soon all this would change.

The ladies were the ones concerned about a proper burial. They had witnessed the crucifixion.

And many women who followed Jesus from Galilee, ministering to Him, were there looking on from afar, among whom were Mary Magdalene, Mary the mother of James and Joses, and the mother of Zebedee's sons. (Matthew 27:55-56)

And now they desire to honor Jesus by anointing His body with spices, in line with Jewish custom. Having taken note where Joseph and Nicodemus laid Jesus' body, Mary Magdalene and Mary purchase the necessary spices to take to the tomb at dawn on the first day of the week, Sunday. As they make their way there they discuss the problem of the large stone covering the entrance to the tomb. "Who will roll away the stone for us from the door of the tomb?"

From a distance, Mary sees that the stone has already been rolled away. She makes an immediate assumption and runs to tell Peter and John.

Then she ran and came to Simon Peter, and to the other disciple, whom Jesus loved, and said to them, "They have taken away the Lord out of the tomb, and we do not know where they have laid Him." Peter therefore went out, and the other disciple, and were going to the tomb. (John 20:2-3)

The other ladies continue on to the tomb and are greeted by the angel. But that, later.

Mary has run to Peter and John, and now Peter and John run to the tomb, to be followed by Mary later. John records that he arrived first but did not go into the tomb. Peter, in Peter-like action, rushes past John and enters the tomb to be joined by a timid Son of Thunder. And, wonder of wonders, the tomb is empty; the grave clothes of Jesus are neatly arranged, with the napkin for His head rolled up in a separate place. If the glorified body of Jesus could pass through doors (as we shall see), the newly resurrected body would have no difficulty in passing through the linen shroud that enwrapped Him. And Jesus, upon arising from death, made His bed! Unlike Lazarus He needed no one to unwrap Him and set Him free! "Then the disciples went back to their home." Later, we will meet the ten apostles as they huddle together in a locked room in fear of the Jews, perhaps the same Upper Room used for the final Passover.

But back to Mary. Peter and John have left and Mary Magdalene now returns to the tomb, where she sees two angels in white, one sitting at the head and the other at the feet where Jesus had lain. Unlike most angelic encounters, which produce initial fear, Mary responds in a coherent way to their questions. Perhaps the fact that she had not noticed that the angels were angels would explain her non-recognition of Jesus.

> *Then they said to her, "Woman, why are you weeping?" She said to them, "Because they have taken away my Lord, and I do not know where they have laid Him." (John 20:13)*

She turns and sees Jesus standing there, and yet she doesn't "see" Him. Her eyes are clouded with tears. Both the angels and the resurrected Jesus ask, "Woman, why are you weeping?"

Jesus advances the questions of the angels by adding, "Whom do you seek?" Again, Mary makes an incorrect assumption. She concludes that the man speaking to her is the cemetery gardener, and that he has relocated the precious body of Jesus.

Mary hears her name! The resurrected Jesus speaks to her in that same tone of voice familiar to her on the other side of the cross. No longer a strange voice of a supposed gardener, but the familiar voice of the Savior; of the One who had cast out seven demons; of the One she and the other ladies had supported during His public ministry.

> *Now it came to pass, afterward, that He went through every city and village, preaching and bringing the glad tidings of the kingdom of God. And the twelve were with Him and certain women who had been healed of evil spirits and infirmities-Mary called Magdalene, out of whom had come seven demons, and Joanna the wife of Chuza, Herod's steward, and Susanna, and many others who provided for Him from their substance. (Luke 8:1-3)*

These are the ladies of first appearances, and Mary is the first of the firsts. "Mary!" Her response is immediate: "Teacher." And with that she takes hold of His feet as if to secure His presence. Jesus informs her of His ascension, His return to His Father and God.

> *And as they went to tell His disciples, behold, Jesus met them, saying, "Rejoice!" So they came and held Him by the feet and worshiped Him. Then Jesus said to them, "Do not be afraid. Go and tell My brethren to go to Galilee, and there they will see Me." (Matthew 28:9-10)*

These honored supporting ladies see the resurrected Lord first, and they report to the Eleven—and their message of great joy is rejected as an idle tale.

87

On the Road to Emmaus

Luke 24:13-33

Now behold, two of them were traveling that same day to a village called Emmaus, which was seven miles from Jerusalem. And they talked together of all these things which had happened. So it was, while they conversed and reasoned, that Jesus Himself drew near and went with them. But their eyes were restrained, so that they did not know Him. And He said to them, "What kind of conversation is this that you have with one another as you walk and are sad?" Then the one whose name was Cleopas answered and said to Him, "Are You the only stranger in Jerusalem, and have You not known the things which happened there in these days?" And He said to them, "What things?" So they said to Him, "The things concerning Jesus of Nazareth, who was a Prophet mighty in deed and word before God and all the people, and how the chief priests and our rulers delivered Him to be condemned to death, and crucified Him. But we were hoping that it was He who was going to redeem Israel. Indeed, besides all this, today is the third day since these things happened. Yes, and certain women of our company, who arrived at the tomb early, astonished us. When they did not find His body, they came saying that they had also seen a vision of angels who said He was alive. And certain of those who were with us went to the tomb and found it just as the women had said; but Him they did not see."

Then He said to them, "O foolish ones, and slow of heart to believe in all that the prophets have spoken! Ought not the Christ to have suffered these things and to enter into His glory?" And beginning at Moses and all the Prophets, He expounded to them in all the Scriptures the things concerning Himself. Then they drew near to the village where they were going, and He indicated that He would have gone farther. But they constrained Him, saying, "Abide with us, for it is toward evening, and the day is far spent." And He went in to stay with them. Now it came to pass, as He sat at the table with them, that He took bread, blessed and broke it, and gave it to them. Then their eyes were opened and they knew Him; and He vanished from their sight. And they said to one another, "Did not our heart burn within us while He talked with us on the road, and while He opened the Scriptures to us?" So they rose up that very hour and returned to Jerusalem, and found the eleven and those who were with them gathered together. (Luke 24:13-33)

An idle tale, this joyful story of the resurrection of Jesus! The emotional ladies were confused. And the result of the apostles' deliberation? They did not believe them! This official verdict of the apostles brought discouragement to the other disciples, and two of them decided to go home.

Home was a small town, seven miles from Jerusalem, Emmaus by name. It was not a long walk, a couple of hours under normal conditions. But this walk home was a long one, interrupted by questions and discussion about the death of Jesus. A slow pace for contemplation with intermittent stops of despair.

And Jesus Himself drew near to them. At their slow pace, they were easily overtaken by Jesus with His newly glorified body. Jesus joins the two disheartened disciples in their slow walk home. They could not recognize Jesus—a miracle of impaired vision prevented them at this time. Soon they would see!

And the conversation begins.

"What kind of conversation is this that you have with one another as you walk and are sad?" (Luke 24:17)

Jesus heard some of the conversation as He drew near to them, and their body language communicated sadness. The response of Cleopas is both reasonable and amazing in this setting.

"Are You the only stranger in Jerusalem, and have You not known the things which happened there in these days?" (Luke 24:18)

It is reasonable in that the crucifixion of Jesus had been the event which had dominated the life of Jerusalem that week! How could this man not know? But, it is also an amazing question. Jesus, above all people, knew what had happened. He knew it before it happened! Not only that, He was the principal participant! He was the only one in Jerusalem who really knew what had happened in the great event of the crucifixion. And yet, in supposed ignorance, He asks, "What things?"

The response of the disciples is accurate but understated.

"The things concerning Jesus of Nazareth, who was a Prophet mighty in deed and word before God and all the people, and how the chief priests and our rulers delivered Him to be condemned to death, and crucified Him. But we were hoping that it was He who was going

to redeem Israel. Indeed, besides all this, today is the third day since these things happened." (Luke 24:19-21)

The Son of God had become merely a great prophet. The Messiah had not redeemed Israel. With the death of Jesus, their hopes disappeared. And to add to this, the ladies had seen a vision of angels who related a strange message of resurrection—a message rejected by the apostles. A real appearance became a vision. No wonder there is discouragement. Reality is fading to doubt.

With a gentle rebuke Jesus begins to teach the two disciples. They should have understood the prophecies concerning the Messiah—that His glorification would follow His suffering, as Peter explains in his epistle:

> *Of this salvation the prophets have inquired and searched carefully, who prophesied of the grace that would come to you, searching what, or what manner of time, the Spirit of Christ who was in them was indicating when He testified beforehand the sufferings of Christ and the glories that would follow. To them it was revealed that, not to themselves, but to us they were ministering the things which now have been reported to you through those who have preached the gospel to you by the Holy Spirit sent from heaven. (1 Peter 1:10-12)*

The prophets who wrote on the other side of the cross could not understand, but the disciples on this side of the crucifixion should have understood. So for the rest of the walk home, Jesus taught from the Old Testament.

> *And beginning at Moses and all the Prophets, He expounded to them in all the Scriptures <u>the things concerning Himself</u>. (Luke 24:27)*

All of the prophecies concerning the Christ, all the typology of the tabernacle and sacrifices, all of the covenants made with Israel—these are "the things concerning Himself." Oh, that the walk home could be longer! But they came to the village of Emmaus. And Jesus pretended that He was going to go further.

Notice the communication approach of Jesus. First of all their eyes were kept from functioning normally, a slight miracle. Second, He feigned ignorance of the happenings in Jerusalem; and finally, He pretended that He was continuing the journey. Divine disguise and pretense is acceptable by the Master Teacher.

The Teacher was invited home for an additional time of teaching, a meal, and overnight lodging. As they were at the table, Jesus took the bread and blessed it and gave it to them. He had done this before in the feeding of the five thousand and of the four thousand. Specifically, He had done this in the Upper Room, and now the two Emmaus disciples were witnessing the Lord doing so in their own midst—the significance of the Breaking of Bread increases. Having recognized Him, He vanished out of their sight—a concluding miracle in the brief Emmaus experience.

The two Emmaus disciples immediately set out on a return trip to Jerusalem and to the apostles, even though it was "toward evening and the day was far spent." Perhaps some male credibility would cause the apostles to believe in the resurrection. We shall see.

88

Jesus Appears to the Ten and Then to the Eleven

John 20:19-31; Luke 24:33-43

Then, the same day at evening, being the first day of the week, when the doors were shut where the disciples were assembled, for fear of the Jews, Jesus came and stood in the midst, and said to them, "Peace be with you." When He had said this, He showed them His hands and His side. Then the disciples were glad when they saw the Lord. So Jesus said to them again, "Peace to you! As the Father has sent Me, I also send you." And when He had said this, He breathed on them, and said to them, "Receive the Holy Spirit. If you forgive the sins of any, they are forgiven them; if you retain the sins of any, they are retained." Now Thomas, called the Twin, one of the twelve, was not with them when Jesus came. The other disciples therefore said to him, "We have seen the Lord." So he said to them, "Unless I see in His hands the print of the nails, and put my finger into the print of the nails, and put my hand into His side, I will not believe. And after eight days His disciples were again inside, and Thomas with them. Jesus came, the doors being shut, and stood in the midst, and said, "Peace to you!" Then He said to Thomas, "Reach your finger here, and look at My hands; and reach your hand here, and put it into My side. Do not be unbelieving, but believing." And Thomas answered and said to Him, "My Lord and my God!" Jesus said to him, "Thomas, because you have seen Me, you have believed. Blessed are those who have not seen and yet have believed." And truly Jesus did many other signs in the presence of His disciples, which are not written in this book; but these are written that you may believe that Jesus is the Christ, the Son of God, and that believing you may have life in His name. (John 20:19-31)

At last, Jesus appears to His chosen disciples. Two were missing. Judas, the Son of Perdition, had gone as was determined. Better for him if he had never been born—so said Jesus. Thomas the Twin was absent, alone and doubting.

Thomas had a tendency to pessimism. Earlier, when Jesus was returning to Bethany to resurrect Lazarus, Thomas thought they were all going to die because of the previous hostility they had met in Judea, when the people had tried to stone the Lord.

Then Jesus said to them plainly, "Lazarus is dead. And I am glad for your sakes that I was not there, that you may believe. Nevertheless let us go to him." Then Thomas, who is called the Twin, said to his fellow disciples, "Let us also go, that we may die with Him." (John 11:14-16)

Jesus' purposes were not clear to Thomas in the Upper Room. It was Thomas who had asked the great question leading to the wonderful response of Jesus:

Thomas said to Him, "Lord, we do not know where You are going, and how can we know the way?" Jesus said to him, "I am the way, the truth, and the life. No one comes to the Father except through Me." (John 14:5-6)

Thomas doubted and questioned, and he was not there with the Ten.

But the Ten were there, and the two Emmaus Road disciples found them and others gathered together. They shared the amazing news and the events of the Emmaus Road experience.

So they rose up that very hour and returned to Jerusalem, and found the eleven [the group was known as the Eleven even though Thomas was absent] and those who were with them gathered together, saying, "The Lord is risen indeed." And they told about the things that had happened on the road and how He was known to them in the breaking of bread. (Luke 24:33-35)

In the process of sharing the good news, Jesus appeared in their midst. Remember, the doors were shut for fear of the Jews. The grave clothes, the stone on the door to the tomb, and now the closed door—no barriers to the resurrected Lord. He passed through the closed door and stood among them. Glorious resurrection!

They were barricaded for fear of the Jews, and now they were frightened by the unexpected presence of Jesus.

But they were terrified and frightened, and supposed they had seen a spirit. And He said to them, "Why are you troubled? And why do doubts arise in your hearts? Behold My hands and My feet, that it is I Myself. Handle Me and see, for a spirit does not have flesh and bones as you see I have." (Luke 24:37-39)

A frightening specter—that's what they thought initially. They were frightened, they wondered—and worse, they disbelieved. Even when He showed them His wounded hands and side they disbelieved. How to overcome this disbelief? Jesus requested some food, and He was given a piece of broiled fish. The resurrected Jesus ate a piece of fish. Now the disciples are glad because they have seen the risen Lord. The resurrection of Jesus Christ is as real as a piece of broiled fish! He would eat fish with them again, later.

In a preliminary commission and giving of the Holy Spirit Jesus ministers to His disciples and again vanishes.

> *So Jesus said to them again, "Peace to you! As the Father has sent Me, I also send you." And when He had said this, He breathed on them, and said to them, "Receive the Holy Spirit. If you forgive the sins of any, they are forgiven them; if you retain the sins of any, they are retained." (John 20:21-23)*

The ladies are rejoicing, they have seen the Lord! Thomas is still doubting, but that is about to change. Thomas makes a strong statement of doubt.

> *So he said to them, "Unless I see in His hands the print of the nails, and put my finger into the print of the nails, and put my hand into His side, I will not believe." (John 20:25)*

Doubt will turn to faith in eight days. Again the disciples were in the closed house, and Thomas was with them this time. Jesus passes through the door and again gives His greeting of peace. And then He quotes the statement that Thomas made eight days earlier, confronting him directly.

> *"Reach your finger here, and look at My hands; and reach your hand here, and put it into My side. Do not be unbelieving, but believing." (John 20:27)*

Thomas's doubt was strong. He, with the other disciples, did not believe the ladies initially. And he would not believe the newly believing Ten. "I will not believe." Truly, Thomas was *Doubting* Thomas. But Jesus confronts him with his own words, and Thomas believes. From the deep doubt of Thomas comes the clearest statement of the deity of Jesus Christ in the Scriptures:

> *And Thomas answered and said Him, "My Lord and my God!" (John 20:28)*

"My Lord and my God!" These great words of faith are addressed to Jesus, resurrected Jesus—fully God and fully Man.

And so it is written, "The first man Adam became a living being." The last Adam became a life-giving spirit. However, the spiritual is not first, but the natural, and afterward the spiritual. The first man was of the earth, made of dust; the second Man is the Lord from heaven. As was the man of dust, so also are those who are made of dust; and as is the heavenly Man, so also are those who are heavenly. And as we have borne the image of the man of dust, we shall also bear the image of the heavenly Man. (1 Corinthians 15:45-49)

Thomas saw and believed. Jesus commends those who believe without seeing. And the confession of Thomas, born out of doubt, has become a major text to demonstrate the deity of Christ—the stated purpose of the gospel of John. Even failure is used for the glory of God. Thank God for Thomas!

Now Jesus did many other signs in the presence of the disciples, which are not written in this book; but these are written that you may believe that Jesus is the Christ, the Son of God, and that believing you may have life in His name. (John 20:30-31)

89

Peter Goes Fishing and Is Restored by Jesus

John 21:1-23

After these things Jesus showed Himself again to the disciples at the Sea of Tiberias, and in this way He showed Himself: Simon Peter, Thomas called the Twin, Nathanael of Cana in Galilee, the sons of Zebedee, and two others of His disciples were together. Simon Peter said to them, "I am going fishing." They said to him, "We are going with you also." They went out and immediately got into the boat, and that night they caught nothing. But when the morning had now come, Jesus stood on the shore; yet the disciples did not know that it was Jesus. Then Jesus said to them, "Children, have you any food?" They answered Him, "No." And He said to them, "Cast the net on the right side of the boat, and you will find some." So they cast, and now they were not able to draw it in because of the multitude of fish. Therefore that disciple whom Jesus loved said to Peter, "It is the Lord!" Now when Simon Peter heard that it was the Lord, he put on his outer garment (for he had removed it), and plunged into the sea. But the other disciples came in the little boat (for they were not far from land, but about two hundred cubits), dragging the net with fish. Then, as soon as they had come to land, they saw a fire of coals there, and fish laid on it, and bread. Jesus said to them, "Bring some of the fish which you have just caught." Simon Peter went up and dragged the net to land, full of large fish, one hundred and fifty-three; and although there were so many, the net was not broken. Jesus said to them, "Come and eat breakfast." Yet none of the disciples dared ask Him, "Who are You?"—knowing that it was the Lord. Jesus then came and took the bread and gave it to them, and likewise the fish. This is now the third time Jesus showed Himself to His disciples after He was raised from the dead. So when they had eaten breakfast, Jesus said to Simon Peter, "Simon, son of Jonah, do you love Me more than these?" He said to Him, "Yes, Lord; You know that I love You." He said to him, "Feed My lambs." He said to him again a second time, "Simon, son of Jonah, do you love Me?" He said to Him, "Yes, Lord; You know that I love You." He said to him, "Tend My sheep." He said to him the third time, "Simon, son of Jonah, do you love Me?" Peter was grieved because He said to him the third time, "Do you love Me?" And he said to Him, "Lord, You know all things; You know that I love You." Jesus said to him, "Feed My sheep. Most assuredly, I say to you, when you were younger, you girded yourself and walked where you wished; but when you are old, you will stretch out your hands, and another will gird you and carry you where you do not wish." This He spoke, signifying by what death he would glorify God. And when He had spoken this, He said to him, "Follow Me." Then Peter, turning around, saw the disciple whom Jesus loved following, who also had leaned on His breast at the supper, and said, "Lord, who is the one who betrays You?" Peter, seeing him, said to Jesus, "But Lord, what about this man?" Jesus said to him, "If I will that he remain till I come, what is that to you? You follow Me." Then this saying went out among the brethren that this disciple would not die. Yet Jesus did not say to him that he would not die, but, "If I will that he remain till I come, what is that to you?" (John 21:1-23)

This appearance of Jesus was for Peter. It is a lesson in restoration to fellowship and service for a failing apostle and for all who fail. Seven out of the eleven disciples were present for this post-resurrection appearance of Jesus. But Peter is the object of the story. Peter decided to "go fishing," and the rest joined him in the night fishing venture. Remember, the sons of Zebedee—John and James—were professional fisherman, but they caught nothing that night.

An unknown person standing on the beach in the dim light of dawn calls across the water, "Children, have you any fish?" He then counsels the men to cast the net on the right side of the boat. They do so and immediately catch 153 large fish. The miracle catch of fish identified the person on shore. John said, "It is the Lord!" Peter abandons ship to swim quickly to Him. The rest bring the boat to shore with the fish in the nets. At the Lord's direction, Peter takes some fish to Jesus.

Jesus, the Divine Chef, prepared a charcoal-broiled fish breakfast for the apostles who had been fishing. And He invites them to dine. They knew it was Jesus. And they finished the breakfast.

Now it was time to restore Peter, the apostle who three times denied the Lord. Jesus opens with a question, "Do your love Me more than these?" Do you love Me more than the fishing business, or more than you love your disciple friends, or more than the other disciples love Me? If we could see the

Lord's gestures, we would know clearly what He meant. The living nature of language could include all these options. It seems best, however, to choose the third option. Peter had boasted that he would not deny the Lord even if the other apostles did; he said that he loved the Lord more than the other apostles loved the Lord. And now *that* love was questioned by the Lord three times.

Two words translated "love" are used in the text: love that is related to decision, and love that is related to affection and warmth. Both are positive words and used of the love of the Father to the Son, of the Son to the Father, and of believers to one another and to God.

> *He said to him the third time, "Simon, son of Jonah, do you love Me?" Peter was grieved because He said to him the third time, "Do you love Me?" (John 21:17)*

The question was asked three times by Jesus, with two different words for love, emphasizing the similarity of the words. Peter used only the second word throughout the interaction. The nuanced meaning reveals a warm affection of Peter for Jesus, but also a personal understanding of the weakness of his will and his decisions. He learned that through his failure. Being restored, Peter is told to "feed [Christ's] lambs," tend [Christ's] sheep," and "feed [Christ's] sheep." And Peter obeyed His Lord.

He obeyed Him even to the point of death—the promise He had previously made to Jesus. This death, like Peter's denial, was another thing Jesus prophesied about him.

> *"Most assuredly, I say to you, when you were younger, you girded yourself and walked where you wished; but when you are old, you will stretch out your hands, and another will gird you and carry you where you do not wish." This He spoke, signifying by what death he would glorify God. And when He had spoken this, He said to him, "Follow Me." (John 21:18)*

Arising out of the prophecy came an objection from Peter. He was still Peter! Peter said, "Lord, What about this man?" He was referring to the apostle John. The Lord's response is a critical lesson for all Christians.

> *Jesus said to him, "If I will that he remain till I come, what is that to you? You follow Me." (John 21:22)*

"What is that to you?" The Father has a different plan for each individual, and that is God's prerogative. The responsibility of each disciple is to follow the Lord, not look at others as they follow Christ. This is true in successes and failures, in joy and sorrow, and in life and death. Peter continues to learn.

90
•
•
•

The Commission of the Apostles, and Christ's Ascension

Matthew 28:16-20; Luke 24:44-53; Acts 1:1-11

Then the eleven disciples went away into Galilee, to the mountain which Jesus had appointed for them. When they saw Him, they worshiped Him; but some doubted. And Jesus came and spoke to them, saying, "All authority has been given to Me in heaven and on earth. Go therefore and make disciples of all the nations, baptizing them in the name of the Father and of the Son and of the Holy Spirit, teaching them to observe all things that I have commanded you; and lo, I am with you always, even to the end of the age." Amen. (Matthew 28:16-20)

Then He said to them, "These are the words which I spoke to you while I was still with you, that all things must be fulfilled which were written in the Law of Moses and the Prophets and the Psalms concerning Me." And He opened their understanding, that they might comprehend the Scriptures. Then He said to them, "Thus it is written, and thus it was necessary for the Christ to suffer and to rise from the dead the third day, and that repentance and remission of sins should be preached in His name to all nations, beginning at Jerusalem. And you are witnesses of these things. Behold, I send the Promise of My Father upon you; but tarry in the city of Jerusalem until you are endued with power from on high." And He led them out as far as Bethany, and He lifted up His hands and blessed them. Now it came to pass, while He blessed them, that He was parted from them and carried up into heaven. And they worshiped Him, and returned to Jerusalem with great joy, and were continually in the temple praising and blessing God. Amen. (Luke 24:44-53)

And being assembled together with them, He commanded them not to depart from Jerusalem, but to wait for the Promise of the Father, "which," He said, "you have heard from Me; for John truly baptized with water, but you shall be baptized with the Holy Spirit not many days from now." Therefore, when they had come together, they asked Him, saying, "Lord, will You at this time restore the kingdom to Israel?" And He said to them, "It is not for you to know times or seasons which the Father has put in His own authority. But you shall receive power when the Holy Spirit has come upon you; and you shall be witnesses to Me in Jerusalem, and in all Judea and Samaria, and to the end of the earth." Now when He had spoken these things, while they watched, He was taken up, and a cloud received Him out of their sight. And while they looked steadfastly toward heaven as He went up, behold, two men stood by them in white apparel, who also said, "Men of Galilee, why do you stand gazing up into heaven? This same Jesus, who was taken up from you into heaven, will so come in like manner as you saw Him go into heaven." (Acts 1:4-11)

T he Lord has completed His ministry on earth and He is to return to His Father as He promised and prayed. He now addresses His eleven apostles with what is now commonly termed the Great Commission. There is a very significant change in this commission given to the apostles. Notice the instruction given to them previously.

These twelve Jesus sent out and commanded them, saying: "Do not go into the way of the Gentiles, and do not enter a city of the Samaritans. But go rather to the lost sheep of the house of Israel. And as you go, preach, saying, 'The kingdom of heaven is at hand.'" (Matthew 10:5-7)

The clear instruction during the ministry of Jesus limited the message to the Jews only. The literal, earthly, political kingdom of David had been offered to Israel. First it was offered in Galilee, then in Judea, and then in Perea. The offer of the kingdom was rejected in that same order. Finally, on Tuesday of Passion Week, Jesus withdrew the offer.

"Therefore I say to you, the kingdom of God will be taken from you and given to a nation bearing the fruits of it." (Matthew 21:43)

The nation of Israel confirmed the action.

When Pilate therefore heard that saying . . . he said to the Jews, "Behold your King!" But they cried out, "Away with Him, away with Him! Crucify Him!" Pilate said to them, "Shall I crucify your King?" The chief priests answered, "We have no king but Caesar!" (John 19:13-15)

Remember, in the Teaching of the Twelve, Jesus revealed His death and resurrection. He also prophesied the beginning of the church. Israel's predicted rejection now gives opportunity for that new era. And Jesus gives new instructions to the apostles—make disciples of *all nations!* Those apostles and that yet-to-be-named apostle (Paul) accomplished their commission, one upon which subsequent generations of believers have continued to build.

A second important instruction is set forth for the apostles: baptism.

> *"Go therefore and make disciples of all the nations, baptizing them in the name of the Father and of the Son and of the Holy Spirit." (Matthew 28:19)*

Jesus had already established the ordinance of the Lord's Supper; now He establishes the second ordinance of the church, baptism. Just as John's baptism marked the initiation of the offer of the kingdom, so baptism in the name of the Trinity marks the church era. And John, who introduced water baptism, also spoke of the baptism of the Spirit, which marks the beginning of the church as well. The difference between the baptism of John and the Great Commission baptism is seen in the following.

> *And it happened, while Apollos was at Corinth, that Paul, having passed through the upper regions, came to Ephesus. And finding some disciples he said to them, "Did you receive the Holy Spirit when you believed?" So they said to him, "We have not so much as heard whether there is a Holy Spirit." And he said to them, "Into what then were you baptized?" So they said, "Into John's baptism." Then Paul said, "John indeed baptized with a baptism of repentance, saying to the people that they should believe on Him who would come after him, that is, on Christ Jesus." When they heard this, they were baptized in the name of the Lord Jesus. (Acts 19:1-5)*

John's baptism relates to the kingdom; the Great Commission baptism relates to the church. The Lord's Supper and baptism have continued as the two ordinances of the church to this day.

Only Luke records Christ's ascension. Although he himself did not witness it, he consulted with the apostolic witnesses and recorded complementary segments in his gospel and the book of Acts. Just as there was a preliminary giving of the Holy Spirit in an earlier appearance, Jesus now instructs the apostles to remain in Jerusalem where, in a few days, they will be baptized with the Holy Spirit. *They* were thinking about the kingdom; *He* was thinking of the church.

> *And being assembled together with them, He commanded them not to depart from Jerusalem, but to wait for the Promise of the Father, "which," He said, "you have heard from Me; for John truly baptized*

with water, but you shall be baptized with the Holy Spirit not many days from now." Therefore, when they had come together, they asked Him, saying, "Lord, will You at this time restore the kingdom to Israel?" (Acts 1:4-6)

Jesus had promised to send the Holy Spirit once He returned to the Father. He instructs them to remain in Jerusalem until the Holy Spirit is given. Once the Holy Spirit is sent and the church is formed through the baptism by the Spirit, the witness of the church can begin, fully empowered by Him. The teaching on earth by Jesus is concluded. All that remains is His return to heaven.

Now when He had spoken these things, while they watched, He was taken up, and a cloud received Him out of their sight. And while they looked steadfastly toward heaven as He went up, behold, two men stood by them in white apparel, who also said, "Men of Galilee, why do you stand gazing up into heaven? This same Jesus, who was taken up from you into heaven, will so come in like manner as you saw Him go into heaven." (Acts 1:9-11)

Jesus Christ has ascended into heaven. And He will return—first, in the clouds to rapture the church, and then to earth after the tribulation, to establish His kingdom!

"Your kingdom come, Your will be done on earth, as it is in heaven."

Jesus Shall Reign

Jesus shall reign where'er the sun, does its successive journeys run;
His kingdom spread from shore to shore, till moons shall wax and wane no more.

To Him shall endless prayer be made, and endless praises crown His head;
His name like sweet perfume shall rise, with every morning sacrifice.

People and realms of every tongue, dwell on His love with sweetest song;
And infant voices shall proclaim, their early blessings on His name.

Blessings abound where'er He reigns; all prisoners leap and loose their chains;
The weary find eternal rest, and all who suffer want are blest.

Let every creature rise and bring, honors peculiar to our King;
Angels descend with songs again, and earth repeat the loud amen!

–Isaac Watts

Just A Minute...

DID YOU KNOW that within the next 60 seconds, two ECS Ministries Bible correspondence courses will be distributed? That's over 1,000,000 Bible courses . . . or two courses **EVERY** minute of **EVERY** hour of **EVERY** day of the year!

That's a lot of correspondence courses . . . and a whole lot of studying of God's Word. Perhaps this very minute a student in Abilene, Texas will start a foundational course such as "What the Bible Teaches" or perhaps a student in the Orissa province of India will start "Basic Bible Doctrines" in their native language.

With courses available in over 125 countries and languages, ECS Ministries is faithfully bringing *the Word to the World*.

66 I never learned so much about the Bible until I studied your courses. I can honestly say that I have learned more in this one year than at any other time in my life! 99

– student in Colorado

Every minute . . . every 60 seconds . . . two more students begin studying God's Word. Why not make that you? Go ahead, join a student body of over 400,000 and start on the Emmaus Road to Bible Knowledge.

phone: 563-585-2070
website: www.ecsministries.org
email: ecsorders@ecsministries.org
PO Box 1028, Dubuque, IA, 52004-1028